Ruined Village Map
Scenery

- Piles of timber (page 92, LMG)
- Old walls (page 94, LMG)
- Steep slope (page 91, LMG)
- Rubble (page 95, LMG)

Old Ford Map
Scenery (page 91, LMG)

- Boulders
- Knee-deep water
- Shallow slope

Gloomy Fold Map
Scenery

- Crags (page 90, LMG)
- Boulders (page 91, LMG)
- Steep slope (page 91, LMG)
- Shallow slope (page 91, LMG)

Adventures in Middle-earth™

Wilderland Adventures™

– CREDITS –

Written by: Gareth Ryder-Hanrahan, Francesco Nepitello, Jon Hodgson, and Steve Emmott
Development by: Jon Hodgson, David Rea and Jacob Rodgers
Creative Direction by: Jon Hodgson
Art by: Jon Hodgson and Tomasz Jedrusek
Edited by: Francesco Nepitello and Dominic McDowall-Thomas
Graphic Design and Layout: Paul Bourne
Maps by Paul Bourne
Proofreading: Amado Angulo, David Rea, Jacob Rodgers, Luke Walker

Based on *The One Ring Roleplaying Game* by Francesco Nepitello and Marco Maggi

© Sophisticated Games Ltd 2017   © Cubicle 7 Entertainment Ltd 2017

To find out more about *Adventures in Middle-earth*, and
to subscribe to our newsletter, please go to: www.cubicle7.co.uk

Product Identity: The following items are hereby identified as Product Identity, as defined in the Open Game License version 1.0a, Section 1(e), and are not Open Content: All trademarks, registered trade-marks, proper names (characters, place names, etc.), new rules, classes, items, virtues, backgrounds, places, characters, artwork, sidebars, and trade dress. Open Game Content: The Open content in this book includes material taken from the Systems Reference Document. No other portion of this work may be reproduced in any form without permission.

Published by Sophisticated Games Ltd, 3 Andersen Court, Newnham Road, Cambridge CB3 9EZ, UK and
Cubicle 7 Entertainment Ltd, Suite D3, Unit 4, Gemini House, Hargreaves Road, Groundwell Industrial Estate,
Swindon, SN25 5AZ, UK

The One Ring, Middle-earth, The Hobbit, The Lord of the Rings, and the characters, items, events and places therein are trademarks or registered trademarks of The Saul Zaentz Company d/b/a Middle-earth Enterprises and are used under license by Sophisticated Games Ltd and their respective licensees. All rights reserved. No part of this publication may be reproduced, stored in a retrieval system, or transmitted, in any form or by any means, electronic, mechanical, photocopying, recording or otherwise, without the prior permission of the publishers.

~ contents ~

Introduction — 4
How to Use this Guide — 6
Level Range — 6
The Passing of Years — 6

Don't Leave the Path — 7
Adventuring Phase — 7
Part One – Where Rivers Run With Gold — 7
Part Two – The Edge of the Woodland Realm — 10
Part Three – The Long Road — 11
Part Four – Castle of the Spiders — 12
Part Five – The Hermit — 15
Part Six – The Well in the Wood — 17
Epilogue – The Forest Gate — 19

Of Leaves & Stewed Hobbit — 20
Adventuring Phase — 20
Part One – The Easterly Inn — 20
Part Two – Searching the High Pass — 25
Part Three – Battle at the Ringfort — 27
Part Four – Into The Mountains — 31
Part 5 – Prisoner of the Goblins — 33
Epilogue – Back To The Inn — 36

Kinstrife & Dark Tidings — 37
Adventuring Phase — 37
Part One – A Funeral Boat — 38
Part Two – Beorn's Hall — 39
Part Three – The Chase — 43
Part Four – Kinstrife — 44
Part Five – The Chase Continued — 48
Part Six – Cruel, Ill-Favoured men — 49
Part Seven – The Outlaw Boy — 52
Part Eight – Grim Tidings — 55
Part Nine – Judgement at the Carrock — 57
Aftermath — 58

Those Who Tarry No Longer — 59
Adventuring Phase — 59
Part One – The Borders of the Forest — 60
Part Two – Weary of the World — 62
Part Three – The Hill of Woe — 64
Part Four – A Guest of Eagles — 66
Part Five – The Ruins — 67
Part Six – Dark Dreams — 72
Part Seven – Dawn in the West — 75
The Journey Home — 76

A Darkness in the Marshes — 77
Adventuring Phase — 77
Part One – Wizard's Counsel — 78
Part Two – Across the River — 80
Part Three – The Harrowed Hall — 82
Part Four – The Passage of the Marshes — 87
Part Five – Slave & Hunters — 89
Part Six – By Secret Ways — 90
Part Seven – Fly, You Fools! — 95
Epilogue – The Shadow of the Future — 98

The Crossings of Celduin — 99
Adventuring Phase — 99
Part One – The Gathering of Five Armies — 99
Part Two – A Golden Prize — 104
Part Three – An Ill-Made Party — 108
Part Four – Raven's Tidings — 110
Part Five – The Journey South — 113
Part Six – The Calm Before The Storm — 115
Part Seven – The Battle Begins — 118
Part Eight – The Last Day — 120
Aftermath — 124

The Watch on the Heath — 125
Adventuring Phase — 125
Part One – Council Under The Mountain — 125
Part Two – Across the Trackless Waste — 129
Part Three – The Grey Mountains — 132
Part Four – Zirakinbar — 133
Part Five – The Scourge of the North — 134
Part Six – The Watchtower — 137
Epilogue – A Renewed Spring of Joy — 142

Appendix — 143
Introduction to the Journey Rules — 143
Journey Event Tables — 144

Index — 157

- Introduction -

This guide contains seven ready-to-play adventures for your company of heroes, complete scenarios that can be played separately, or as a mini campaign spanning across a number of years. All adventures are set in the years after 2946, and take place in Wilderland. A wealth of background material expands the setting information contained in *Adventures in Middle-earth*, and will prove useful to Loremasters and players alike, even after all the adventures have been played through.

The first adventure takes the companions from Lake-town across the breadth of Mirkwood, while the following four are set west of the forest. The last two take place in Dale and the northern regions beyond the Lonely Mountain. The adventures are presented in order of increasing difficulty: while the first four adventures can be tackled by a group of relatively inexperienced adventurers, the last three offer a greater challenge. A suggested level range is given for each adventure. These suggestions are based on a company with four members of varied skills. The seven adventures are:

◆ Don't Leave the Path (Levels 1 or 2)
The companions find adventure outside Lake-town and are given the chance to discover why even the hardiest of adventurers shun the forest of Mirkwood and its depths. In the process, they go and see Elves, meet a crazed hermit, and stumble into a wood of ancient and angry trees.

◆ Of Leaves & Stewed Hobbit (Levels 2 or 3)
The company discovers the Easterly Inn, a piece of the Shire in the land of the Beornings. But the Wild is still the Wild, and it takes more than Hobbit cooking to keep adventures at bay; in no time, the companions find themselves involved in the search for a missing trade caravan. Their quest will put them on the road to the High Pass, and see them go over hills and under hills.

◆ Kinstrife and Dark Tidings (Levels 3 or 4)
A sorrowful discovery along the banks of the Anduin brings the characters to Beorn's Hall. A terrible crime has been committed, but the culprit has now escaped his captors and fled into the Wild. Beorn charges the adventurers with finding the lawbreaker and bringing him to judgement – but as the company searches for their quarry, they learn that right and wrong are not always as clear-cut as one might hope.

◆ Those Who Tarry No Longer (Levels 3 or 4)
The company is honoured beyond measure when asked to escort an Elf-woman across Wilderland to the High Pass. Irimë of the House of Gil-Galad is heading West, to leave the shores of Middle-earth. But the passing of such a bright light under the shadow of the mountains doesn't go unnoticed, and the company is waylaid by an evil spirit. This powerful shade tries to wield Irimë's sorrow as a weapon against her. If the adventurers cannot restore her hope, then the spirit will devour a light that has shone since the First Age!

◆ **A Darkness in the Marshes** (Levels 4 or 5)
Troubled by recent news, Radagast the Brown sends the company west across the Great River, to seek the counsel of the Woodmen of Mountain Hall. There, they receive tidings that lead them south, into the Gladden Fields. Eventually, they find and explore the Dwimmerhorn, a dark fastness where a dark plot is hatching. This is a danger beyond the company's ability to defeat alone, and they flee. But in their attempt to return to Woodland Hall, they risk bringing a great evil with them.

◆ **The Crossings of Celduin** (Levels 5 or 6)
Black treachery shakes the great festivities held in Dale for the Gathering of Five Armies! Warriors are poisoned, and the next day brings news of an army approaching from the south. With many of his soldiers sickened by the poison, King Bard turns to the adventurers and sends them to hold the Crossings of the River Running for as long as they can. If the Enemy host crosses the bridge too soon, then Dale will burn.

◆ **The Watch on the Heath** (Level 6 or Higher)
The Battle at Celduin didn't end the threat to the North. The army menacing Dale was but one of the many threads woven into a foul scheme. As the Free Folk of the North are enjoying a respite, the plot is secretly coming to fruition among the dreary peaks of the Grey Mountains: an ancient and unstoppable enemy is being summoned out of the frozen wastes. Luckily, not everyone is fooled, and the company is sent to the north by the King under the Mountain, to investigate the suspicious theft of records held in the Chamber of Mazarbul under Erebor. Will the adventurers learn about the impending threat in time and find a way to prevent it before it is too late?

The Gibbet King

The main villain of adventures 4 to 7 is an evil spirit whose true name is lost and forgotten. Called the Gibbet King by his servants, he is a wraith-creature, felt by mortals only as a passing shadow, a whisper on the wind. He served for centuries as the torturer and jailer of the Necromancer of Dol Guldur, bound to its pits by the will of his Master.

When the Necromancer left his fortress in Mirkwood, he forsook his many servants and slaves - the Gibbet King among them. The spirit hid in the deepest recesses of the stronghold, and escaped notice. When he finally left Dol Guldur, he was no more than a shapeless spectre of hate and malice. In time, he learnt to use sorcery to take possession of dead bodies and thus interact with the physical world.

Today, the Gibbet King hates Sauron as much as he hates all living things, but in his wickedness he is bound to seek similar ends.

How to Use this Guide

Most of the adventures presented in this guide are self-contained, and can be played as single quests without reference to any past or future adventure. You can pick the most appropriate adventures to run based on the composition of your players' company and their journeys across the Wild.

Don't Leave the Path, Of Leaves & Stewed Hobbit, Kinstrife & Grim Tidings and *Those Who Tarry No Longer* have no direct links to the other adventures, save whispers of the Gibbet King's influence. *A Darkness in the Marshes, The Crossings of Celduin* and *The Watch on the Heath* are all interlinked, but a Loremaster can pick the connections apart easily. (For example, instead of the Gibbet King at the head of the army that attacks Dale in *The Crossings of Celduin*, make the villain an Orc-chieftain or an Easterling warlord). *A Darkness in the Marshes* and *The Watch on the Heath* are more closely linked still. Alternatively, you can combine all seven adventures into a short campaign. The adventures should be played in the order they are presented in this guide.

Experience Awards

Throughout this volume you'll see symbols in the margin. These indicate a chance for the Loremaster to award Experience Points for overcoming challenges. These opportunities are optional, to be made at the Loremaster's discretion and in accordance with the method of levelling they have chosen. They might form a direct, numerical award, or a silently observed instance that counts towards gaining a whole level if enough are checked off.

Every game will vary, but these Experience Awards have been calculated to offer a good chance for a typical company to level up in accordance with the pace we suggest for this campaign.

Wilderland Adventures makes use of the Experience Rewards by Challenge table for non-combat encounters. Just as a combat encounter should be scaled to reflect the size of your company, so too should these Awards be scaled to match your group of adventurers.

The symbols **in red** represent an individual achievement. Those **in green** are intended to be divided amongst the party.

Experience derived from battle is calculated according to the core rules – for the sake of simplicity and consistency there is no change there.

Challenge	XP	Challenge	XP
1/8	25	3	700
1/4	50	4	1,100
1/2	100	5	1,800
1	200	6	2,300
2	450		

Individual Award **Group Award**

The Passing of Years

If you want to follow the default pacing of gameplay suggested in *Adventures in Middle-earth*, playing all the adventures contained in *Wilderland Adventures* should take several years. Every scenario offers plenty of opportunities to keep the companions busy for a year of game time, as the players can easily follow their Adventuring phase with a fruitful Fellowship phase, or even start a supplemental Adventuring phase building upon the consequences of the previous one. (Some suggestions concerning the follow-up to each adventure are presented at the end of each scenario).

Even if you don't feel comfortable with playing one adventure per year of game time, we suggest that you at least let one year pass for every two adventures. A tight pace of gameplay could be as follows:

Don't Leave the Path and *Of Leaves & Stewed Hobbit* could be run over the course of the same year. *Kinstrife & Dark Tidings* is suited to be the opening adventure of a new year, while *Those Who Tarry No Longer* can be followed aptly by a Fellowship phase marking the end of that year.

A Darkness in the Marshes is well suited to be the first adventure of any given year, with *The Crossings of Celduin* taking place the following November.

The Watch on the Heath should follow closely for an intense campaign finale.

- don't leave - the path

for heroes of level 1 or 2

- **When:** The company may undertake this quest at any time during the spring, summer or autumn.
- **Where:** The quest begins in Lake-town, on the Long Lake.
- **What:** The company are hired to escort a merchant's caravan across Mirkwood. The journey begins at the Halls of the Elvenking.
- **Why:** The Battle of Five Armies and the ensuing peace means that there is more trade and travel across the North. A Merchant of Dale intends to capitalise on this by bringing Dalish smithcraft and jewels across Mirkwood to Woodland Hall.
- **Who:** Baldor Rivergold is the name of the merchant. He travels with his son Belgo, a youth of ten years.

Adventuring Phase

This adventure is divided into six parts, covering the journey from Esgaroth to the Forest Gate.

Part One - Where Rivers Run With Gold
The company rescue Baldor the merchant from three ruffians, and he asks them to serve as his caravan guards on the crossing of Mirkwood.

Part Two - The Edge of the Woodland Realm
Baldor has friends in Thranduil's court, so the first part of the journey is on board the Elven rafts up the Forest River. The company are escorted to the edge of the forest kingdom and warned not to leave the path.

Part Three - The Long Road
The company set off for the west, braving the perils of the dark wood.

Part Four - Castle of the Spiders
As the company make camp, Baldor falls afoul of the enchanted stream that runs through Mirkwood. Temporarily deprived of his memories, he flees into the woods and is trapped by Spiders in a ruined castle.

Part Five - The Hermit of Mirkwood
The company find shelter with a crazed hermit. Can they convince him to aid them, or is he planning to murder them in their sleep?

Part Six - The Well in the Wood
The last danger of the woods comes from the trees themselves. Their contempt for everything that goes on two legs threatens to turn into a deadly trap.

Epilogue - The Forest Gate
Where the company exits Mirkwood, and possibly reaps the benefits of their deeds.

- Part One - Where Rivers Run With Gold

The company are out in the countryside near the Long Lake. Perhaps they are returning from a previous journey, or out fishing, or simply walking by the shore. The ruins of the old Lake-town are visible in the water. Blackened poles poke out like ribs, and when the water is very, very still, one can sometimes spot the bones of Smaug the Dreadful. Sometimes gemstones from the dragon's fabled diamond waistcoat wash up on the shore.

The company hear someone running, and shouts of *'help! help!'*. A young boy about ten years old bursts out of the rushes ahead of them. He spots the company and runs towards them, waving his arms. Tears run down his cheeks.

"Help! Please help! My father – his guards – they're going to kill him! We're going to Mirkwood and they're going to kill him! He told me to run! Find help! Help!"

Belgo's words tumble out in a terrified flood. The company can piece together the story: his father Baldor is a merchant of Dale. He has a caravan of trade goods, and intended to bring it across Mirkwood. He hired three guards for protection, but these guards have now turned on him. The caravan is nearby – if the company hurry, they can rescue Baldor.

Playing Baldor

Baldor is tired and careworn, and more than a little out of his depth. He is too old and soft for long journeys, but he lost his fortune in the destruction of Lake-town and so he is forced to return to the road. Don't be a burden to the company. Try to help the player characters.

Worry about everything, especially Belgo. Speculate about the dangers in the wood.

Speak softly but try to be persuasive. Pretend to lean on a walking-staff.

Playing Belgo

Young Belgo is ten years old, on the cusp of becoming an adult.

Take care of the ponies. Show that you are as useful as any of the company.

Never argue directly with your father, but second-guess him when talking to the player characters.

Look up at the players to give them the impression that you are smaller than they are.

Saving Baldor

Baldor and the three thugs are only a short distance away, on the path that led from old Lake-town into the forest. This path is now mostly overgrown – few people pass this way now, as the site of the town was moved after the death of the dragon. Baldor stands with his back to a tree and a heavy branch in his hand. His three treacherous caravan guards surround him with drawn swords. One of the three has a nasty fresh welt on his face, where Baldor struck him with the branch. Refer to the Path Map on the front end papers.

Anyone from Dale or Esgaroth recognises the three guards as Jonar, Kelmund and Finnar, three notorious troublemakers from Lake-town. A few years ago, they were thugs in the service of the old Master. The new, wiser Master dismissed them from service, and they are now thieves and sell-swords. Obviously, they decided that murdering Baldor and taking his caravan was more profitable and a lot safer than braving the wilds of Mirkwood.

When the company arrive, Jonar – the biggest of the trio – tries to convince them to leave. *"Be off!"* he shouts, *"This is none of your business!"* He claims that Baldor cheated them, and that they are only taking what is due to them. When it becomes clear that the company do not believe him, he tries to appeal to their greed. All they need to do is turn their backs for a minute, and keep their mouths shut afterwards, and he'll give them a cut of the stolen goods.

Intimidating the Thugs

The trio are craven at heart – the company can intimidate them into leaving with an **Charisma (Intimidation)** check before the fight begins. If the character beats a DC 15, the thugs depart but nurse grudges against the company, and may prove to be trouble in future should the company ever return to Lake-town. If the character beats a DC of 20, the thugs are so terrified that they never dare cross the company again.

Fighting the Thugs

Where words do not serve, then swords must out. The thugs are not an especially difficult group of foes, and try to surrender if reduced to half their starting Hit Points.

During the fight, Baldor harasses the thugs by taking wild swings with his tree-branch; each round, randomly pick one player character fighting the thugs. That player character has Advantage on their attacks this round.

Use the Thug statistics on p. 73 of the *Loremaster's Guide*.

Baldor's Offer

Once the thugs are dealt with, Baldor throws down his branch and embraces his son. He then expresses his thanks for the company's prompt rescue.

"Thank you! Thank you! You arrived in the nick of time."

He explains that he set out from Lake-town with his son and the three thugs. He is a merchant and a travelling trader, and his four ponies are carrying iron tools and toys from Dale that he intends to sell to the folk of Woodland Hall. He has arranged with the Elves for passage through their lands. He knows that Mirkwood is dangerous, and so he looked in Esgaroth for guards who were brave enough to risk the crossing of the forest. It seems that he chose poorly.

He offers the job of guarding the caravan to the company instead. He promises to pay them in coin and goods (totalling 50 silver pennies each) once they reach the Forest Gate.

Baldor's History

If the company question Baldor, they can learn the following as they travel:

- He was once a rich merchant of Lake-town, but he lost a great deal when the dragon fell on the city.
- Not only was his fortune destroyed, but his wife Halla also perished. He carried his young son out of the flames, but could not find his wife.
- While others have found prosperity in the years since the Battle of Five Armies, he has not been so lucky. He moved to Dale when its reconstruction started, but he has yet to rebuild his former wealth.
- Young Belgo is a good lad, his father's pride and joy.

The Journey

Baldor has already planned the journey, although well-travelled companions can make suggestions. He plans to meet with Elvish friends of his at the edge of Mirkwood, and these Elves will accompany the caravan up the river on paddle-boats. From the Elvenking's hall, the company will set off down the Forest Path to the west side.

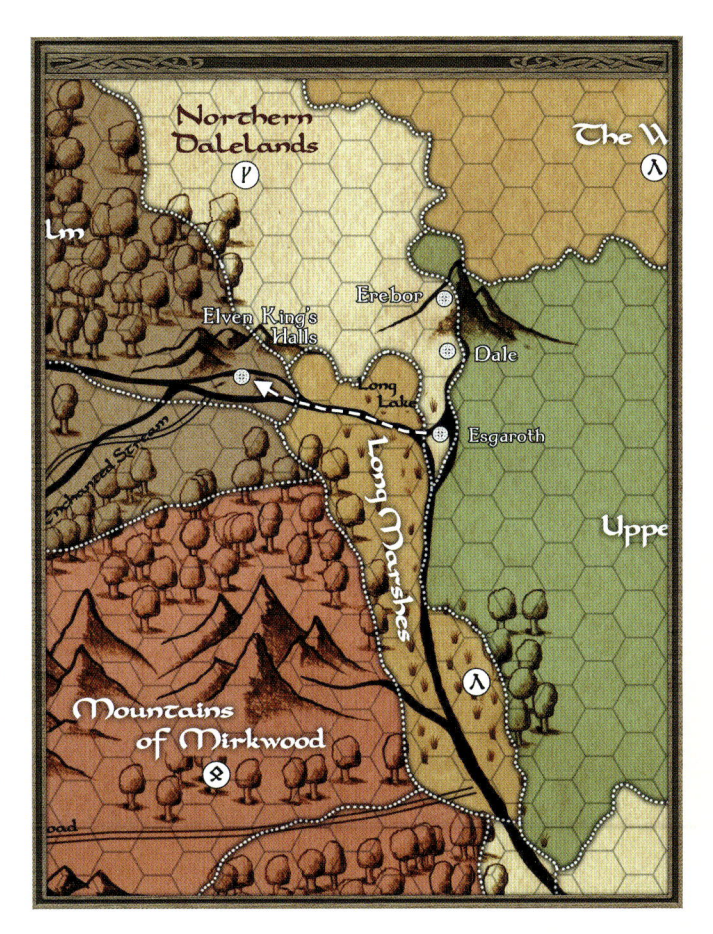

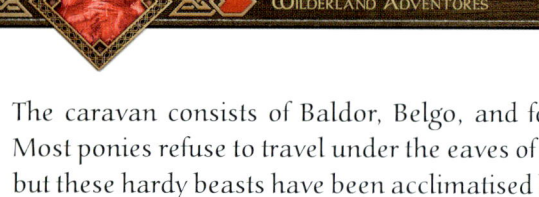

The caravan consists of Baldor, Belgo, and four ponies. Most ponies refuse to travel under the eaves of Mirkwood, but these hardy beasts have been acclimatised by arduous training, and will at least consent to be dragged along the Elf-Path. He already has plenty of travelling supplies for the company. Baldor leads the company along the banks of the Forest River, taking a well-travelled path that runs alongside the waters.

- Part Two -
The Edge of the Woodland Realm

At twilight, a trio of rafts emerge from the mists on the river. Green-cloaked figures punt these rafts to the shore. The Elves greet Baldor and the company warmly – the merchant is well known to them. The Elves are amused and fascinated by Belgo; they say there are few children among them in these days.

The ponies are unloaded and their burdens transferred to the rafts. The animals are initially wary about getting onto the rafts, but one of the Elves whispers in the ponies' ears and instantly all four of the animals become perfectly calm, happily trot onto the rafts and stand stock-still in the middle.

Once departed, the Elves expertly pilot their rafts against the current of the Forest River. After several days of slow travel, the land on either side of the rafts rises and turns stony and wooded, and the company pass into the shadow of the trees. It is as though the rafts are sailing up a dark tunnel, as the branches interlace overhead into a dark canopy. The company glimpse tall hills in gaps between the trees, until the river widens and the trees grow thinner once again. Here, a bay opens, and huts cling close to a shingly shore. The Elves steer up a stream which flows out of a rocky canyon. The canyon walls grow higher and higher, until the rafts pass a portcullis and suddenly they find themselves in the caves of the Elvenking.

Guests of the Elves

Sadly, the company see little of the Elvenking's halls. Baldor is met by a friend of his, an Elf named Lindar who is master of the king's cellars. Baldor is welcome here – the other characters may not be so lucky. If the company are unable to convince Lindar of their good character, they are obliged to wait under guard in the cellars until the caravan is ready to depart. Elves of Mirkwood are of course allowed to wander the halls as they wish.

Motivation

Lindar's sole motivation is to ensure that the player characters keep the peace within the Elf-King's halls.

Expectations

+2: If the player characters are especially polite and courteous, or bring interesting news from afar
+1: If there are any Elves in the Company.
-1: If there any Dwarves in the company.
-2: If the characters demand better accommodation or complain about the guards.

Introduction

In the halls of the Elven-king, it is expected that one makes a **DC 15 Intelligence (Traditions)** check. Less educated heroes might attempt a **DC 20 Charisma (Persuasion)** check instead.

Interaction

Lindar suggests that as the Elves do not know the company, they should remain here to 'guard the supplies'. In two days, the Elves will bring the company to the edge of Thranduil's realm. In the meantime, they can remain here in the caves; Lindar promises to send down some bread and *wine*.

Outcomes

Failure: Insulted, Lindar demands that the company leave immediately. It's a *Fell and Forboding Start* to their crossing of Mirkwood, and they automatically get that result without having to roll on the Embarkation table.

Success by 0-2: Lindar permits the adventures to reside in the caves until they are ready to depart.

Success by 3-4: Lindar sends down excellent meals from the Elf-King's kitchens, and the adventurers are welcome to visit again in future.

Success by 6 or more: The characters are permitted to stay in better quarters in the upper caves, and may even hear the Elves singing. The combination of soft beds and good company ensures the characters depart *With Hopeful Hearts and Clear Purpose* when the journey begins without needing to roll on the Embarkation table.

The Journey Begins

After two days, Lindar and some other Elves escort the company out of the caves by a secret route, and bring them some miles down the Elf-path. This part of the wood is not so oppressive; the path is lined with beeches, and sunlight filters through the trees to dapple everything with green-gold light. This region still preserves the beauty and peace of Greenwood the Great. Lindar warns that the company will soon enter more perilous regions, and he gives them one key piece of advice – don't leave the path! The path is mostly clear of trouble, but the same cannot be said of the woods to either side.

Loading the Ponies

Companions can profit from the fact that they are travelling with ponies and load some of their gear upon them. Heroes travelling with ponies can ignore the first level of exhaustion incurred on a Journey. See page 166 of the *Adventures in Middle-earth Player's Guide*.

– Part Three –
The Long Road

Lindar and the Elves have led the company to the point where the Enchanted Stream crosses the Elf-path. They bring the company across by boat – the ponies are temporarily relieved of their load – and the Elves warn the characters not to drink from the stream. Once their feet are firmly set on the path, Lindar bids them good luck, and vanishes into the shadows of the trees. The company are now on their own, and face a long journey.

The Journey

The companions must follow the Elf-path across almost the whole width of Mirkwood. While walking on the path eases the toll of the journey somewhat (the forest doesn't darken their hearts as grievously as if they were leaving the trail), being parted from the light of the sun and the open air for so long is going to put the company to the test.

- Travel through Mirkwood, even along the Elf-Path, is arduous. This journey has a Peril Rating of 3.
- The road from the Enchanted Stream to the Forest Gate is 160 miles, making it a Medium journey. Roll 1d2+1 for the number of challenges. The DC for any journey events is 15.

- The darkness of the forest weighs heavily on the company's spirits. Travellers in wild lands like the forest must make two **DC 15 Wisdom** saving throws; each failed saving throw gives 1 point of Shadow.

While the truly perilous parts of the forest are away down to the south, in the Heart of Mirkwood and around Dol Guldur, that does not mean that travelling in Northern Mirkwood is a pleasant stroll through the woods.

- Refer to the **Wilderland Adventures Journey Events Table** starting on Page 143 for the events that may occur during this journey.

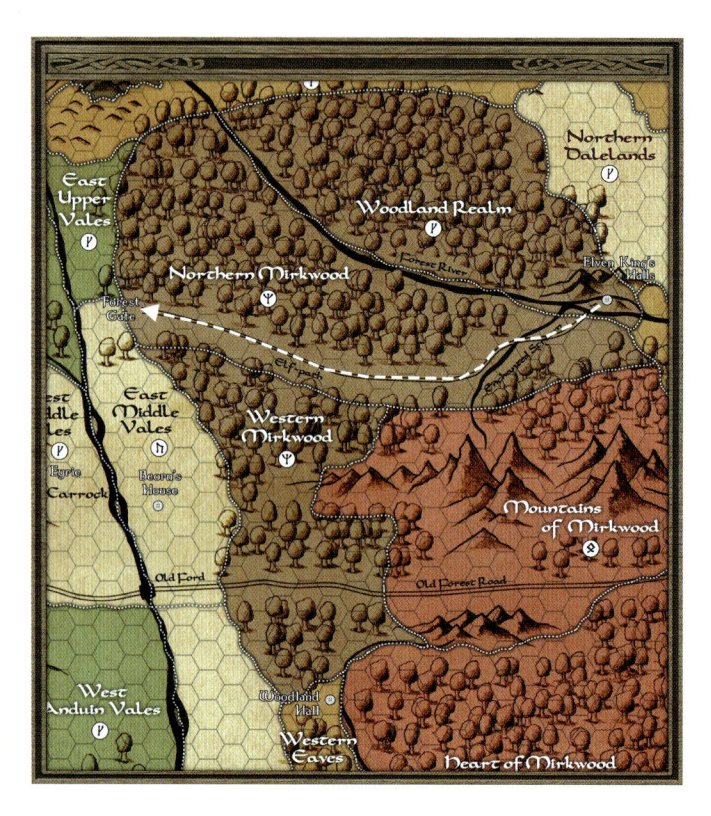

Belgo's Talisman

As noted on page 15, Belgo wears a talisman around his neck as a reminder of his lost mother. This talisman plays a key role in the final part of this adventure, so the Loremaster should establish its existence earlier in the game. For example, if the company are attacked by spiders, then Belgo could drop the talisman in the struggle, and one of the other characters could spot it.

- PART FOUR -
CASTLE OF THE SPIDERS

The Enchanted Stream runs through Mirkwood, and the main course of the waters crosses the Forest Path far to the east of the company's present location. There are other streams in Mirkwood, though, and they too are not always wholesome to drink from.

This part of the adventure begins when the company make camp. Their Scouts find an excellent place to rest for the night, where the path opens into a pleasant, grassy forest clearing. Any Elf in the party recognises this spot as one of the open-air feast-halls of the Elvenking, although this particular field has not been used in many years. A sparkling stream of fresh water runs along the edge of the clearing. The company make camp – if the player characters mutter about wanting to push on, then young Belgo throws himself down on the grassy floor and announces that he is much too tired to travel any more that day.

Presumably, the company set watches during the night.

BALDOR'S ERROR

During the night, Baldor the merchant wakes up. He leaves his bedroll and exchanges a few words with whoever is on watch, and complains about bad dreams. He is still half-asleep, but his mouth is dry so he wanders over to the stream to take a drink of water. Moonlight shimmers on the dancing waters, and what was safe and pure during the day is not always unchanged at night.

When Baldor drinks from the stream, it robs him of his memories. The last five years fall away from Baldor's mind. He forgets where he is, and who he has become. Suddenly, he believes he is back in Esgaroth on that terrible night five years ago, when the dragon came to the Long Lake.

He sees the company and mistakes them for bandits who have kidnapped him. All he knows is that he has to get back to Lake-town, to save his wife and child from the dragon. He does not even recognise Belgo – in his mind, Belgo is a laughing five-year-old, not a prematurely serious boy of ten. Belgo looks into his father's eyes, and sees no spark of recognition or love. His father looks at the boy as if he was a stranger.

"Who are you? Where am I? Where... there is fire under the Mountain! Those fools have woken the dragon! I must find Halla! I... you've kidnapped me! You rogues! Where is Belgo?"

A **DC 10 Wisdom (Insight)** check makes it clear that Baldor is not in his right mind – his eyes burn with crazed intensity, and he clearly does not recognise the company. If anyone approaches him, he turns and sprints headlong in the forest.

- Baldor -

- Belgo -

Following Baldor

The company need to decide what is to be done quickly. The longer they wait, the farther Baldor strays from the path. Will they all go after him? Will they take the ponies? Belgo volunteers to remain behind to watch the animals, while the characters rescue his father.

The most likely solution is that they leave the boy to guard the ponies, as this clearing seems like a safe place. If one or more player characters stay behind, then the Loremaster could have the clearing attacked by spiders to put them in peril.

Normally, tracking someone through the forest would require a **Wisdom (Survival)** check, but in this case Baldor trampled through the muddy ground near the stream, leaving big deep footprints that even a blind Dwarf could follow. However, the characters have to hunt around for the trail with torches until dawn breaks, so it takes them several hours to follow Baldor's route. The trail plunges into the dark woods, until it just suddenly stops, as if Baldor vanished into thin air. Searching around reveals a few strands of webbing hanging from two trees nearby.

A successful **DC 10 Intelligence (Investigation)** check determines that Baldor blundered into a spider-web at such speed that he pulled the web off the trees it was anchored to. Looking around finds drag marks on the ground. He must have gotten tangled up in the web, then something dragged him off deeper into the woods.

Following the trail brings the company to another clearing.

The Castle

A castle stands on a low hill amid the sea of green trees. It's anybody guess if it was Elves or Men who built this castle, but it has fallen into ruin. No trace remains of the defensive walls or outbuildings; all that remains are a single round tower and part of what must have once been the keep. The keep has crumbled and collapsed in on itself, leaving only one corner still standing as an L-shaped wall. Both tower and wall are covered in a dense shroud of cobwebs, and web-strands run between tower and wall.

Hanging from the very top of the wall is a wriggling bundle of webbing. It must be Baldor.

There is no sign of any spiders at first glance, but there are any number of places where they could be hiding. The only sound is the occasional thump as Baldor wrestles and struggles against his bonds. To get to Baldor, the company need to climb the wall, or else climb the still-intact spiral staircase in the tower and then clamber across the webbing to the top of the wall. Refer to the Castle Map on the front end papers.

Climbing the Wall

The wall is thirty feet high and is tricky to climb, as the character must be careful to avoid getting stuck on the cobwebs.

- Climbing the wall requires a **DC 15 Strength (Athletics)** check.

If the test fails, the character gets stuck on the cobwebs (becoming Restrained) and must cut their way free, which attracts the attention of the spiders – see *The March of the Spiders*, below. Cutting through the web requires a **DC 10 Dexterity (Sleight of Hand)** or **DC 13 Strength (Athletics)** check. If the test fails by 10 or more, then the character falls from the wall and suffers 2d6 damage.

The Tower Stairs

The spiral staircase in the tower is mostly intact, so the characters can easily make their way up to the top. From there, they can see a 'bridge' of spider-webs running from the tower to the top of the wall – but they can also see dozens of spiders nesting on the far side of the ruined keep. The spiders seem to be sleeping, but any vibration on the web will alert them.

- Crossing the bridge requires a **DC 15 Dexterity (Acrobatics)** check..

Failing the test alerts the spiders; failing by 10 or more alerts the spiders *and* means that the character is caught by the webbing again; the hero is Restrained and must make a **DC 10 Dexterity (Sleight of Hand)** or **DC 13 Strength (Athletics)** check to get free.

Rescuing Baldor

Once a character reaches Baldor, they can drag his body to the top of the wall with a **DC 13 Strength (Athletics)** check and then cut him loose. Baldor is Stunned, but can move or climb with a hero's assistance. Both Baldor and the assisting hero move at half speed during this process. Baldor and the heroes must make another **Dexterity** check to cross the bridge and another **Strength** check to descend the wall.

March of the Spiders

If the companions manage to reach Baldor, cut him loose and escape the scene without failing a single skill check, then they successfully rescue the merchant out from under the noses of the spiders (if spiders have noses) without being seen. However, if one of the characters pulls on the wrong strand, then the spiders come marching.

- In the first round, the characters feel the web moving, but no spider appears. In the second and subsequent rounds, a single Attercop arrives to menace the heroes. Each Attercop that joins the fight gains the same Initiative as its brethren.

While one Attercop (page 105, *Loremaster's Guide*) is not a deadly threat to a group of well-rested adventurers, unlucky dice rolls might mean that the company is soon outnumbered. If there are more spiders than heroes, they are in terrible danger. The Attercops target characters who are stuck in the web.

> ### Doomed!
> If luck turns against the characters and it seems as though they are about to be defeated by the spiders, then the Loremaster can rescue them by having the hermit show up with a bow. The hermit laughs and shouts nonsense while he fires deadly accurate shots at the biggest of the spiders.

Escape!

After the characters rescue Baldor, they still need to make their way back to the path, and they must do so with a host of brown hairy spiders scuttling after them. The spiders move with unnatural speed, leaping from tree to tree and trailing strands of webbing like fishing lures as they try to snare the companions. Baldor is still confused after drinking from the Enchanted Stream, but even in his witless state, he recognises that he is better off with these strange companions than as a spider's supper. After several minutes' running, the characters arrive back at the clearing, where they meet Belgo and the ponies. The spiders do not dare cross the path.

Baldor recovers most of his memories after a few hours' rest and conversation with his son. He seems unsteady and wary for the rest of the journey. He tells the characters that he thought that he was back in Esgaroth when Smaug attacked, and relates the tale of how his wife Hilla was lost when the dragon fell on Lake-town. Baldor was able to carry his young son out of the flames, but never saw Hilla again.

Gathering Darkness

During the rest of the journey, show that there is now a wedge between Baldor and Belgo. The boy feels betrayed and lonely, and Baldor is too confused and nervous to comfort his son – the memory-erasing stream washed away most of Baldor's memory of the last five years, and he finds it hard to reconcile his surviving memories of his son with the present situation.

- In game terms, poor Belgo has picked up several Shadow points due to anguish and terror. Belgo spends more and more time toying with the amulet he wears around his neck.

– Part Five –
The Hermit

The Hermit of Mirkwood had a name once, but he lost it in the dungeons of Dol Guldur. He remembers only parts of his life before the darkness. He was a Woodman, a warrior, a hero. He remembers sun on the trees, the weight of an axe in his hand, the smoke rising from the cooking fires at the end of a long hunt, the warmth of the Great House when the winter winds howled outside. All that was lost when he was captured. For many years he suffered in the dungeons, tormented by Orcs and other horrors. Then, five years ago, the Shadow was driven from the Hill of Sorcery. The Hermit heard the noise of a tremendous storm overhead, a storm so loud it woke him in his gaol cell deep underground. He found the door was unlocked, and he fled through the endless warren of tunnels until he came to a drain that opened into sunlight. He fled, naked and shrieking and quite quite mad, into the forest, and here he has lived alone since that day.

The Thunderstorm

The company are travelling along the Elf-path when a sudden storm descends on Mirkwood, turning the forest as dark as midnight. High winds tear through the tree-tops, sending a hail of leaves and twigs down on the company. Larger branches creak ominously, and rotten boughs crack and tumble. The clouds open as though some great hand picked up the whole of the Long Lake and dumped it on the forest. Thunder and lightning crash overhead, incredibly loud and perilously close, and water starts trickling along the trees more and more copiously until dozens of little streams and rills start winding their way through the forest floor. Further travel is impossible – the company must find a dry place within sight of the path.

- As lightning flashes, one of the company's Scouts spots an unusual sight at some distance from the path. There is a huge dead hollow tree up ahead, and a thin plume of woodsmoke rises from the top. Someone is living inside the hollow tree! Searching around the base of the tree lets the characters find a tunnel that runs between the roots into the tree's interior.

There is no sign of anyone around or inside, but they cannot be far away if they left a cooking fire unattended. Even if the company are willing to brave the weather and travel on, neither Baldor nor Belgo is strong enough to keep going in the teeth of the storm. The hermit's tree is the only source of shelter to hand.

The Hermit's Tree

The hermit's tree is hollow on the inside. The entrance tunnel opens into a single round room. The walls are the dead wood of the tree, and the roof is a mix of bark and thatch that keeps most of the wind and rain out. It is not as snug as a hobbit-hole, but it's better than being outside in Mirkwood in the storm. There is a ring of stones in the middle of the room, and a small cooking-fire burns there, with some hunks of meat (one hopes a rabbit or a squirrel) cooking on a spit. Other unidentifiable bits of meat hang from the ceiling on long black strings. There is a single bed of leaves and furs near the fire. Jars of water and baskets of fruit sit in a cool muddy hollow at the back of the room. Any Woodmen recognise the style of the handiwork. Looking around leads to a grim discovery, though – the walls are covered in woodcarvings depicting horrible faces and monsters of all sorts. Whoever lives here is tormented by nightmares.

Encountering the Hermit

After a few minutes, the company hear scratching outside, as someone arrives at the entrance tunnel and wriggles their way into the hollow tree. The characters smell the hermit before they see him; an incredibly rank smell wafts from his filthy rags and scarred, rail-thin body. His wrists and ankles are scarred. The hermit shrieks in alarm when he finds the company in his home, and levels a spear at them, but he does not attack.

Playing the Hermit

Talk to yourself. Argue with yourself.
Mutter random nonsense.
You're crazy, but you know you're crazy. Get irritated if the characters try to soothe you. Hunch your shoulders, chatter your teeth, sniff the air like an animal.

Motivation

Get the strangers out of your tree! Drive them away! But wait… you remember, long ago… better days, sun on your face. Maybe… friends?

Expectations

+2: If the company treat the hermit with respect and kindness; if there is a Woodman in the company
+1: If threatened effectively
-1: If anyone asks questions about the carvings; if there are any Elves or Dwarves in the company
-2: If threatened ineffectively

Introduction

The company must explain who they are and why they have trespassed in the hermit's home.

Interaction

The first thing to do is to ask for permission to stay. This requires a **DC 13 Charisma (Persuasion)** check, though **Intelligence (Riddle)** may also be used. Offering the hermit food and drink helps win him over – he is obviously starving and gobbles down anything the company offer him. If the company ask who the hermit is, he shrugs.

"Don't need a name, do I? There's only me, I know who I am. I'm me. You need name, though. You're not me. Had a name once, but they took it."

Asking about the carvings on the walls alarms him. He made those to scare away his nightmares. There is a darkness in the wood, he insists, a great shadow. The light drove it away, but it is growing again. He hears it creep up on him as he sleeps. That's why he hides in this tree, and why he stays away from Men. He knows that the Shadow crawls into the hearts of Men and turns them into beasts. Why, any of the company could be servants of the Shadow.

- Unless the company reassure him that they are enemies of the Necromancer, he attacks them (see below).

Outcomes

Failure: The Hermit screams at them to leave his house. If they agree to do so, then they find that the worst of the storm has passed, but the company still suffer a -1 penalty to their Arrival roll. If they refuse, then the Hermit attacks; (If needed, use stats for Town Guard, *Loremaster's Guide* pg 69, with a club for weapon.) killing the Hermit in his own home is a Misdeed worth at least 3 Shadow Points.

Success by 0-5: After a few minutes, the Hermit grows tired of the conversation, and falls asleep. The company can stay in the hollow tree (gaining a long rest), but must depart in the morning once the storm has passed.

Success by 6+: If the company win his trust, then the hermit reaches into his tattered rags and produces a broken piece of metal. It is the remains of a once-magnificent axe-head. The Hermit presses it into the hands of a companion, saying that the Shadow hides in things and it is better to have nothing of value, because the darkness could be hiding in a stone or an egg-shell or a gemstone or a ring. He carried this axe-head for too long, and now he wants the characters to take it away.

- A successful **DC 15 Intelligence (Lore)** check identifies the piece of metal as a shard from a famous axe called *Wolfbiter* (Woodmen heroes recognise the item right away). The weapon was an heirloom of the folk of Woodland Hall, but was lost long ago when one of their chieftain's sons was captured by Orcs.

- Part Six -
The Well in the Wood

The western reaches of Mirkwood are grim and dangerous. Some woods were inhabited by Men once, and the trees still remember the bite of the axe. This part of the forest is far from the Shadow in the south, but its depths are unwelcoming nonetheless and have no love for anything that walks on two legs.

Still, the air in some places is not so stagnant and heavy, and the light is brighter. Sometimes, through gaps in the canopy, the company can see the open sky above. In the filtered sunlight, the company see stones scored with runes, or piled rocks that show that Men once lived in these parts. One day soon, they will come around a bend in the path and see the end of the road and the Forest Gate as the land slopes down towards the Vales of Anduin.

The Ancient Wood

The day after the storm sees the sun rising on a warm morning (unusually warm if it's autumn). Even if the company is still in the shadow of Mirkwood, they feel the temperature rising. As the company marches on, the companions begin to feel very hot. Towards midday, a sense of sleepiness seems to creep out of the ground and up their legs. Flies buzz round their ears, and water trickling from a hundred rills sounds like a half-whispered lullaby.

A short distance ahead of the company there is an old stone well, and at the bottom of that well lives something nameless and malignant. The ancient trees living in this area have struck a deal with the thing, and lure to it any traveller who dare tread upon their roots.

- When the company is in the area close to the well, call for a **DC 16 Wisdom** saving throw. All those who fail gain a Shadow point as they start feeling downhearted and worn out. If at least half of the companions fail the roll, the company agrees to stop for a midday break.

If the company stop, they choose a place a short distance from the path. Close by, the mouth of the old well opens. The well is not readily visible, as it is simply a low ring of stones around a hole in the ground, currently covered by fallen leaves and thick undergrowth. Those companions who do not act as Look-outs feel compelled to take a nap after a quick meal. As soon as they close their eyes, they start having vivid dreams. If the companions do not agree to stop (less than half the company failed their roll), those who failed the saving throw begin to have strange intuitions instead.

Dreams and Intuitions

The wood that the company is travelling across is weaving a spell to send the companions towards the Thing lurking at the bottom of the well. Whether they are sleeping or still marching, the heroes who failed the saving throw receive suggestions from the ancient and malevolent trees.

- The companions dream or feel that something of great importance is nearby, if only they can find it. Tie these dreams or visions into the characters' Shadow Weaknesses. A Scholar might dream that there is a book describing many secrets of the Enemy at the bottom of a well nearby; a Treasure Hunter might glimpse gold inside it, while a Wanderer is strangely drawn to leave the path and explore the nearby woods.

Under the Spell

If any character succumbs to a Bout of Madness while near the well, they run towards it. If none of the characters has such a fit, then it falls to young Belgo to be the victim. The boy is tormented by dreams that his mother's ghost is nearby, calling him from the trees. With his father half-lost to him because of the Enchanted Stream's theft of memories, Belgo is uniquely vulnerable to the lure of the trees. He runs off into the wood, calling out for his mother and holding his talisman tightly.

If Belgo, or a companion, is drawn into the woods, he crashes through the trees, leaving the path. Their companions can either try to Restrain the victims, or else follow them into the woods to the well.

The Old Well

The well itself is some twenty feet deep. A stone ledge juts out of the wall half-way down, and the bottom of the shaft is choked with ropy plant growths, like thick roots or the tangled stems of a monstrous creeper vine. Among the ropy vines are many old bones, the remains of previous victims of The Thing in the Well. An old rotten rope hangs down into the well, but putting any weight on it snaps the rope instantly. Refer to the Well Map on the front end papers.

- The first victim to reach the well throws himself into it. If it is Belgo, he lands heavily on the stone ledge. A player character who jumps into the well falls all the way to the bottom and lands among the vines, falling for the full twenty feet.

The Creature Attacks

When someone falls into the well, or is at least within 20 feet from its mouth, the ropy vines unfold and attack. The lashing tentacles are all guided by one purpose, and try to wrap around the companions to strangle and crush them.

The companions who failed the saving throw are still under the power of the spell set upon them by the wood: they don't see the creature as a horrible monster, but as whatever dream or vision drew them here. Belgo sees his mother embracing him; a character who came here in search of gold sees gold coins and jewels at the bottom of the well, and thinks he is digging them out of the ground, when he is actually being strangled by the creature.

- As a consequence, they cannot attack the creature in any way, and cannot be persuaded to stay away from it.

Victims are freed from their madness if the creature is wounded, or if another character helps them snap out of it. For example, if Belgo's talisman is torn from his grasp, then he sees the creature for what it really is.

Fighting the Creature

Characters inside the well have Disadvantage on their attacks on the creature, while the creature has Advantage against them.

- Climbing out of the well requires a **DC 15 Strength (Athletics)** check. Characters hit while climbing might be knocked back down.
- Companions outside the well can fight normally. The companions harm the thing by hacking at its many tentacle-like arms. If the creature is reduced to 27 or fewer hit points, its gnarled tentacles slither back into the well and vanish into the mud at the bottom.

The Thing in the Well

There are older and fouler things than Orcs in the deep places of the world.

Not even the Wise might guess whether the creature in the well is a part of the wicked wood or something that crept out of dark waters under Mirkwood.

The Thing in the Well
Medium Aberration (Nameless Thing)

STR	DEX	CON	INT	WIS	CHA
15 (+2)	14 (+2)	13 (+1)	6 (-2)	10 (+0)	9 (-1)

Armour Class 12
Hit Points 55 (10d8+10)
Speed 0 ft

Condition Immunities: Blinded, Prone
Skills Perception +2, Stealth +4
Senses darkvision 60 ft, passive Perception 12
Challenge 2 (450 XP)

Many Tentacles (Recharge 6). The Thing in the Well may use its action to make a tentacle attack on all creatures within 20 feet of it.

Actions

Tentacle. *Melee Attack:* +4 to hit, reach 20 ft. *Hit:* 6 (1d8+2) bludgeoning damage. If the target was attempting to climb out of the well, it must make a **DC 13 Strength** or be knocked back into back into the well. If the target is outside the well, it must make a **DC 13 Dexterity** saving throw or be pulled into the well.

- Epilogue - The Forest Gate -

From the well, it is only a short few days travel to the edge of the woods. The company emerge into blazing sunlight and a refreshing breeze. From here, Baldor intends to travel south to trade with the Woodmen and the Beornings; these lands are protected by Beorn's folk, so there is little danger of bandits and he no longer needs the company's services. He thanks them and pays them what he promised. The company have passed through Mirkwood and lived to tell the tale. Wilderland lies before them!

Fellowship Phase

If a Fellowship Phase follows this adventure, then the company could continue with Baldor to Woodland Hall and stay there, to possibly turn the hall into a sanctuary. Once there, they might consider returning the shard of the axe *Wolfbiter* to their rightful owners, the Woodmen of the House of Woodland Hall. If they do so, they are invited to meet their Council of Elders, and then presented with gifts worth 20 silver pennies each. Moreover, from now on they can consider both Woodland Hall AND the nearby Woodmen-town as Sanctuaries.

– Of Leaves –
& Stewed Hobbit

for heroes of level 2 or 3

- **When:** This quests fits best at any time during summer or autumn, in any year from 2946 onwards.
- **Where:** The adventure begins at the Easterly Inn, a new establishment on the road from the Old Ford to the Forest Gate of Mirkwood, and then leads across the Great River to the High Pass.
- **What:** A caravan of goods and supplies from the Shire has failed to arrive on time, and the innkeeper, one Dodinas Brandybuck, Esq., newly arrived in the Wild, fears for his brother's safety. The characters are asked to look for signs of the caravan and ensure the safety of Dinodas Brandybuck and the trade goods.
- **Why:** The new Easterly Inn could be a haven for travellers or even a Sanctuary for the player characters if it survives, so protecting the inn is a good deed for all who adventure in the Wild. More prosaically, Dodinas offers a small sum of money and other treasures if the companions find his brother.
- **Who:** The object of the quest is Dinodas 'Dindy' Brandybuck, the younger brother of the innkeeper.

Adventuring Phase

This adventure is divided into six parts, comprising the initial Audience at the inn, the journeys to and from the High Pass and the dangers encountered there.

Part One – The Easterly Inn
The first part of the adventure describes how it came to pass that a Hobbit opened an inn in the middle of the Wild, the history of the Brandybuck brothers, and the fate of the missing Dinodas. The Easterly Inn is described in detail, as the company may return here again and again on their travels.

Part Two – Searching The High Pass
This section deals with the journey across Wilderland to the foothills of the Misty Mountains and the High Pass. The company encounter several dangers on this journey, and pass through the ruins of a town built many centuries ago. They find signs that the caravan was attacked.

Part Three – Battle at the Ringfort
The company comes upon the survivors of the caravan, and aid them in a desperate battle against a Goblin host. The company is victorious (or else perish in the battle!), but discover that the Goblins carried off Dinodas as they fled.

Part Four – Under the Hills
Following the Goblin kidnappers brings the adventurers into the tunnels under the Misty Mountains. After braving these dark passages, they find that the Goblins have imprisoned Dinodas with an unbreakable chain.

Part Five – The Goblin Feast
The reputation of Hobbit cooking has reached even the caves of the Goblins, and they demand that Dinodas cook them a feast. The adventurers can use this feast to trick the Goblins into fighting amongst themselves, or to steal the key and free Dinodas from his bonds.

Epilogue – Back to the Inn
After rescuing Dinodas, the companions return to the Easterly Inn for their reward.

– Part One –
The Easterly Inn

In a hole in the ground there lived a Hobbit. Four Hobbits, in fact, with a fifth coming to join them. The Hobbit in question was one Dodinas Brandybuck, formerly of Buckland in the Shire, but now a resident of Wilderland. Above the newly-dug hole there was a newly-built inn, so new it still smelled of sawdust and paint, and the whitewashed walls were actually white and not yellowed with pipe-smoke and spilled beer. He lived in the hole with his wife Agatha and his two young sons, and there was a branch of the hole awaiting the arrival of his brother Dinodas.

Dodinas – or Dody, as his friends called him (and he had a knack for making friends) – once considered himself to be a well-travelled Hobbit. He had gone as far as Bree, which for most Hobbits constitutes about twice the journey of a lifetime, and dined out on his tales of strange, exotic folk and unusual customs. On one trip to Bree, in the common-room of the Prancing Pony, he met another Hobbit – the famous (or infamous) Bilbo Baggins.

The two fell to sharing stories, and for once Dody was the one who was flabbergasted and entranced by the other's stories of distant lands. Compared to Bilbo's journey There and Back Again, Dody had hardly stepped outside his front door. After several hours and several pints, Bilbo invited Dody to visit him at Bag End for dinner the following Sunday. Dody brought his younger brother Dindy and his wife Agatha along.

The dinner involved several bottles of wine and more tales of Wilderland, as well as innumerable courses. Dodinas declared that he was determined to outdo Bilbo, Dinodas climbed on the table and sang a story about giants, Bilbo enthusiastically showed them his collection of maps and diaries, and Agatha... well, Agatha sipped her wine and thought about practicalities. When Agatha Took married Dody Brandybuck, everyone assumed that the steely young Hobbit-maid would drum some sense into the notoriously eccentric and wild Brandybuck, and ensure that he found a business or craft to occupy his days. However, Agatha was a Took, and there is a latent streak of adventure and wanderlust in that family.

None of the three Hobbit gentlemen could quite remember how it came to pass – again, a good deal of wine was involved – but a curious plan was formed. Since the successful Quest of Erebor and the defeat of the Dragon, a new era of peace and prosperity had fallen on the North. There was much more traffic on the Forest Road than before, thanks to the watchful eyes of the Beorning-folk and the revived Kingdom of Dale. These travellers and merchants would need somewhere to stay along the road. The plan was that the two brothers would build, open and run an inn on the road between the Old Ford and the Forest Gate – quite close to Beorn's Hall, where no evil thing dared go.

Bilbo gave the two brothers some money to start the inn, as well as several letters of introduction to various dignitaries and persons of importance that he had met on his travels. The two brothers set off from Buckland a few weeks later, still slightly dazed. They crossed the Misty Mountains without incident, and presented themselves at Beorn's house. Beorn ignored the letter of introduction, but was amused by the Hobbits' presumptuousness (the barrel of beer carried all the way from the Golden Perch might also have helped matters), and gave them leave to build their inn.

A Homely house

The Easterly Inn is situated near a little brook that flows out of Mirkwood towards the Great River, approximately twenty miles south of where the Forest gate opens along the eaves of the wild wood. A small stone bridge arches over the babbling waters, and just beyond that stands the inn. The Easterly Inn (Dindy jokes that it is the eastern-most outpost of the Shire) consists of a small but comfortable wooden inn containing the common room and a few guest rooms for Big Folk, some outbuildings and stables, and the Hobbit-hole beneath, where Dindy, Dody, Agatha and Dody's two young sons live.

Although it only opened a few months ago, the inn is gaining a reputation as a good stopping point for journeys west of Mirkwood. The beer is good, the food is excellent, and Hobbits make wonderful hosts (even when their homes are invaded by thirteen dwarves and a wizard, as Bilbo proved some years previously). In truth, the success of the inn has less to do with Dody's beer or even Agatha's delicious food, and owes more to Beorn's promise of protection and the curiosity of travellers come to see the strange Halflings. Still, if someone comes to shelter from bandits, and stays for the food and the soft feather beds, that is still silver in Dody's pocket.

Indeed, if the inn survives, it may become the heart of a new village, just as Bree sprang up at the crossroads around the Prancing Pony.

Folk of the Inn

Dody Brandybuck: The owner and bartender of the inn, Dody is exceptionally gregarious and friendly, even for a Hobbit. He could talk the hind legs off any creature in Middle-earth; if Dody had ended up in Gollum's cave instead of Bilbo, then he would have lost the Riddle-Game, but the Dwarves would have found Dody by following the noise of a drunken Gollum singing about fish. He is everybody's best friend.

Dindy Brandybuck: Dody's younger and more nervous brother. Unlike his garrulous sibling, Dindy never wanted to travel in the Wild. He always dreamed of opening an inn, but assumed it would be in Buckland or maybe the Eastfarthing, not over the edge of the Wild. Still, if things keep going smoothly, then the Easterly Inn could make the fortune of both Brandybuck brothers, and he could move back to the Shire in a few years with chests of silver and gold, just like Bilbo Baggins.

Last spring, Dindy returned to the Shire to obtain vitally needed supplies, such as handkerchiefs, umbrellas, spice-racks, silverware, barrel-spigots, feather-bolsters and round doors, as well as trade goods like pipe-weed and Shire-beer (which, to be honest, could also be counted as 'vitally needed supplies').

Agatha Brandybuck: Dody's wife, a quiet woman of Tookish blood. She is much more sensible and hard-working than Dody; she lets him keep the customers entertained while she organises the rest of the business. For example, she buys supplies off the Woodmen and the Beornings – and even, rarely, the Elves – and sees to the security of the inn. Underneath her businesslike, bustling demeanour, she's absolutely enchanted to be out here in the Wild meeting all sorts of strange folk.

Her two sons **Dando** and **Rodry** both run wild around the inn and the surrounding countryside. She intends to send them to foster with relatives in the Shire in a few years.

Frier: Frier is a Dwarf tinker-smith who has travelled the roads between the Misty Mountains and the Iron Hills for years. He helped build the inn, and has signed on as their carpenter/blacksmith/farrier/assistant bartender/woodcutter and general axeman in residence. Frier is fond of the Hobbits and fonder still of the money they pay him. After many years of wandering, the Easterly Inn is a good place for him to rest his feet.

Shadrach: A stray dog that was 'adopted' by the Hobbits – or, more accurately, that adopted them. Shadrach is actually one of the wonderful dogs who serve Beorn; Beorn asked the dog to keep an eye on the Hobbits and bark if anything truly dangerous menaced the inn. Shadrach spends his days playing with the Hobbit boys or lazing in front of the fire, but always keeps one ear cocked for danger.

The Adventure Begins

The adventure begins when the company arrive at the Inn. News of the new inn has likely reached them as they travel through the Wild, as wayfarers often share news of good stopping places and shelters. This may be the first time any of them have visited the inn. Hobbit adventurers may know the Brandybuck brothers already (and may have even travelled with them in the past, or even be part of this madcap scheme to open an inn in the Wild). The lights of the Easterly Inn shine with a warm welcoming light in the gloom as the company approaches. It is late summer, but the dusk air has a chill in it that heralds the changing of the seasons. A dog strolls out of the twilight to sniff the characters' hands and see if they are worth barking about. Inside, the inn is half-full. At one table, there are a trio of Beornings with great tankards of ale and a big plate of Agatha's sausage rolls; these Beornings are hard, fierce men, forged by long years battling for survival in the wild, but Agatha still insists they use napkins. At another table, the innkeeper Dody is talking to some Dwarf travellers. He leaps up and greets the company when they enter.

A good bed for the night can be had for 2 silver pennies, and heroes of lesser means can sleep in the common room as long as they're buying food (5c a plate) or drink (3c a pint). Hobbit adventurers will be offered rooms in the smials beneath the Inn. Anyone succeeding at a **DC 10 Charisma (Performance)** check gets a drink bought for them by the Beornings, who appreciate music.

Rumours at the Inn

A successful **DC 10 Charisma (Persuasion)** check gets the characters some gossip. The Dwarves just crossed over the mountains from the west, and they bring stories about Goblins. It seems that Orcs are creeping south once more from their fortresses under Mount Gram and Mount Gundabad, and travellers in the High Pass are once again under threat of their attacks. One of the Dwarves speculates that something will have to be done about the matter, and wonders aloud if King Dáin or one of the other rulers of the North will act. The victory won at the Battle of Five Armies should not be thrown away through lack of vigilance. A more cynical Dwarf argues that the Misty Mountains are far away from Dale, and that this new era of prosperity and brotherhood will soon wither away and the Free Peoples will once again grow suspicious and insular. A successful **DC 13 Wisdom (Insight)** check notices that the innkeeper seems concerned by this news, and while he remains jocular and friendly, his demeanor now conceals his worry. In time, Dodinas approaches the company.

1 Dodinas' Plea

This encounter is weighted in favour of the adventurers, as the innkeeper wants a favour from them. It follows the standard format for Audiences.

Motivation

Dodinas wants the adventurers to go looking for his missing brother.

Expectations

+2: Heroes do heroic things (the Company agree to aid him without asking about a reward)
+1: Hobbits stick together (+1 if there is a Hobbit in the party, or if anyone mentions the deeds of Bilbo Baggins)
-1: 'Tis Evil in the Wild to fare (anyone suggests that Dindy is already dead)
-2: Big folk are greedy (the Company demand a larger reward than he can readily afford)

Introduction

Once the company is comfortably sitting in the inn, and they have eaten, Dodinas approaches them with a tray of drinks. He carefully selects the drinks from his cellar to appeal to the different adventurers, so Hobbits get a pint of beer from the Shire, Elves are served fine wine, Beornings get mead and so on. He is clearly trying to curry favour. The characters can introduce themselves with either a **DC 13 Intelligence (Traditions)** or **Charisma (Persuasion)** check.

Interaction

Dodinas then inquires about what business might have brought such a company of adventurers to visit his inn. He listens attentively to what the companions have to say about themselves. The Hobbit is preparing for his own speech, the one he will deliver as soon as he thinks he has figured the adventurers out; he will adjust his words depending on how the characters presented themselves: if during the introduction they used **Intelligence** to recite their deeds and lineages, then he approaches them formally with what amounts to a business proposal; if they used **Charisma**, then he introduces his request as a favour between friends.

Dody gives the company a brief history of the Easterly Inn. He name-drops shamelessly, referring to Bilbo Baggins as his 'business partner and chief investor'. He explains that his brother Dinodas ('Dindy') went West earlier in the year, and was supposed to return by late summer. Dindy sent word some months ago, saying that he had arrived and was gathering supplies for the long journey east. Since then, Dody has heard nothing of Dindy.

Dodinas asks the company if they are travelling west, and if so, will they set his mind and ease and look for signs of his brother. If they seem willing to help him, he offers the companions a reward, a prize proportional to the impression they made on him. Use the Expectations given above, and modify the Final Audience Check accordingly.

The hero can once again use **Intelligence (Traditions)** or **Charisma (Persuasion)** as modifiers.

Outcomes

Failure: Dodinas isn't in a position to say no, so he offers the characters 40 silver pennies each. However, the negotiation is so fraught and bitter that all characters gain a point of Shadow.

Success by 0-1: Dodinas needs the adventurers, but he fears he is wasting his money on them: he offers a small purse of coin, 20 silver pennies each.

Success by 2-3: The Hobbit adds some family silverware to the recompense, bringing the reward up to 40 silver pennies for each companion.

Success by 4-5: Apply the results of 2-3 below; moreover, Dodinas trusts the company and adds free lodgings for all companions and their direct relatives at the Easterly Inn for the winter. He also promises that he will consider their future employment as caravan guards.

Success by 6 or more: Dody is impressed. Apply the results of 4-6 below; additionally, Dodinas gives them the letters of introduction written by Bilbo (see box below). If asked, Dody shows the company the letter he received from his brother earlier in the year. In it, Dindy describes how he has arrived in a village called Bree and started

---

Letters of Introduction

Bilbo wrote several letters for the Brandybuck brothers before they left the Shire. These are very impressive legal-looking documents, sealed with red wax on fine paper and written in Bilbo's best handwriting. The letters start off with lengthy greetings to the recipient, reminding them of their past associations with Mr. Baggins, and then ask that the recipient 'give aid, shelter, hospitality, assistance, friendship, trust and all manner of like good favour to the bearer of this missive'. Four such letters remain in Dody's keeping – one addressed to King Dáin, one to the Master of Lake-town, one to King Bard, and the last addressed to 'Gandalf the Wizard, also called the Grey Wanderer, of No Fixed Abode But Usually Where There's Trouble, Middle-earth'. The other letters (to Elrond, Beorn and the Lord of the Eagles) were already used or lost along the way. The bearer of such a letter may use it in an Audience to use the starting attitude of the letter-writer in place of their own. For example, a Letter from Bilbo would allow a character to be treated as a Hobbit for the purposes of determining starting attitude (it should be noted that Gandalf considers Hobbits Favoured). Furthermore, the letter ensures that the Audience will, at minimum, be counted as a success - even if the bearer of the letter fails the final check, they will still get something as a reward. Each letter can only be used once.

to gather supplies and guards for his journey. Based on the date, Dindy should have arrived at the Easterly Inn if he set off within a month of writing the letter as he intended to do; adventurers know that journeys rarely go smoothly, and that Dindy may have suffered unexpected but quite ordinary delays. Still, if he does not arrive within the next few weeks, then something may indeed have happened to him. It is dangerous to go travelling in the Wild when the autumn wind blows, and even more so when winter comes. According to the letter, Dindy should be travelling with half-a-dozen Men.

- Part Two - Searching the High Pass

If the companions agree to look for Dindy, then Frier the Dwarf suggests they set out by heading south to the Old Ford, and then march due west to the High Pass.

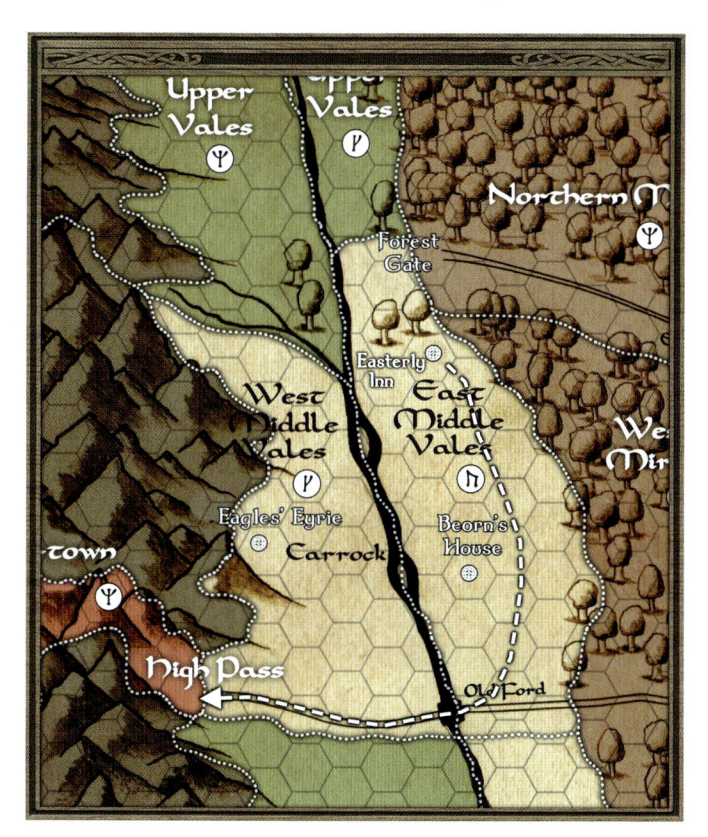

The Journey
The first leg of the journey covers ninety miles south to the Old Ford, but the going is easy as the company marches through the grassy plains and gentle countryside of the Beornings. Alternatively, they can travel west and take boats down the Great River; boats can be obtained from the Beornings, but doing so is expensive (5 silver pennies per boat for the hire) and requires a **DC 15 Charisma (Persuasion)** check.

After the long trek south, the company must cross the river and travel another seventy miles or so west along the road. The distance between the Easterly Inn and the Old Ford is 90 miles, requires about five days, and will provoke 1d2 Journey Events.

The trek from the Old Ford to the High Pass is 60 miles, takes two days to complete (thanks to the road), and will generate 1d2-1 Journey Events.

From The Easterly Inn to The Old Ford
The first few days of the journey are pleasant and easy. An unexpected last gasp of summer brings a series of warm days, and the path leads through the rushes and meadows of the river's flood plain. When the companions come upon the Old Forest Road, they will know it is time to turn west towards the distant grey haze of the Misty Mountains.

The journey has a Peril Rating of 1; roll 1d2 for the number of Events at **DC 13**. Refer to the **Wilderland Adventures Journey Events Table** starting on page 143.

Upon Reaching the Old Ford
The crossings of the Old Ford are kept by Beornings. The company may pass after paying a small toll (5c per head, any Beornings can make a **DC 10 Intelligence (Traditions)** check to waive the fee for themselves only). The guards remember the strange Hobbit-folk, but have heard no word of the caravan.

Don't make an Arrival roll yet; wait until the Company arrive at the High Pass.

From The Old Ford to The High Pass
After crossing the river, the travel becomes harder in places. The route passes through several marshy sections, and the companions can see that the road – such as it is – is supported by piled stones. In some places, though, the old road has succumbed to the bog and the company must follow a newer, more winding path that navigates

around muddy pools and bog land. Sometimes they come upon lines of stones or even walls that mark some ancient border. The Beornings keep the road in repair as best they can, but they cannot build as well as Men once did.

The Peril Rating for this part of the journey is 2; again, roll 1d2-1 for Challenges on the way. Refer to the **Wilderland Adventures Journey Events Table** starting on page 143.

The Mountain Ruins

After their long journey, the company arrives in a region marked by ancient walls and ruined arches. Most of these walls fell long ago and there are hardly more than two or three stones still piled on each other, but it is clear from marks in the ground and the old lines of the path that a town once stood here.

A **DC 13 Intelligence (History or Lore)** lets a companion guess that these are the ruins of some Mannish town, built earlier in the Third Age. Those cities lasted only a brief span of years – the Necromancer's reach grew long, and tore them down, and the Woodmen returned to the wild. The road leads to what must have once been a wide square in the heart of the town; from the marks of fire-pits, other travellers have made camp here in the past, and there is a mountain-brook nearby to provide water. It looks like a good camp-site, but a successful **DC 15 Intelligence (Shadow-lore)** check gives the character an eerie feeling about this place, as if evil lingers here still.

If the company want to find a better resting place, their scouts need to make a successful **DC 20 Wisdom (Survival)** check to find another campsite. Otherwise, they must stay here.

The Night-Wight

The companions were right to be wary. A horror haunts these ruins, a Night-Wight. If the company lie down to sleep in the ruined square, then they are in danger. In the middle of the night, the Night-Wight creeps out from its lair and sneaks up on the adventurers.

Have the Night-Wight make a **Dexterity (Stealth)** check and compare the result to the Look-out's passive Perception. If the wight wins, it automatically places one of the company in an enchanted slumber and carries him off to its lair. Continue making checks for the Night-Wight until the Look-out spots it or realises that he's the only member of the company left!

Once a Look-out spots the Night-Wight (or if the Look-outs are the only members of the company left) then he realises that some of his companions are missing, and battle is joined.

Fighting the Night-Wight

Few of the weapons that the heroes wield will prove very effective in defeating the Night Wight. But the bright light of torches will do more harm than cold steel. You might foreshadow this by describing the wight as a thing of shadow, with seemingly little substance. It shies away from any fire that the companions have, and attacks with either its **Wicked Spear**, or its **Spells of Despair**. If it seems that any hero is trying to make torches it will viciously attack them with either its long spear or its **Strangling Claws**. Once the heroes begin to overwhelm it with torches, it will flee rather than face the bright light and burning flame.

The Wight's Prisoners

Those kidnapped by the Wight are dragged away to the brook nearby. There, the wight submerges them in the muddy banks of the river, pushing them into boggy graves so that only the victims' faces remain at the surface. They are entombed alive in the clinging mud.

Once battle is joined with the Wight, the victims may use their action in order to make a **Wisdom** saving throw in order to awaken. This starts at **DC 14** and is reduced by 2 at the end of a round. An awake hero may make a **DC 10 Strength (Athletics)** check to escape the mud. Otherwise, the hero remains Restrained by the mud.

A hero who was buried in the mud is considered to be temporarily at Disadvantage when attacking, until he takes a round to scrape off the clinging, chilling grave-dirt.

After the Battle

If the company defeat the Night-Wight, then the next morning they can search for its treasure. A successful **DC 12 Intelligence (Investigation)** check lets the company find the ancient remains of a warrior buried in the bog. Little remains save bones and rags, but there are a few gemstones in what must have once been a fine neck-torc: these gemstones are worth 100sp.

Night-Wight

A shadow came out of dark places far away...

The Night-Wight is a thing of shadow, haunting the remains of a warrior who once fell into corruption. It attacks using a wicked spear with a barbed head, and will resort to using its deadly claws if disarmed.

Night-Wight
Medium undead

STR	DEX	CON	INT	WIS	CHA
12 (+1)	15 (+2)	16 (+3)	10 (+0)	13 (+1)	15 (+2)

Armour Class 14 (Wraith-like)
Hit Points 45 (6d8+18)
Speed 30 ft

Damage Resistances Non-magical bludgeoning, piercing and slashing
Damage Vulnerabilities Fire
Skills Perception +3, Stealth +4
Senses darkvision 60 ft, passive Perception 13
Languages Westron
Challenge 3 (700 XP

Craven. If the Night Wight starts its turn with 22 or less hit points, it must make a DC 10 Wisdom saving throw. On a failure, it is Frightened and must use its Dash or Disengage action to move away from any enemies. If movement is impossible, it will take the Dodge action.
Fear of Fire. The Night Wight is fearful of fire. If a torch or other flame comes within 10 feet of it, the Wight suffers Disadvantage on its attack rolls.

Actions

Wicked Spear. *Melee or Ranged Weapon Attack:* +3 to hit, reach 5 ft or range 20/60 ft, one target. *Hit:* 6 (1d6+3) magical piercing damage or 7 (1d8+3) magical piercing damage if used with two hands to make a melee attack.
Strangling Claws. *Melee Attack:* +3 to hit, reach 5 ft, one target. *Hit:* 4 (1d6+1) magical slashing damage.
Spells of Despair. As an action, the Wight can force one target within 30 feet to make a **Wisdom** saving throw with the DC equal to 10 plus the target's Shadow score. If the target fails the saving throw they become Frightened of the Wight until the end of its next turn.

Searching For The Caravan

After passing through the ruins of the town, the company enter the foothills of the Misty Mountains. The caravan should be nearby. Call for **DC 10 Wisdom (Survival)** checks as the day progresses; if successful, the companions find Goblin-tracks, and later they encounter a pony that has obviously escaped its harness and fled in terror. The pony has a Goblin-arrow sticking out of its hind-quarters. A successful **DC 10 Wisdom (Medicine)** check lets a companion remove the arrow, which fortunately is not poisoned and did not inflict any permanent injury on the poor terrified creature. As twilight comes closer, the company spot a big bonfire on a nearby hilltop – they have found the caravan, and just in the nick of time! Dindy and his guards have taken refuge in an old ringfort on the hilltop, and the Goblins are coming...

– Part Three –
Battle at the Ringfort

The company has only a few minutes to make it to the ringfort and meet with the members of the caravan before battle is joined, so they had best make those minutes count!

The Ringfort

'Fort' is too grand a term – this old fortification consists of a ring-shaped earthen bank around the hilltop. There was once a small settlement here, possibly a watch on the pass or a shepherds' cabin, but it has long since vanished leaving only a few stones as traces. The earthen bank is still in moderately good condition, and will give the characters an advantage when it comes to defence. There are only two easy approaches up to the ringfort, so the Goblins will have to come up those mountain paths, and as long as the company defends these approaches, they stand a good chance of holding the fort against the enemy.

Characters manning the walls of the fort against foes outside have Advantage on their attacks. The walls also give half cover (+2 AC) against enemies coming up the path. Characters blocking the two gaps into the fort do not gain these bonuses, but the gaps are so narrow that only one enemy can engage them at a time.

A successful **DC 12 Intelligence (Investigation)** check uncovers an old souterrain (an underground passage) that runs from the middle of the ringfort to a spot outside the walls. The passage is choked with roots and dirt, but

Wilderland Adventures

the ringfort

One square equals 5 feet

a companion could wriggle through with a successful **DC 12 Dexterity (Acrobatics)** check. The passage is of no use as an escape route in this situation, as the Goblins see better in the dark and would chase any would-be escapees on the hillside, but the discovery of the passageway is important nonetheless. Firstly, the Goblins might try to creep up the passageway and attack from the defenders' rear, so the adventurer may wish to block the entrance with heavy stones. Alternatively, a brave adventurer could use the passageway to sneak out of the ringfort when battle is joined, and attack the Goblins from behind.

The Caravan

There are five travellers in the ringfort. There is no time for proper introductions, so the caravan leader (Iwgar) hastily greets the company and explains the situation.

The Hobbit Dinodas Brandybuck: Poor Dindy is exhausted and terrified by his ordeal, and even the news that his brother sent the company to find him brings him little relief. He is polite, in the way that only a desperate, terrified Hobbit can be. (*"I'm most grateful that you could stop in for tea! Very grateful indeed! But as we've got some uninvited guests coming, I do hope you'll excuse me while I hide under these boxes!"*) It is clear that Dindy will be of little use in the coming battle, so Iwgar has ordered him to keep the fire in the middle of the ringfort blazing.

Iwgar Longleg: The caravan leader and guide, Iwgar is a Beorning who travelled west. He is cursed with a great wanderlust, and has even gone to see the Sea. He wears a cockle-shell in his hat. He led the caravan over the mountains, and is the best warrior and guide in the party. Unfortunately, a poisoned Goblin-arrow caught him in the flank last night, and he is clearly suffering from it. Unless a hero is able to prepare a poison antidote (either a **DC 20 Wisdom (Medicine)** check or an appropriate ability), Igwar cannot fight. If he can, treat him as a Warrior (*Loremaster's Guide*, page 71)

Andy Blackthorn, Bill the Bowman, Tom Lumpyface: Three young men from Bree-land, in the West, hired to protect the caravan. None are experienced warriors, and they are all harrowed by the Goblin attack. They have all sustained some cuts and injuries, and are clearly very tired, but they can still fight. Treat them as Town Guards (*Loremaster's Guide*, page 68).

Their Tale

Dinodas and his travelling companions were late leaving Bree. There are always delays when travelling, especially with a heavy load. They journeyed across the land towards the mountains without incident, and climbed up the slopes to the High Pass. As far as they knew, the mountains were still mostly free of Goblins, so they did not hasten, but instead took the easiest route through the pass. Two nights ago, Iwgar spotted a Goblin spying on them. Since then, they have been beset by Goblin attacks. The worst came last night. They managed to beat the creatures back, but lost their ponies and most of their supplies and trade goods. Fearing that they would not make it to safety if they stayed on the road, Iwgar headed to this easily-defended ringfort to fight.

Their Plight

Now the travellers – and the companions – all face the same danger. This fort is the most defensible spot in the hills around here, and if they can hold it all night, then they can make their escape down the mountainside the next morning in the bright light of day. There are more Beorning warriors in the foothills, and the goblins will not dare pursue the caravan any farther east. The numbers of Goblins have increased each night since the first encounter – one on the first night, many more on the second, and Iwgar expects a whole host of them tonight. Already, in the gathering gloom, the companions can see shapes skulking out there.

Tactics

Iwgar's plan is simple: to keep the fire in the middle of the ringfort burning, and to hold off the attackers for as long possible. The Goblins will mostly approach by the two easy paths up the hillside – Iwgar intended to split his forces between these two points, but now that the companions are here, they can take one side of the fort and he and the Breelanders will guard the other.

A successful **DC 10 Intelligence (Shadow-lore)** check confirms that this is a good plan, although the Goblins will probably send lightly armoured skirmishers around the side, and that it would be wise to dedicate one or two warriors to dealing with these attackers. It also suggests that making a run for it would be suicidal.

The Enemy

From their vantage point on the ringfort walls, the companions can see Goblin-shapes sneaking through the dusk and hear the howling of wolves. There are lots of Goblins out there, mostly smaller scouts (Misty Mountain Goblins, see the *Loremaster's Guide*, starting on page 102), but a few bigger brutes (Orc Soldiers and Goblin Archers, see the Loremaster's Guide pages 103 and 104) and Wolves.

- The heroes will face one Orc Soldier for every companion, plus their leader Ubhurz, who does not join until at least one orc is slain..

- The Goblins and the Orcs are a **Weak-willed Alliance**. If Ubhurz is slain, all goblins automatically flee.

The Challenge

Before battle is joined, the enemy leader – a big Orc – shouts a threat to the defenders of the ringfort.

"Rragh! Trapped in your little circle like rats in a grave! I am Ubhurz, and I am here to kill you – but if you throw out your swords and spears, and give up, then maybe Ubhurz will let some of you go!"

One of the Breelanders, young Andy Blackthorn, moves to throw his sword over the wall and surrender. The adventurers may deal with this as they wish; they might use a **DC 13 Charisma (Persuasion)** check to rally Andy's spirit, or give him Inspiration, or issue a counter-threat to Ubhurz with a **DC 15 Charisma (Intimidation)** check – or just decide the time for talking is over, and fire an arrow at the Orc!

The Goblin Tactics

The Goblins' plan of attack is a simple one – send a wave of sword-fodder to swarm the defenders and drive them back from the wall, and then the big Orcs follow up behind them.

If the company has not discovered the secret souterrain, then the Goblins find the outer entrance as they advance up the hill. The Goblins then send four of their number through the passage, to attack the company from behind at the worst possible moment (or, alternatively, they kidnap Dinodas via the passage – see The Kidnapping, below).

Battle!

With a roar of vile battle-cries and a hail of Goblin-arrows, battle is joined. The goblins toss their spears at Iwgar and the Breelanders and the Orc Soldiers do the same for the heroes. Then they swarm up and over the dirt walls and along the paths, attacking with their bent swords!

Battle Events

The Loremaster should apply the following battle events at appropriate moments.

A Rain of Arrows

Goblins outside the ring fort keep firing arrows over the banks. These attacks are not aimed at any particular target; they are firing to keep the defenders off balance. Each round of combat, pick a player character at random and roll an attack on him (+4 to hit, 5 (1d6+2) piercing damage).

The Wolves Beyond The Walls

The howling wolves do not participate in the battle unless one of the company slips out via the secret passage.

Goblin Skirmishers

If the company have not secured the secret passage, or if the Loremaster wishes to make the fight harder, then a few Misty Mountain Goblins manage to climb over the steeper sides of the hill and climb over the banks. These attackers swarm in and attack the companions from behind, or else cause other problems like kicking over the bonfire and plunging the ringfort into darkness.

Dread Ubhurz

The last Orc to join the fray is dread Ubhurz himself, the Orc leader. He too scales the side walls like the Goblin skirmishers, then charges into the rear of the company wielding his mighty scimitar. Ubhurz is a huge Orc of the Misty Mountains, an infamous hunter and mercenary. Unlike the other Goblins in this host, he does not make his lair in the caves nearby – he travels the mountains in search of blood and gold. Ubhurz is an Orc Guard (page 104 of the *Loremaster's Guide*).

Victory!

If Dread Ubhurz is defeated, the remaining Goblins – if any – flee the hilltop in terror.

The Kidnapping

As the Goblins go shrieking into the night, and the survivors bind their wounds, the company hears a muffled cry of alarm. A pair of Goblin stragglers crept into the ringfort and grabbed Dinodas Brandybuck! The unfortunate Hobbit is half-way down the mountainside before the companions notice he is gone.

The company can chase the Goblins, but before they reach Dinodas, the Goblins duck into a cave mouth and vanish into the tunnels.

> ## Averting the Kidnapping
>
> Some Loremasters prefer to let everything be ruled by the whims of the dice, and always give the players a chance to stop their foes from acting. The advantage of this approach is that the players never feel like their fate is out of their hands; the downside is that if the players are quick and lucky, they can rescue Dinodas before the Goblins get underground.
>
> If you favour this approach, then players who possess Distinctive Qualities like *Keen-eyed*, *Quick of Hearing* or *Wary* might be allowed to make a DC 20 Wisdom (Perception) check to spot the Goblins grabbing the poor Hobbit. Then heroes who are *Nimble*, *Reckless* or *Swift* might be allowed to make a DC 20 Strength (Athletics) check to sprint down the hillside and reach the kidnappers before they enter the cave.
>
> If the companions do thwart the kidnapping, skip Parts Four and Five and move right on to Part Six!

– Part Four – Into The Mountains

After the fight, Iwgar and the Breelanders are all too badly injured and exhausted to pursue Dinodas. They beg the company to rescue the Hobbit.

If the company did not see Dinodas's abduction, a successful **DC 10 Intelligence (Investigation)** check lets a hero find Goblin tracks going into a nearby cave. Iwgar knows these mountains are riddled with tunnels and caves. He suspects that the Goblins are heading for one of their underground halls with the loot they stole from the caravan the night before. He doubts the Goblins will return to the surface tonight, not after the bloody nose they got in the Battle of the Ringfort, but unless the companions rescue Dinodas immediately, the poor Hobbit will doubtless perish.

The Tunnels

There's nothing to do except follow the Goblins. At the back of the cave is a narrow, noisome passage that winds steeply down into the rock. Rivulets of icy-cold water make every footstep treacherous, and the whole place smells of bat droppings. Climbing down the passage leads down to a tunnel that slopes more gently downwards and heads west towards the roots of the mountains – although working out that they are facing West requires a a successful **DC 13 Wisdom (Survival)** check.

It would be very, very easy to get lost down here, but in the distance, the companions can hear grotesque singing echoing up the tunnel. The Goblins are marching back through the tunnels to their Goblin-hall, and they are singing as they go.

> ## The Goblin Song
>
> Goblins live down in the caves,
> Ain't had nothing to eat for days!
> Empty bellies, sharpened teeth,
> Sharp blades in a blackened sheath!
>
> Goblins are a courteous folk
> Always polite and real well spoke!
> After a fight when we're the winner
> Bring the foe back home for dinner!
>
> Dwarves is tough and mostly beard.
> Elves are stringy and taste weird.
> In better times we eat Man-flesh
> Smoke it, cook it or eat it fresh!
>
> Put the Hobbit in the pot!
> Eat him up, we'll have the lot!
> Bring him to the Goblin feast!
> Bring him to the Goblin feast!

> ## Journeys in the Dark
>
> Travelling underground can be more or less dangerous than a journey on the surface, depending on where you are. When passing through Moria, for example, the Fellowship travelled forty miles underground between the evening of the 13th of January and the afternoon of the 15th – and that included their stop by Balin's tomb, Gandalf taking some time to decide which way to go, and the battle with the Balrog! However, Moria was in its day a great thoroughfare between West and East, and travelling though it was comparatively easy in terms of terrain. The Dwarrowdelf is full of long straight passages and staircases. Adventurers in Moria can travel quickly – the problem, of course, is not getting lost!
>
> By contrast, natural caves are extremely difficult terrain. With no light, no sure footing, many opportunities to get lost and lots of narrow passages to squeeze through, a company would be lucky to travel more than a few miles for every arduous day they spent underground.

Darkness and Light

Having a good source of light is vitally important when travelling underground. A companion caught in the pitch darkness is at a great disadvantage. Luckily, Iwgar can supply the company with torches. There are two torches for every hero, but they do not last indefinitely, and can be extinguished accidentally.

The Journey Through the Tunnels

The Goblin hall is only a few miles away, but it still takes the company the better part of a day to make their way through the tunnels.

First, the company's Scouts must pass a **DC 15 Intelligence (Investigation)** check to follow the Goblins. If these tests are failed, then the company is lost for a day in the tunnels. Next, Due to the terrifying conditions, each hero must make a **DC 18 Wisdom** saving throw, gaining 1 Shadow on a failure.. Finally, all companions must make a **DC 16 Wisdom (Survival)** check as they trudge through the echoing passage. Anyone who fails gains a level of Exhaustion. If more than half the company fail, pick one of the following events.

Event Suggestions

Getting Stuck
The tunnel gets narrower, and narrower, and narrower as it branches off several times. In places, the companions have to crawl or squeeze through little gaps. The Guide must make a **DC 13 Intelligence (Investigation)** check to select the correct tunnel branch. Otherwise, any heroes wearing heavy armour find themselves getting stuck and gain a level of Exhaustion as they struggle.

Falling Rocks
The Scout must open a blocked passageby making a **DC 13 Strength (Athletics)** check. If he fails, he accidentally triggers a small rock-fall and the company is pelted with stones, causing 3 (1d6) bludgeoning damage. If the Scout rolled a natural 1, they are buried alive and must be dug out by their companions, slowing the company more.

Cave Spiders
The company passes into a section of caves where huge Cave Spiders lurk. The company Huntsman may make a **DC 13 Wisdom (Perception)** check to recognise signs of the impending danger; if he fails, then the company blunders into spider-webs and are caught. The Cave spiders are similar to the Attercops of Mirkwood (page 105 of the *Loremaster's Guide*).

Wandering Troll
The Look-out hears something huge moving through the tunnel ahead. A Cave-troll is coming this way, blindly snuffling as it shambles through the mountain. The company can fight the monster, or – much wiser – they can hide if the look-out gave them enough warning. First, the Look-out makes a **DC 10 Wisdom (Perception)** check, then everyone in the company must make **Dexterity (Stealth)** checks to hide. The DC for the stealth tests is 8 if the company have adequate warning, and 13 if they do not. If anyone fails the stealth test, the troll spots them.

Tap-Tap-Tap
Ranging ahead in the darkness, the company hear a noise echoing through the rock from far away and far below.

Tap-tap-tap, it says, tap-tap-tap. The noise is unsettling, and everyone must make an immediate **DC 12 Wisdom** saving throw to avoid gaining a point of shadow.

Treacherous Footing

The tunnel opens up into a chasm. A raging underground river plunges into this pit, falling into the uttermost deeps of the world. The tunnel continues on the far side of the chasm, and a narrow ledge runs along the opposite wall of the chasm to the waterfall. The company can – if they dare – clamber along this water-slick ledge to continue their journey. A wise Guide will advise the travellers to rope themselves together, and then have the strongest companion make the first crossing. The first crossing requires passing a **DC 10 Dexterity (Acrobatics)** check. Failure. Failure means the adventurer falls into the depths and perishes, unless he is roped to other companions (if a hero is lost this way, then all his companions must pass a **DC 15 Wisdom** saving throw or gain one Shadow point for the distressing experience - see Anguish on page 181 of the *Player's Guide*.

Goblin Sentinels

At the end of their journey, the companions arrive at a network of caves where the Goblins have clearly made themselves at home – judging by the raucous singing and the smell, there are lots of Orcs up ahead! The map on page 34 shows the layout of the caves.

Watching the cave entrance (map key no. 1) is a pair of Orc Soldiers (page 103 of the *Loremaster's Guide*). The Orcs have a bottle of fine wine from the vineyards of the Southfarthing that was stolen from Dindy's caravan and are passing it back and forth between them and singing a filthy song about dancing bears. The companions need to deal with the Orcs without raising the alarm.

- **Ambushing the Sentinels:** The guards are drunk, so it is easy to take them by surprise. The DC for **Dexterity (Stealth)** checks to ambush them is 5, reflecting the goblins' inattention. The Orcs try to sound the alarm immediately instead of fighting, so the adventurers need to knock the guards out before they can act.
- **Tricking the Sentinels:** A clever adventurer can exploit the guards' drunkenness, either by disguising the party as an Orc patrol, or by convincing the guards to fight each other with a **DC 20 Charisma (Deception)** check.
- **Sneaking Past:** These guards are not very attentive, and can be avoided with a a **DC 5 Dexterity (Stealth)** check.

Alarums!

If a Goblin shouts out a warning, then the alarm is raised. If the Goblins do sound the alarm, then the rest of the tribe come staggering out of the feast. The Goblins are drunk and merry, and armed with dinner forks and steak-knives (1 piercing or slashing damage, respectively) instead of bows and spears, but that does not make them any less dangerous. Quite the contrary, in fact! The Goblins are hungry, and will try to eat the companions alive! Each goblin now has the Biter special ability, see page 118 of the *Loremaster's Guide*. There are countless Goblins in the feast-hall, so standing and fighting is not an option. The company might be able to carve their way through the crowd to the chief, kill him, steal the key, and then escape, but they will be hard pressed to do so. Stealth and burglary are by far the better options here.

– Part Five –
Prisoner of the Goblins

The first turning after the guard post brings the companions to Dinodas's prison (map key no. 2). As jail cells under the mountain go, it is a very comfortable one. The Goblins have stacked most of the provisions stolen from the caravan in this room, which also serves as the Goblins' kitchen and larder. There is a roaring fire with a spit and a stove on it, lots of stolen pots and pans, a spice-rack, roasting-tins and egg-timers, knives and forks and skewers and spoons and all the rest of the kitchen implements that were supposed to end up at the Easterly Inn. Meat sizzles and roasts in a dozen different ways.

In the middle of it all sits a very miserable Dinodas, busily chopping potatoes. Even the arrival of the companions to rescue him does not lift his spirits. "It's very kind of you to try to rescue me," he says, "but I fear it's quite impossible. Look!" He holds up his hairy foot, and the companions see that he is chained to the wall. "The chief Goblin locked me in here. They demand that I cook them a feast... and I think I'm the pudding!"

- **The Chain:** The chain was not forged by Goblins. Any character with the Old Lore specialty, or a Dwarf, can tell this is ancient Mannish work, and the chain is made from forged steel, unbreakable without the proper tools. Picking the lock is equally impossible; the only way to escape the chain is to unlock it, and the chief Goblin has the only key.

If the companions suggest to Dinodas that they cut his foot off, he faints on the spot, and can only be revived with a strong cup of tea, a sit down and a successful **DC 10 Wisdom (Medicine)** check.

Cooking Time!

As the characters are speaking to Dinodas, a Goblin voice roars up the tunnel, "Where's our dinner? 'Urry up, we're starvin'!" If the companions are to avoid raising the alarm, they need to prepare a feast for the Goblins. Dinodas can do most of the work, but anyone with the **Cooking** specialty can help and keep the Goblins from noticing the intruders.

The Goblin Hall

1. Guard Posts: There are two guards standing watch at each of these posts, just like the two the company passed on the way in. Most of the other guards are not quite as sloshed as the first two, though!

2. The Larder: Where poor Dinodas is chained. The small alcoves along the wall contain the gnawed remains of some other prisoners.

the Goblin hall

One square equals 5 feet

3. Wine Cellar: Where the beer and wine from the caravan is stored.

4. Feast-Hall: The main chamber, supported by several rock pillars (see page 96 of the *Loremaster's Guide*). See *The Feast*, below.

5. Goblin-Caves: Small caves where the Goblins live, full of filth and chewed bones and stolen trinkets. These areas have Low ceilings (see page 95 of the *Loremaster's Guide*). Most Goblins are in the feast-hall.

6. Smithy: Where the Goblins forge their knives and arrow-heads.

7. Goblin Chief's Chamber: The Goblin chief resides here, and here is where he keeps the best of his loot. There is a four-poster bed covered in sheep-hides, a fine shield stolen from some dead mountaineer and a Dwarf-made mirror so the chief can admire his toad-like features. The chamber is guarded by three Orc Soldiers, who are more vigilant than the other guards. They are not drunk, but are instead chewing on the thigh-bone of one of the caravan's ponies.

8. Goblin Treasure Hoard: A small pile of silver and gold coins, ranging from crudely-made Goblin coins to ingots of Dwarven silver, as well as a few other ill-gotten treasures; as a whole, it is worth 200 silver.

The Feast

Goblins are naturally wicked creatures. In any situation, they instinctively know the best way to be cruel and hurtful. Mockery and nasty tricks come to them without a moment's thought. So, when they captured a Hobbit, their minds instantly settled on a plan to mock him.

In the feast-hall, the Goblins have erected long trestle tables for their feast. All the Orcs have napkins, wine glasses, fine silverware, and are behaving like Hobbit gentlemen at a dinner (or rather, how Goblins imagine gentle-hobbits behave). They have looted Dinodas's wardrobe, and some are now wearing torn waist-coats, burst breeches and even a top-hat (a gift from Dinodas's uncle). At the head of the table, the Goblin Chief sits on his throne, giving self-important speeches and toasting everything from Mount Gundabad to the warts on his toes.

- The key to Dinodas's chain is in the Goblin Chief's pocket. He takes it out and toys with it every few minutes when giving a speech.

More Meat!

As soon as the Goblins devour one course, they want more! Every few minutes, a few of the more sober Goblins stumble down to the larder and pick up whatever dishes Dinodas has cooked. Some of this food even makes it back to the feast-hall. Clever adventurers could intercept the Goblins in small groups as they go in search of more food, thereby fighting the Goblin horde in bite-sized chunks instead of all-at-once.

More Drink!

The caravan was laden down with barrels of beer and bottles of wine from the Shire, and the Goblins are drinking their way through them. They have hacked open some of the barrels and watered the beer down shamefully. Only the Goblin Chief's chosen warriors get the good beer and the wine. If the companions want to trick the Goblins into getting even drunker, they can swap the watered-down beer for full-strength barrels or wine. Drunken Goblins wobble over to the wine cellar for refills every few minutes.

Rescuing Dinodas

To save the Hobbit, the company need to obtain the key from the Goblin Chief, free Dinodas, then escape the way they came. Here are three of the likely methods for obtaining the key; the players may invent other schemes to save the day.

Stealing The Key

Stealing the key is, on its own, an impossible task. The companions need to distract the Goblin Chief. They could get the chief drunk by tampering with his wine-cup, or cook a meal so outrageously heavy that the chief gets sleepy after eating it, and then steal the key from his sleeping chambers. They could cause a distraction, say by starting a fight or demanding that the chief give an after-dinner speech, or disguise one of their number as a Goblin, so he can get close enough to pick-pocket the chief.

- Stealing the key requires two **Dexterity** tests (**Stealth** to sneak up, **Sleight of Hand** to steal the key) at a DC of 10 to 15 depending on how cleverly the companions have arranged their scheme.

Sabotaging The Feast

An adventurer would never stoop to using poison, and anyway, Goblins happily eat far worse things than poison. The company could sabotage the feast by making the food so rich it puts the Goblins to sleep, or mixing in strong spices to ruin their digestion. They could sow dissent among the Goblins by putting all the meat on one side of a roasted goat, leaving nothing but skin and gristle on the other, and waiting until the Goblins start fighting over the unfair portions. They could break out the strong wine and get all the Goblins drunk, or distract the Goblins by rolling the barrels of wine down the sloping exit tunnel nearby.

Surprise Attack

Militant companions can take advantage of the situation by charging into the middle of the feast and attacking the Goblin Chief. The company automatically starts with Advantage and the Goblins are Surprised (and possibly Poisoned if they are drunk).

- Most of the Goblins here are Misty Mountain Goblins (see page 102 of the *Loremaster's Guide*), with a few Orc Soldiers (see page 103 of the *Loremaster's Guide*). The Goblin Chief himself is an Orc Chieftain (page 103 of the *Loremaster's Guide*) and likely beyond the strength of the company to defeat after they have dealt with his guards.

Escape!

Once the companions have the key, they can free Dinodas and escape the Goblin Hall. The journey back through the caves is much easier, and within a few hours the company emerges back on the hillside in the bright sunlight.

Epilogue – Back To The Inn

If they survived, Iwgar and the Breelanders were not idle while they waited. They found the scattered ponies, repaired the carts, and loaded up the supplies that could be salvaged. Once reunited with the company, the whole caravan can depart again. The road lies straight east, and the going is easy. Ten days after rescuing Dindy, the company reaches the Easterly Inn and the warmest welcome east of the mountains.

Dody throws a feast in the company's honour. Dindy is shaken by his ordeal, but a few days of good food and soft beds soon put him right. If the company managed to steal some of the Goblins' treasure, they can spend a few coins at the inn buying food and drink for the Beornings and visiting Dwarves, and so improve their reputation in the local area.

The loss of some of the supplies means that Dindy will have to return to the West next year to purchase replacements. If any of the company wish to travel with him, they can find ready employment as caravan guards or guides. For now, though, the beer is good and the company is merry at the Easterly Inn, a little outpost of the Shire in the Wild!

Fellowship Phase

If the company spend a Fellowship Phase completing the *Open Sanctuary* undertaking at the Easterly Inn, then they may count the inn as a Sanctuary in future adventures.

However, if they do not, then the inn falls prey to the growing darkness of Wilderland in future years. By 2951, the inn is destroyed by Orcs out of Southern Mirkwood. Outposts like the Easterly Inn exist on a knife's edge in Wilderland, and it is only through the actions of heroes like the companions that they can survive and prosper.

Kinstrife & Dark Tidings

for heroes of level 3 or 4

- **When:** The company may undertake this quest at any time from the year 2946 onwards.
- **Where:** The adventure begins on the Great River or one of its tributaries, within a short distance of Beorn's Hall. From there, the adventurers travel down the river and search the Beornings' territory for an escaped prisoner.
- **What:** The company finds the bodies of two slain Beornings in a boat on the river. Investigating their deaths brings the company to Beorn's Hall, where Beorn asks them to recapture the prisoner. Travelling to a nearby village, the companions discover that the villain murdered a kinsman and has now fled into the woods, where he has fallen in with evil men from the South.
- **Why:** Beorn himself asks the adventurers to bring the villain to justice. For a Beorning, capturing the escaped prisoner is a matter of honour.
- **Who:** The prisoner was a young warrior named Oderic, and his crime was one of passion. He accidentally killed his kinsman Rathfic in a quarrel over a woman. Now, Oderic has fled into the woods and joined a band of outlaws, who plan to attack the land of the Beornings. Sorrow is piled on sorrow and tragedy breeds more tragedy as the curse of the kinstrife works its baleful influence.

Adventuring Phase

This adventure is divided into nine parts.

Part One – A Funeral Boat
The company happens upon a boat that has run aground on the banks of the Great River. The corpses of two Beorning men lie within, both pierced by many Orc-arrows. The companions discover that there was a third man in the boat, a prisoner, and that the Beornings were warriors bringing him back for trial.

Part Two – Beorn's Hall
The company travels to Beorn's House and delivers the news. The next morning Beorn confirms their suspicions and asks them to find this escaped prisoner and bring him to justice. The companions may choose to wait a few hours before beginning the chase in order to pay their respects to the fallen.

Part Three – The Chase
The company travels south for several days, looking for signs of the prisoner.

Part Four – Kinstrife
The trail leads to the village of Stonyford, where the company learns the tale of Oderic's crime and his strange history. They question the witnesses, and learn that Oderic returned to the village a few nights ago, and may still be nearby.

Part Five – The Chase Continued
The hunt brings the companions across the Great River into wilder lands.

Part Six – Ill-Favoured Men
The company finds signs that a band of outlaws is nearby, and learns that Oderic has fallen in with them. By spying on the outlaws, they see that Oderic is guiding the outlaws – but has he turned traitor, or is he being forced to serve them?

Part Seven – The Outlaw Boy
The companions recapture Oderic, either by appealing to his better nature, by trickery, or by force of arms.

Part Eight – Grim Tidings
With Oderic's aid or without it, the company must choose what to do about the outlaw band.

Part Nine – Judgement at the Carrock
The company returns to Beorn's Carrock and the player-heroes speak at Oderic's trial.

- PART ONE -
A FUNERAL BOAT

While travelling along the Great River in the proximity of Beorn's house, either on the shore or by boat, the company's Look-out spots another boat that has run aground in the thick rushes and weeds on the east side of the stream. Flies buzz around two slumped shapes that lie over the edge of the boat, and a limp arm trails in the water. As the company come closer, they can see the black shafts of arrows sticking out of both corpses and the frame of the boat.

> ### Foreshadowing
> You can make the discovery of the boat creepier by describing it in the right way. Talk about carrion-crows circling overhead, or describe how the arm of one of the dead men beats against the hull of the boat as the current buffets it, thumping like the sound of a drum. Maybe the company come upon the boat in the twilight, where the gathering darkness makes everything uncertain and ghostly, or perhaps a character with a Virtue like Woeful Foresight, Night-Goer or Natural Watchfulness sees signs of the Orc-attack before the boat is discovered.

Investigating, they find:

- The boat is a simple wooden one, and the dead men were clearly making their way up the Anduin. They have few supplies left, suggesting they were nearly at their destination (a **DC 13 Intelligence (Riddle)** check yields the above information).
- The two bodies are both those of male Beornings. From their weapons and clothing, they were warriors of good standing and both of them have silver cloak-pins in the shape of a bear's head. Any Beorning, or a hero that makes a **DC 10 Intelligence (Traditions)** check, recognises these badges as being of a sort given to men trusted by Beorn. They serve as his thanes, his wardens and watchmen.
- A Beorning might recognise one of the dead men as Merovech the Mighty, one of the first warriors to pledge allegiance to Beorn. Merovech was one of Beorn's must trusted allies. Merovech's duty was to travel from village to village, hearing cases and resolving disputes. Furthermore, in cases of serious crimes, it was Merovech's duty to bring the accused to Beorn for justice.
- A successful **DC 10 Intelligence (Shadow-lore)** check identifies the arrows as Orc-arrows.
- Searching the boat lets the companions find several lengths of rope cut jaggedly with a blade. By making a **DC 10 Intelligence (Riddle)** check, heroes can

deduce that someone was tied up in the boat, and escaped by cutting their bonds and jumping into the river. Merovech's sword is missing — maybe the prisoner took it with him as he fled.

- If the companions search the west bank of the river with a successful **DC 10 Intelligence (Investigation)** check, they come upon the remains of two Orcs lying in the mud. Both Orcs were impaled on the same spear! Merovech must have thrown his spear across the breadth of the river with enough force to punch clean through one Orc and kill another one behind the first. That was a mighty throw indeed.

Beorn's house is not too far away from this spot on the river-bank. Any Beorning will know, or a successful **DC 12 Wisdom (Traditions)** check will reveal, that the right thing to do is to bring the bodies of his thanes to Beorn. The easiest thing to do is to use the boat as a makeshift bier, and carry the bodies in it.

Alternatively, they can bury the bodies, mark the graves, and just bring the bear-pins as tokens to Beorn.

Ignoring the Dead

An unworthy band of adventurers, or a party already on a quest, might decide that the fate of some dead Beornings is none of their concern and ignore the boat. If you want to gently nudge the players into investigating the boat, then just have one of the companions suffer from nightmares about being attacked by Orcs while boating on the Anduin. A few nights of guilty, broken sleep should be enough to prompt the companion into visiting Beorn. Another possibility is that the companions go straight after the escaped prisoner, and do not bother visiting Beorn's house. If they do so, skip to Part Three immediately.

- PART TWO - BEORN'S HALL

The hall of Beorn is a day's easy walk from the river, although the company may be weighed down with the burden of the dead. In the middle of the afternoon, the companions find themselves walking across vast patches of clover of different colours; the air is fragrant with the flowers' sweet scents and is droning with the sound of dozens of large bees. Several homesteads can be seen to the north and south, the residences of those who have come to live under Beorn's protection.

By sunset, the company arrives in sight of an ancient belt of mighty oak trees; beyond it rises the high thorny hedge that surrounds Beorn's Hall. A tall and wide wooden gate opens in the thorn-hedge to the north, beyond which a wide track leads south towards Beorn's house and the surrounding outbuildings.

Beyond the Gate

If the company has chosen to carry the dead Beornings with them, when they push open the heavy creaking gate and start making their way towards the house of Beorn, they feel as if they were returning home after a lengthy absence. Their spirits feel uplifted, and even the bodies of the Beornings seem suddenly easier to carry — if they turn to inspect the bodies they are surprised by the expressions on their faces: their facial features are no longer twisted by pain and suffering, but composed and seemingly at peace, as if they were simply asleep. The companions feel the bonds of mutual friendship that ties together their company reinforced by the experience: each hero who is not already Inspired gains Inspiration.

The company is met along the track by dogs, who sniff them and bark excitedly at first, but then grow momentarily quiet as they notice the burden carried by the adventurers. These dogs knew and loved Merovech, and start howling mournfully once they realise he is dead. The adventurers are accompanied by the wailing dogs until they reach the courtyard outside Beorn's hall – a long, low building with several wings and out-houses. Bees buzz sleepily as the dusk sets it. Beorn himself sits on the porch of his house, whittling a piece of wood. Observant characters notice that he is not using a knife to carve the wood – his fingernails are tougher than oak.

Encountering Beorn

The companions are starting at a disadvantage – they are bringing bad news, and that is never the best way to start a conversation. By far the safest thing to do is to deliver the bodies, explain what happened, and wait for Beorn to decide what to do. Failing to meet Beorn's expectations or, worse, demanding a reward is unwise.

Motivation
Beorn wants an honest, direct account of what happened, not weasel-words and guesses. He just wants the facts.

Expectations
+2: I will be shown respect without flattery, courtesy without honeyed words
+1: The customs of the Beornings are to be respected. (Specifically, he expects that the characters brought the bodies of the dead Beornings with them, as opposed to just taking the bear-pins and burying the bodies.)
-1: Strangers are not to be trusted. (Beorn distrusts Elves, Dwarves, and Men from lands he does not know like Rohan or Gondor).
-2: The dead will not be left to the crows. (If the characters brought the bear-pins and didn't even stop to bury the bodies.)

Introduction
Beorn brings the company into his hall and bids them sit down on benches on either side of the long table, while he settles his massive frame into an equally massive wooden chair. Beorn is a giant of a man, dressed in a woollen tunic tied with a simple belt. He wears no jewellery or silver to mark his high standing, and the axe at his side is a plain, unadorned weapon, notched and scraped with a lifetime of use. The only sign that he is a great leader of men and not a lone woodsman is the fact that his hair and flowing black beard are now combed. Those who knew Beorn of old notice a few flecks of grey in his beard, although whether this is due to the advance of age or worry over his new responsibilities is impossible to tell.

If a company spokesman makes a brief introduction of the company, then gets onto more important matters, call for a **DC 15 Intelligence (Traditions)** check. If other heroes wish to add to the formal introduction, Beorn grows visibly impatient.

Interaction
The interaction with Beorn is divided into four sections – *telling the tale, the exchange of news, dinner,* and *arrangements for the night.*

Telling the Tale

Beorn asks for one companion to describe what they saw at the river. The difficulty for this test is based on how the player roleplays; a clear, organised account adds a +1 modifier to the Final Audience Check. If the hero instead spends too much time guessing, speculating or hiding information from Beorn, a -1 modifier to the check is applied instead. Beorn is troubled by the tale.

"Orcs so close to my house – they were either greatly daring, or very, very foolish. Either way, they have killed my men, and that I will not allow. I sent Merovech south, to the other villages along the Great River. I told him to sort out arguments and make sure all was well. I guess, from the sounds of it, that he and Odo were bringing a prisoner back to me for judgement."

Beorn shrugs his hairy shoulders and then continues.

"I never wanted to be a ruler of men, but if they choose to follow me, then they must keep to my laws, and them that break my laws must come before me for a trial at the Carrock."

He then asks about Merovech's purse of silver. Beorn gave Merovech a purse of silver coins when he left on his journey – did the company find it? The purse was already gone when they arrived, taken by the escaped prisoner, but the companions do not know this. Beorn takes any Beornings or Woodmen at their word, but any other strangers must pass a **DC 15 Charisma (Persuasion)** check to give a convincing protestation of honesty:

- If a character fails at the roll, Beorn frowns and looks at him suspiciously, and any further check attempted by the same character will be considered a failure (without the player knowing it), as Beorn now thinks the companion might be a thief and a liar.

Exchange of News

Next, Beorn asks the company for news of the wider world, and offers his own stories in exchange. The heroes can gain a further +1 modifier to the Final Audience Check by telling stories of fighting Orcs or other creatures of the Shadow. Alternatively, if they tell amusing tales of the Hobbits at the Easterly Inn they might receive a +1 bonus as well.

For his part, Beorn relates that he has been troubled lately by news of Orcs crossing his lands from the east, coming out of Southern Mirkwood and making for the Misty Mountains. Some travellers claimed that the growing strength of the Free Peoples has driven the Orcs out of their old hiding places and forced them to flee Wilderland, but Beorn does not think they are so lucky, nor so strong. Something else is behind the movements of these Orcs. (This foreshadows the adventure *A Darkness in the Marshes* on page 77).

Dinner

"All this talking is hungry work!" declares Beorn. He claps his hands, a door at the back of the hall opens, and in comes a whole flock of sheep and several shaggy hounds. The sheep have trays of food on their backs, and the dogs can stand on their hind legs to serve their master. The food consists of fresh-baked bread, a stew of herbs and vegetables, mead, and then honey-cakes for dessert.

The companions are joined at dinner by other Beornings coming from the nearby homesteads. They have been warned of the recent events, and have come to pay their respects to the dead. As wooden drinking-bowls are raised in toast, tales are told of Merovech, Odo and other famous Beornings.

The heroes are part of the wake, and might steer the Beornings away from becoming too grim or mournful. If not, then some begin to weep and other stare glumly into their mead-bowls as everyone remembers the dead. If this occurs, add a -1 modifier to the Final Audience Check.

As the feast ends and people retire to bed, Beorn stands and declares that he must go and think. *"What is to be done? What is to be done?"* he mutters to himself. Call for a Final Audience Check of **Intelligence (Traditions)** from one of the player characters; if that character succeeds, he or she knows that the thing to do is step back and say nothing, and let Beorn come to his own decisions.

Arrangements for the Night

If the companions haven't angered their host, Beorn offers them beds in his hall. Otherwise, he stalks out the door at nightfall, and one of the other Beornings tells the characters they can sleep in the stables. The companions can raise a fuss about this treatment if they wish with a **DC 15 Charisma (Persuasion)** check; if they succeed, then the Beornings let them sleep in the hall. If they fail, then one of Beorn's wonderful horses closes the barn door in their faces, and they have to sleep outside.

During the night, wherever the company sleeps, they hear the noise of some tremendous animal growling and snuffling somewhere by the house of Beorn. Before they can do something about it, the sound swiftly dies away.

- Any hero forced to sleep outside must pass a **DC 15 Constitution** saving throw. Adventurers who fail this saving throw sleep horribly and gain one level of Exhaustion.

The Next Day

The following morning finds Beorn in a much better mood. One of his dogs leads the characters back to his hall, where they find the big man happily making toast and cheese for breakfast. A dozen Orc-helms lie piled on the table; anyone who examines one notices that it is dented as if struck with immense force. Outside the stead, there are a dozen pikes with fresh Orc-heads on them. Beorn puts plates of toast and cheese down in front of the company, and then takes a huge iron kettle off the fire and fills a strange teapot made of some greenish metal and decorated with pictures of birds.

"I was busy last night. A dozen Orcs in my land without so much as a by-your-leave, not that they would ever have gotten my leave to do so. The deaths of a thousand Orcs might pay for the deaths of Merovech and Odo. I would sooner have my friends back, but at least some justice has been done."

"Now, I also found signs – footprints, scents, the night-speech of bird and beast – that there was a third man on the boat. As you guessed, he was a prisoner, and it looks like he escaped when the Orcs attacked. He went south, and he must be found."

Beorn asks the companions to undertake this quest. The circumstances and the offered reward vary depending on how successful they were during the previous audience with him.

Failure: Beorn grumbles that the companions are stormcrows who bring nothing but bad news, and that if they are ever to be welcome in his lands again, then they

A Nightly Adventure

A Beorning companion possessing a virtue like Brothers to Bears or Night-goer (or simply a curious adventurer!) will almost certainly try to investigate the snuffling and join Beorn in his nocturnal hunt in bear-form. This escapade is up to the Loremaster to improvise, but Beorn will most likely ignore and leave behind any hero not in spirit form, or will attempt to confound any pursuer and get them lost in the wild. A hero possessing the Night-goer virtue might be in for an unforgettable experience, as he joins a troop of spirit-bears as they dance and hunt with Beorn all through the night for traces of what happened to Merovech and Odo. The Next Day (above), contains some information about what Beorn did during the night that might need adjusting to reflect the events of your game.

must complete Merovech's mission. Obviously, fate put the company on the path to finding that boat, and he is in no mood to be picky with fate's offerings!

Success by 0-2: Beorn grudgingly offers a purse of coins as bounty on the escaped prisoner. If the companions find him and bring him back alive, Beorn will distribute that silver among them to a value of 50 silver for each companion, and then send them off.

Success by 3-5: Beorn is impressed with the companions. Apply the results of 0-2 above; additionally, he asks them to undertake this quest as a favour to him, and he will one day do them a favour in return. He bestows his blessing upon them and asks if the companions wish to leave immediately, or if they will attend the funeral.

Success by 6+: Beorn is very impressed. Apply the results of 3-5 above; additionally, Beorn asks that they attend the funeral and speak in memory of Merovech and Odo's final stand. Finally, at the end of the adventure Beorn will be available to be selected as a patron for the company.

The Funeral

The funeral of Merovech and Odo is held that evening. Neither of the two men were married, although Odo was betrothed to a young shield-maiden named Avila who stands quietly with red-rimmed eyes, refusing to weep. If the bodies were brought back to the hall, then they are taken to a line of burial mounds nearby to be interred. Beorn honours his thanes by covering their bodies with two funeral cloths decorated with golden bees. If they were left by the river, then only the first day of the ceremony takes place here, and the next day the mourners will travel down to the river to gather the dead.

The full funeral rites take several days, but the first night is devoted to honouring the fallen. The Beornings tell stories and sing songs of the thanes' heroism and bravery. Beorn watches over the ceremony in silence, but nods gravely when the tales please him. As the companions know the most about how the two warriors died (even though they only found their bodies), they are invited to speak.

- A successful **DC 15 Charisma (Persuasion)** check impresses the crowd, mentioning the spear throw that killed the two orcs reduces the DC to 10. A failed roll means the character cannot find the right words, or exaggerates. The Beornings do not mind boasting, but hate lies.

If the companions act respectfully at the funeral, then they win friends among the Beornings; they are treated as Favoured in interactions with Beornings in the coming year.

– Part Three –
The Chase

Beorn scented the trail of the prisoner on the banks of the Great River – he emerged from the water a short distance downstream, and then headed south along an ancient path. As the companions are unsure how many days passed between the deaths of Merovech and Odo and the discovery of the boat, they do not know how much of a head start the prisoner has. Beorn suggests that the prisoner might return to the lands he came from, the Beorning settlements south of the Old Ford, on the edge of the land of the Woodmen.

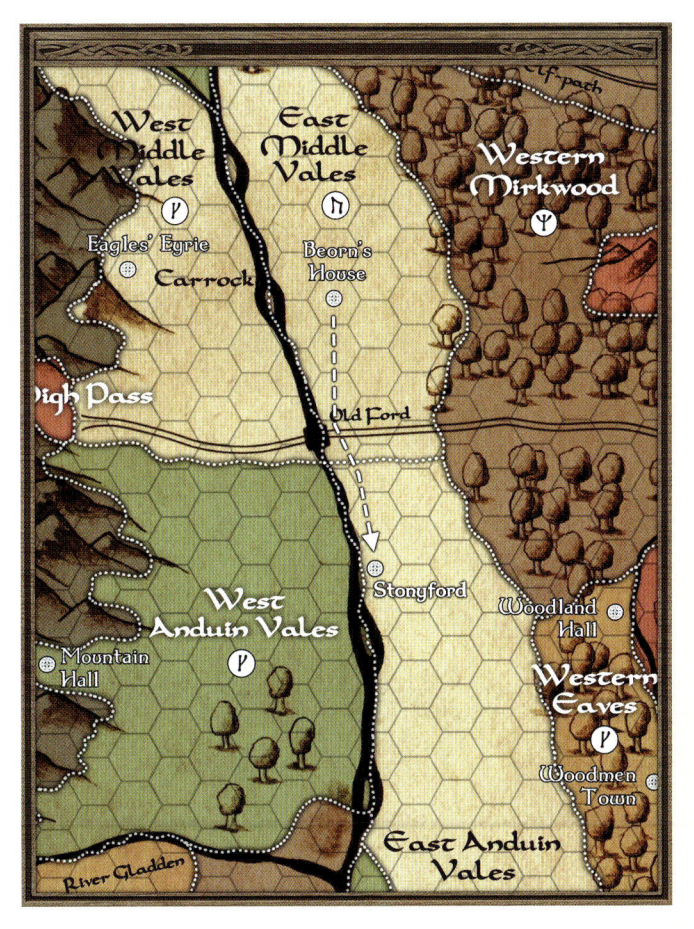

- The journey south is around sixty miles, along open terrain in Free lands. On foot, this should take around three days; if the companions are travelling with mounts or are given them by Beorn, they can make it south in two days. The Peril Rating is 1, and there will be 1d2-1 Events on the way.

In the morning of the second day of travel the company should cross the Road near the Old Ford, where a great bridge of stone once stood, built of old by Men from the south, they say. Another day of marching will bring the company to the vicinity of the Beorning village of Stonyford, and *Part Four* of their adventure.

Planning the Route

The lands around the Old Ford are, in recent days, some of the safest and most-travelled in Wilderland. The Beornings protect this region, and have driven out the Orcs and outlaws who once preyed on the few travellers who passed this way. These are green, bright lands, untrammelled by farms or fences. They are mostly empty, but there are a few isolated homesteads in sheltered dales along the river.

Event Suggestions

The land of the Beornings is usually safe, so the company might expect to face no Events worth the name. However, the Orc band that Beorn fought the night before was not entirely defeated, and there are still a few scattered Orcs abroad in the wild. These Orcs might attack the company at night, or try to sneak up and cut the Look-out's throat so they can murder the rest of the company as they sleep.

Searching for the Fugitive

The company is not travelling with a destination in mind, so there is no set time for an Arrival roll. Instead each Player-hero is allowed to make two skill checks each (using either **Intelligence (Investigation)** or **Wisdom (Perception or Survival)**, each at **DC 15**: every successful check yields some traces of Oderic and lets the company stay on the track. Most of these signs are subtle ones – a footprint here, a path through the meadows there, marks of a campfire and so on, but three are of special note.

- **Dead Orc:** The corpse of an Orc lies at the bottom of a stony gully. The Orc was one of those who attacked the boat; Oderic slew the monster and kicked its body down into this pit. Examining the Orc's filthy remains shows that its head was chopped clean off with a sword, possibly even the same sword of Merovech that went missing from the boat.

- **The farmstead:** The company passes an isolated Beorning farmstead. There, they meet an old man called Geral. If questioned, a successful **DC 10 Charisma (Persuasion)** check reveals that a young adventurer stayed with him a few days ago, and left after one night leaving a silver coin as payment. Geral remembers the young man's name as Oderic and says he was an odd sort, but respectful and generous.

- **Rumours on the road:** The company meets a small band of Woodmen, travelling to Mountain Hall in the far west. They passed through the village of Stonyford recently, and heard tell there of a bloody murder. Some Beorning named Oderic murdered another hunter, an older man called Rathfic. According to the tale, Rathfic caught Oderic in bed with his wife, the two fought, and Rathfic was mortally wounded.

- Part Four -
Kinstrife

There has not been a ford at Stonyford for hundreds of years. The river was passable here once, but no longer. The tumbledown pile of stones atop a low hill were once a watchtower that guarded the road in a time when kings ruled the land. The village remains, though; a few wooden huts that cluster around the foot of the mound by the river. The folk here survive by fishing and hunting, as they have done for many generations. The trail of the escaped prisoner leads to this village, and the circumstances behind his crimes can be discovered here. Unless the company travels by night and avoids the path by the river, the villagers spot them long before they arrive, and the village's elders come out to meet them. The Beornings do not welcome visitors to their lands with ease, so the company must convince the elders to let them enter the village.

Encountering the Village Elders

The three Beornings who face the company are: **Hartwulf**, a greybeard who leans heavily upon a staff, and mumbles when he talks. The villagers call him their wiseman, and believe he knows all sorts of magical secrets – but who knows what he means when he mutters to himself. **Ava** is Hartwulf's daughter and one of the strongest personalities in the village. She is the clan's diplomat and spokeswoman when trading and dealing with outsiders. She mistrusts visitors, and always tries to dissuade them from coming too close to the village. **Williferd**, a warrior who, with the recent death of Rathfic and the disgrace of Oderic, is now the most experienced warrior of Stonyford. He is very nervous about this new honour, and is clearly jumpy. He keeps one hand on his axe-handle at all times.

Motivation

Hartwulf just wants to get through the encounter without too much fuss.
Ava wishes to give a good impression of her village to the strangers.
Williferd is nervous, and desperate to show strength.

Expectations

+2: Beornings can be trusted; other folk less so. (If the companions declare they are on a mission for Beorn immediately or if the company has Beorn's blessing, they are counted as Beornings.)
-1: (Ava only) Affairs are to be kept private. (Ava grows worried if the characters seem too eager to pry into the events that led to Oderic's arrest.)
-1: (Hartwulf only) Discussions are to be kept short. (Hartwulf grows tired if the characters are evasive or longwinded.)
-1: (Williferd only) Swords come easily to the hands of strangers. (He's looking for a fight.)

Introduction

The three villagers introduce themselves first, with Ava doing most of the talking.

"Strangers we do not welcome to our homes. Unless you have business here, you must move on. Woodland Hall is but a few days travel east of here; doubtless you will find better hospitality there. We have suffered enough sorrow in recent days. I beg you, leave us in peace."

Ava is a hardened diplomat and difficult to impress. She imposes Disadvantage upon the **DC 15 Intelligence (Traditions)** introduction check.

Interaction

The first thing the companions need to do is to get permission to enter the village. If they provide a thorough telling of how Oderic escaped and how the companions have tracked him back here, they receive a +1 bonus modifier to the Final Audience Check. If they instead barge into the village without explaining themselves, they gain a -1 modifier. In either case, Ava directs them to an empty house near the river-bank, this was Oderic's house.

- Unless persuaded otherwise, Ava demands they hand their weapons over to Williferd before entering the village.

Once they have permission to enter the village, they can share news. On hearing that Oderic has escaped, the Beornings are alarmed. Ava shakes her head.

"These are grim tidings. Oderic is a murderer and kinslayer. We thought that by sending him to the Carrock for judgement, we were done with his evil."

Her aged father mutters something into his beard about curses and ghosts, while Williferd grips his axe even tighter and looks around warily as if expecting Oderic to jump out from behind a tree. The company can get the same story from Ava as they receive in *Sorrows Old & New*, below, although Ava's version of events is less charitable than some. Ava tells the company that she has heard nothing more of Oderic since he was taken away up the river by Merovech and Odo, but it is possible that someone in the village saw him and said nothing.

Barred From The Village

If the company fail the audience and are not permitted to enter the village openly, then their adventure can continue if they search the lands around the village. They meet one of the villagers, a boy named after Beorn, who tells them that he saw Oderic steal a boat and cross the Great River a few days ago. The adventure continues in Part Five, but the companions now have little hope of redeeming Oderic without knowing how he came to be outlawed.

Sorrows Old & New

The goodwill of the villagers depends on how they did meeting the elders. Choose one hero to make a Final Audience Check using any appropriate skills (**Traditions** or **Persuasion** most likely).

Failure: The villagers offer no welcome, and barely acknowledge the travellers' existence. They are given stale bread to eat. The difficulty for all interactions in the village is set at **DC 15**.

0-4: The villagers give a grudging welcome, and invite the company to share their fires. They are given fish to eat, and the DC for interaction rolls stays at the level of **DC 10**.

5 or more: The villagers greet the travellers as welcome guests! A deer is roasted, and the whole village gathers around to hear news and tell tales. The DC of Interaction rolls is reduced to **DC 5**.

Village Stories and Rumours

Asking about what happened is like opening a floodgate. Everyone in the village has their own opinions about Oderic, Rathfic and Brunhild. Use **Intelligence (Riddle)** checks to get the following information and **Wisdom (Insight)** can be used to weight its truthfulness. Entries in bold are true facts, whereas those in italics are opinions.

Oderic's family were killed by outlaws when he was a young child.
He's been strange since then.
He never stopped practising fighting since that day.

Oderic was fostered by an old warrior called Helmgut, father of Brunhild.
Helmgut treated Oderic like his son.
Helmgut never liked Oderic; he only took him in to honour Oderic's dead father
Helmgut was the best warrior in the village, and he was training Oderic to follow in his footsteps. When Rathfic came to live here, Oderic was jealous
Oderic and Brunhild lived like sister and brother.

Oderic was very close to Brunhild.
Oderic was obsessed with Brunhild, and would follow her around the village.
He would do anything to protect her.
If he came back to the village, she would know about it.

A few years ago, Rathfic came down from the mountains to settle here.
He became the village's chief warrior, and was betrothed to Brunhild.
Rathfic bought Brunhild from her father.
Helmgut was pleased to have Rathfic as a son-in-law.
Rathfic was a great warrior, and an honourable man.
Rathfic was a great warrior, but he was often cruel. He cared only about himself, and treated his wife like a servant.
Oderic always hated Rathfic because he took Oderic's place in Helmgut's heart.
Oderic always hated Rathfic because Rathfic married Brunhild.

One night, Oderic and Rathfic fought, and Oderic killed Rathfic.
Oderic crept into Rathfic's house and murdered him while he slept.
Rathfic caught Oderic in bed with Brunhild.
Rathfic caught Oderic spying on him.
Oderic broke into Rathfic's house and challenged him to a fight.

After killing Rathfic, Oderic surrendered to his foster-father Helmgut, and Helmgut sent Oderic to the Carrock.
Oderic would have fought his way out, but he couldn't bring himself to kill his foster-father.
Oderic would have fought his way out, but Brunhild begged him to stop.
The fighting-madness left Oderic, and he realised what he had done.

The Foster-Father's Tale

Old Helmgut, Oderic's foster-father, lies in his hut with a skin of wine, staring at the woven rushes of the ceiling. Since the murder of Rathfic by his foster-son, he has fallen into a deep despair. The company can question him, but doing so is risky. The old warrior has refused to leave his house since Oderic left the village; he's drunk, emotional and armed with a big axe. If the company go in there to question him, they make get more cloven heads than answers.

Helmgut really doesn't want to talk to anyone other than his wineskin. Courtesy and riddling talk don't work on him; it takes a **DC 15 Charisma (Intimidation** or **Persuasion)** check to convince him to talk.

Helmgut exclaims that he heard his daughter scream, and came to investigate. He found Oderic standing over Rathfic's body, and he immediately assumed that Oderic had killed Rathfic out of jealousy. He struck Oderic, knocking the dagger from the boy's hand. Oderic, he sobs, was always a difficult, angry young man, and while Helmgut tried to raise the boy, he has failed. Now his son-in-law is dead, his foster-son is a murderer, and his daughter refuses to speak to him.

- If the company fail to convince Helmgut to speak, he tries to attack them in a drunken rage - but the old man is too drunk and exhausted to put up a proper fight; he just swings his axe wildly before collapsing into a wine-sodden heap.

The Widow's Tale

Since the death of her husband and the arrest of her foster-brother, Brunhild has attended to her duties as a grieving widow. Every day, she puts fresh flowers on the grave-mound of Rathfic, and lights candles at night to guide his soul to whatever doom awaits mankind. She has become cold and brittle, like a woman of ice.

As the only witness to Rathfic's murder, questioning Brunhild is vital if the company are to discover the truth about what happened. So far, Brunhild has been icily polite but evasive when anyone questioned her, saying only that Oderic had committed a crime and would be judged at the Carrock. This icy demeanour hides her own guilt and confusion – she blames herself for Oderic's actions.

What happened that night?

Brunhild explains that her brother Oderic came to her and said that he was tired of the village, and that he intended to leave and seek his fortune in the wild. No-one in the village other than Brunhild really trusted him, he said, and he was sick of the place. He asked her to come with him – she hesitated, and then Rathfic came home.

The two men never liked each other, and they immediately began arguing. She tried to stop them, and Rathfic struck her in the face, knocking her down. Oderic attacked him, one of them drew a knife, they struggled – and then the knife was in Rathfic's chest, and there was blood everywhere. She screamed.

Shortly afterwards, her father Helmgut came running. He saw Oderic standing there over Rathfic's body, and hit his foster-son with the flat of his axe. Oderic did not even try to fight back; he just dropped the knife and fell.

Was Rathfic a good husband?

Not especially, but neither was he a monster. He and Oderic quarrelled, but Oderic fought with everyone in the village. She loves her foster-brother, but he has a talent for making enemies. Still, the person who is most to blame, she thinks, is herself – she wishes she could have stopped the fight. No-one needed to die that day.

Has she seen Oderic since then?

She hesitates, then nods. Oderic visited her one night, a few days ago. He explained that Merovech and Odo were killed by Orcs, but that he managed to slip away in the confusion. He believed that fate had given him a second chance, and that he now intended never to return to the land of the Beornings. He went west, across the Great River. She does not expect to see her brother ever again.

Optional Complication: Brunhild's Crime

Playtesters suggested an interesting added twist to the dilemma – what if Brunhild was the real murderer? She could have stabbed her husband to protect her foster brother. In this variation, Oderic is protecting Brunhild by taking the blame and fleeing. If the company are unwilling to defend Oderic at the Carrock, then he could confess the truth to them (see page 57).

– PART FIVE –
THE CHASE CONTINUED

If the companions have found the right clues in the village of Stonyford, they will have learned something about Oderic's whereabouts from Brunhild. If they failed to find anything of interest, they might discover that Oderic crossed the river from the fact that a boat has gone missing (see **Signs of the Prisoner** below).

If they are set on the right track, this second chase will take them across the Great River and then south into the woods north of the Gladden Fields. These are ill-omened woods, long a dwelling-place of evil and misfortune.

ACROSS THE GREAT RIVER

The company must first cross the Anduin. If they are on good terms with the Beornings of the village, they can be ferried across. Otherwise, they must either find a way to be granted passage or else brave the river. The frantic current of the Anduin slows as it approaches the morass of the Gladden Fields, so a strong swimmer may be able to cross the water.

- The chase takes the company southwest and then south for forty miles in the wilderness and across sparse woods in the West Anduin Vales (moderate terrain). The route is 40 miles long, and takes roughly three days of march. It has a Peril rating of 2, and will provoke 1d2 Journey Events with a DC of 14.

Planning the Route

As the characters have no set destination, the Embarkation roll will determine how well the search will progress. Use the following chart to generate modifiers to the tests made during the search:

Embarkation Roll Result	Modifier to DC
1-2	+2
3-4	+1
5-8	0
9-10	-1
11-12	-2

For Journey Events, refer to the **Wilderland Adventures Journey Event Table** starting on page 143.

SIGNS OF THE PRISONER

This time, **DC 13 Intelligence (Investigation)** or **Wisdom (Perception** or **Survival)** checks are needed to search for signs of Oderic's movements. Every hero is allowed to make two skill rolls each day, with every successful check revealing a significant sign of Oderic's passage. Every clue leads the company progressively to the south, towards the woods north of the Gladden Fields.

- **The Boat:** One of the first clues found by the travellers is along the banks of the Great River. Oderic stole a boat and rowed several miles downstream before he abandoned it on the west bank. The companions come upon this boat as they search the riverside.

- **The Broken Knife:** Oderic made camp one night on the rolling plains between the river and the wood, and while trying to prize a stone from his boot he accidentally snapped the blade of a knife he stole from Odo's body. The broken shards of a Beorning-made knife lie in a sheltered dell, near the ashes of a campfire.

- **The Fight:** A day or two before the company arrives, Oderic was taken prisoner by outlaws, and the signs of the fight are still visible to those who can read them, at a short distance from the woods. Trampled grasses, splinters hewn from a shield and a broken spear-haft speak of a battle between one warrior and several others. A successful **DC 13 Intelligence (Investigation)** check reveals that the lone warrior put up a brave fight, but was outnumbered and overwhelmed. An especially good roll may reveal that his foes spared his life, bound his hands, and led him off into the woods. A clear trail leads into the forest.

Signs of a Host

When the company finally arrives at the eaves of the forest, a successful **DC 12 Intelligence (Investigation)** check reveals clear signs that a number of armed men are nearby. There are tracks in the mud, trees have been hacked down for firewood and there is no game within several miles. These strangers are not wood-wise and so are unlikely to be Woodmen from Mountain Hall. A successful **Intelligence (Lore** or **Traditions)** or **Wisdom (Perception)** check at **DC 12** suggests that these might be strangers from the south.

- Part Six -
Cruel, Ill-Favoured men

The bandits hiding in the woods are cruel and malicious men, lawless souls who have been easily seduced by the growing power of Mordor. They are thieves, marauders and slavers, with no common cause save wickedness and greed. Some are exiles cast away from the Horse-lords to the South, some come from the east, some from the Woodland tribes, and still others call no place home save the open road. They have come to Wilderland in search of treasure and conquest. Their leader, though, is no mere bandit. Valter the Bloody believes that he is a king.

Valter the Bloody

Valter's ancestor Valind was a knight and close kin to Girion, Lord of Dale, before the Dragon came. When Girion fell, Valter's ancestor took a fast horse and fled the burning city. He travelled to the East, and sired a child on some tavern girl. His son took up his father's sword and armour, as did his son, and his son after him, and with the sword came the dream of kingship. Valter desires to make his own kingdom in the wild, and to rule over lesser men.

For many years, this dream was nothing but an idle fancy, until some dark fate guided his steps and he fell in with a company of outlaws in the south. He rose to lead the band, and brought them north into Wilderland, promising them that they would have land, women, gold, respect and honour when he came into his new kingdom.

Valter is a born leader of men. He can be charming and well-spoken, but he believes that honour and truth are delusions born of listening to too many stories. Only strength and desire matter.

He has a talent for worming out secrets and for finding weaknesses in the character of others. If you secretly nurse some grudge, if some niggling desire gnaws at your soul, if you ever felt that you were not given your proper due, then Valter knows it and promises that he will make everything right – if you follow him.

When his men captured a sullen-eyed Beorning spy, Valter did not have the boy put to death or tortured as some advised. Instead, he freed Oderic from his bonds, fed him, returned his sword and asked him where he came from and how he came to be wandering in the wilds.

Valter intends to begin his conquest with the village of Stonyford. Oderic knows that village as well as anyone, and Valter believes that the young Beorning will be key to his conquest of Wilderland. Today Stonyford, tomorrow more of the land of the Beornings... and who knows what the next year will bring? The Dragon conquered Dale and robbed Valter's ancestor of his rightful place; now Valter is the conqueror!

Valter and the Spirit

If the Loremaster is using the linking story for the adventures (see page 5), then Valter is serving the will of the Gibbet King, who plans to use Valter's attacks on the Free Peoples as a distraction.

Should the company slay Valter, then they find a mummified human head among his possessions (the spirit used the head to let his will be known to Valter).

VALTER THE BLOODY

Valter claims to be the descendant of noble kings, but he would be a bloody-handed tyrant if he ever won his kingdom. His smile is the last thing his foes ever see.

VALTER THE BLOODY
Medium human

STR	DEX	CON	INT	WIS	CHA
16 (+3)	12 (+1)	14 (+2)	13 (+1)	12 (+1)	15 (+2)

Armour Class 16 (corselet of mail, shield)
Hit Points 65 (10d8+20)
Speed 30 ft

Skills Intimidation +4, Survival +3, Traditions +3
Senses darkvision 60 ft, passive Perception 11
Languages Westron
Challenge 3 (700 XP)

Craven. If Valter starts his turn with 32 or less hit points, he must make a **DC 10 Wisdom** saving throw. On a failure, he becomes Frightened and must use his Dash or Disengage action to move away from any enemies. If movement is impossible, he will take the Dodge action instead.

Survivor. If Valter is outnumbered, he always uses the Dodge action. When an opponent misses him, he may use his reaction to make a single melee attack.

Actions

Multiattack. Valter makes two attacks with his longsword.
Longsword. *Melee Weapon Attack:* +5 to hit, reach 5 ft, one target. *Hit:* 7 (1d8+3) slashing damage or 8 (1d10+3) slashing damage if used with two hands to make a melee attack.
Disarming Strike. Valter can aim to strike blows to knock whatever his opponent is holding out of its hand. On a successful roll to hit, his opponent must make a **DC 12 Dexterity** saving throw or drop whatever they are holding. The attack does no other damage.

Reaction

Commanding Voice. Valter can shout inspiring words to his allies. He may use his reaction to utter a command or shout a warning when a non-hostile creature, that he can see within 30 feet, is about to make an attack roll or a saving throw. The target can add a d6 Command Die to that roll, provided it can hear and understand the message. A creature can benefit from only one Command Die at a time, and creatures that possess Commanding Voice cannot benefit from this effect.

Outlaw Archers

Mean, ill-favoured men from the South, armed with bows and knives. Some ride ugly, half-starved horses.

Outlaw Archers
Medium human

STR	DEX	CON	INT	WIS	CHA
13 (+1)	13 (+1)	11 (+0)	11 (+0)	12 (+1)	8 (-1)

Armour Class 12 (leather jerkin)
Hit Points 18 (4d8)
Speed 30 ft

Skills Survival +3, Perception +3
Senses passive Perception 13
Languages Westron
Challenge 1/4 (50 XP)

Actions

Short Bow. *Ranged Weapon Attack:* +3 to hit, range 80/320 ft, one target. *Hit:* 4 (1d6+1) piercing damage.
Knife. *Melee Weapon Attack:* +3 to hit, reach 5 ft, one target. *Hit:* 3 (1d6+1) piercing damage.

Outlaw Warriors

Grim-faced men, veterans of many battles.

Outlaw Warriors
Medium human

STR	DEX	CON	INT	WIS	CHA
14 (+2)	10 (+0)	15 (+2)	11 (+0)	11 (+0)	8 (-1)

Armour Class 14 (hide, shield)
Hit Points 32 (5d8+10)
Speed 30 ft

Skills Perception +3, Survival +3
Senses passive Perception 13
Languages Westron
Challenge 1/2 (100 XP)

No Quarter. When an enemy is reduced to 0 hit points that enemy is considered to already have failed one death save.

Actions

Hand-Axe. *Melee or Ranged Weapon Attack:* +4 to hit, reach 5 ft or range 20/60 ft, one target. *Hit:* 5 (1d6+2) slashing damage.
Spear. *Melee or Ranged Weapon Attack:* +4 to hit, reach 5 ft or range 20/60 ft, one target. *Hit:* 5 (1d6+2) piercing damage or 6 (1d8+2) piercing damage if used with two hands to make a melee attack.

The Bandit Camp

The bandits are encamped in the shelter of the forest, twenty miles north of the Gladden River. There are some fifty warriors in their camp, and more will come from the south if Valter's plans come to fruition. Add in followers, wives, children and slaves, and the full group numbers nearly one hundred.

Valter's tent is easily visible at the centre of the camp, and Valter himself can be seen around the main campfire with his cronies and aides. He keeps Oderic close at hand, and makes sure that the young man always has food and drink and a place of honour at Valter's side – he wants to be sure of winning Oderic's loyalty, so the boy will betray the Beornings and tell Valter all their secrets.

Oderic's own bedroll is at the edge of the camp, where he sleeps under the stars.

Outlaw Patrols

The bandits rely on their patrols to warn them of approaching danger. If the companions can evade or defeat one of these patrols, they can sneak up on the camp and observe it from a close distance without grave risk. Each patrol consists of two outlaw archers and two outlaw warriors.

Spotting the patrol in advance requires a passive Perception of 13 or more (the thick forest makes it easier for the patrol to come upon the adventures without warning). If the characters have advance warning of the patrol, they can choose either to hide (a **DC 13 Dexterity (Stealth)** check, with Advantage due to the thick foliage) or ambush their foes (the outlaws will be Surprised).

Watching for Oderic

From a hidden vantage point overlooking the camp – and there are several excellent and leafy trees in the area – the company can watch the outlaws and identify Oderic. A successful **DC 10 Wisdom (Insight)** check reveals the following:

- Oderic is being treated as an honoured guest by the outlaw king, but the other outlaws watch him suspiciously. He is not a prisoner, but he is under guard.

- One of the outlaws shadows Oderic wherever he goes.
- Oderic sometimes goes walking alone in the woods, followed by his outlaw watcher; if the companions can deal with the watcher, then they could talk to Oderic – or take him prisoner.

By Convincing Oderic to Leave Willingly
Again, the company must deal with the outlaw watchman, but they could then choose to appeal to Oderic's better nature and convince him to aid them against the outlaws or come back to the Carrock for trial.

> ### Sending Word to Beorn
> The company may decide that a whole army of outlaws is much more important than one runaway Beorning, and conclude that their duty at this point is to return to Beorn's stead and warn the Beornings and the Woodsmen of this new danger. Point out that their mission is to recapture Oderic, but if the players are adamant, let them retreat. The battle with the outlaws will be even bloodier in this case.

– Part Seven –
The Outlaw Boy

The company have found their quarry, but now must spirit him away from the outlaw band. There are three ways to do this (and many tactics suggested by the players may be reproduced by customising the suggestions given below).

Openly, by Force
A truly valorous (if lacking in wisdom) company could take on the whole outlaw band in a surprise attack and carry Oderic away. This is not quite as suicidal as it sounds if the company have a few doughty warriors and can move fast. They could attack the camp in the night, grab Oderic, then flee into the trees.

This is the least likely option for most companies. If the players choose this approach, then assume that the outlaw camp has six guards at night, and that every five rounds of combat after the attack begins, another 1d6 outlaws join the fray until the whole camp is roused.

Secretly, by Cunning
The company could lure Oderic away, deal with the one outlaw assigned to watch him, and then knock Oderic out or put a sword to his throat.

Playing Oderic Kinslayer
The young Beorning man is the key character in this scene, so let's take a moment to discuss how best to play him. Oderic is a tragic hero – his great gifts are matched by equally great flaws of character. He wants to be loved, but his dark moods and sullen attitude estrange him from everyone else. Back in Stonyford, the villagers mistrusted him from a young age because of his fey moods and the horrible fate of his parents, and Brunhild was his only friend.

He desperately wanted to prove himself to his foster-father Helmgut but, while Oderic is an excellent warrior, he was no leader of men, which is why Rathfic took Helmgut's place instead of Oderic. Oderic, of course, saw this as a betrayal – and was betrayed again when Brunhild married Rathfic. Convinced that there was nothing left for him in the village, he tried to leave, only to be insulted and threatened by a drunken Rathfic. Oderic never meant to kill the man, but a red mist descended upon him…

When he was seized, Oderic sank into a depression that lifted when fate seemed to intervene and the Orcs killed his guards. He thought that he was free of all his previous entanglements, free to prove that he was not the troublesome orphan boy who caused trouble, but a heroic adventurer. Instead of finding adventure, however, he has fallen in with outlaws. He has let himself be enchanted by Valter, and wants to convince himself that Valter is a kingly man who means no ill to the Beornings – but in his heart, Oderic knows that Valter is evil.

Here, then, is Oderic's dilemma. If he stays with the outlaws, he knows he is doing evil, but the outlaws offer him a place in their camp and the promise of glory. If he returns to the Beornings, he faces trial for a murder that he did not intend to commit, and he will be judged by a people who have always mistrusted and feared him.

Some of the time, Oderic is to be pitied; misfortune is piled on misfortune, and everything he touches turns to ill. Some of the time, he is to be admired; he is a brave young warrior, and could become a great hero if given the chance. The rest of the time, the players should just want to slap him – he's a moody teenager with a big sword who is convinced the world is against him!

The Outlaw Watchman

The chief, Valter the Bloody, ordered one of his most trusted henchmen to shadow Oderic. This watchman is a grim trapper and huntsman from Wilderland named Faron. He never talks except when he is scornful, and never smiles except when he plunges his wickedly sharp knife into something living. In his youth, he was silent as a shadow; he is not as lithe as he once was, but he is still cunning enough to shadow Oderic without the younger man spotting him.

If the company are to speak to Oderic alone, they need to deal with Faron. They might:

- Lure the huntsman away with a trick. It is plain to see from looking at him that he is a cruel man, and while he might raise the alarm if he sees a group of intruders, he would prefer to deal with a lone traveller on his own.
- Ambush him and either kill him or knock him out before he can raise the alarm. Heroes might find any Woodland scenery features they like in their chosen ambush spot.
- Use some ability (**Sleight of Hand** plus **Herb-lore**, perhaps) to drug his ale and knock him out.

Once Faron is dealt with, the company may approach Oderic.

Faron, the Trapper
Faron was exiled from his home when he began to hunt two-legged prey…

Faron, the Trapper
Medium Human

STR	DEX	CON	INT	WIS	CHA
14 (+2)	16 (+3)	15 (+2)	13 (+1)	12 (+1)	8 (-1)

Armour Class 14 (Leather corselet)
Hit Points 52 (8d8+16)
Speed 30 ft

Skills Perception +3, Stealth +5, Survival +3
Senses passive Perception 13
Languages Westron
Challenge 3 (700 XP)

Stalker. If Faron spends at least one minute observing his opponents before attacking, he gains Advantage on all his attacks for the first 1d3 rounds of combat.

Actions
Multiattack. Faron makes two melee attacks.
Spear. *Melee or Ranged Weapon Attack:* +4 to hit, reach 5 ft or range 20/60 ft, one target. *Hit:* 5 (1d6+2) piercing damage or 6 (1d8+2) piercing damage if used with two hands to make a melee attack.

Reaction
Deadly Spear-Thrust. Faron may use his reaction to make a single melee attack against a creature that has just attacked him. If Faron inflicts a critical hit with this ability, the target is knocked Prone as the blow strikes a knee or other joint.
Snake-like Speed (Recharge 5-6). Faron is adept at avoiding injury. He can use his reaction to halve the damage from an attack that he is aware of.

Capturing Oderic

The direct approach is to engage Oderic in combat. While the boy is a skilled and determined warrior, driven by a gushing heart-spring of discontent and hatred, he is only one man against the whole company. Oderic fights with the sword he took from Merovech, putting all the skills he learned from old Helmgut into action. To defeat Oderic, the company can either:

- Reduce him to 0 hit points and knock him Unconscious.
- Reduce him to 1/2 his starting hit points and succeed with a **DC 15 Charisma (Persuasion)** check.
- Disarm him.

Oderic

It can be a great misfortune to be born a hero when your own folk fail to recognise your true worth.

Oderic
Medium human

STR	DEX	CON	INT	WIS	CHA
17 (+3)	15 (+2)	15 (+2)	11 (+0)	8 (-1)	13 (+1)

Armour Class 14 (Leather corselet)
Hit Points 52 (8d8+16)
Speed 30 ft

Skills Perception +1, Survival +1
Senses passive Perception 11
Languages Westron
Challenge 3 (700 XP)

Reckless. Oderic may choose to gain Advantage on all attacks he makes in a round, but all attacks on him gain Advantage until the start of his next turn.
Savage Assault. When Oderic rolls a natural 18 or 19 he may use his bonus action to make a single additional melee attack against the same opponent.

Actions

Multiattack. Oderic makes two melee attacks.
Longsword. *Melee Weapon Attack:* +5 to hit, reach 5 ft, one target. *Hit:* 7 (1d8+3) slashing damage or 8 (1d10+2) piercing damage if used with both hands.

Speaking to Oderic

This is an especially tricky encounter. If the company have not visited Stonyford, they are unlikely to be able to convince Oderic to go with them peacefully.

Motivation & Expectations

Oderic's initial assumption is that the adventurers are rivals in Valter's camp who want to murder him, and demands to be released if held captive – or else he threatens them immediately, demanding they leave him alone. The best introduction is at sword-point here: if the company show they could take Oderic prisoner, but want to talk to him instead of just attacking him, then he will listen to them.

+2: Mentioning Brunhild by name gains Oderic's attention
+1: Hinting that the characters sympathise with his murder of Rathfic
+1: Reminding him of Helmgut's sorrow
-1: Insulting Valter – Oderic is under Valter's spell and mislikes it if the adventurers insult his new master.
-2: Treating him as a criminal

Interaction

Oderic is initially suspicious and mistrustful of the companions. The first thing he wants to know is what they are doing here. A **DC 10 Wisdom (Insight)** check reveals that the boy is fighting against himself; he wants to believe that the outlaws are his friends, but he knows they are bandits and murderers. The company need to make him confront this truth.

Inquiring about Oderic's involvement with the outlaws

Oderic admits that Valter wants him to reveal the secret defences and strongholds of the Beornings. He knows that Valter intends to attack the Beornings, but refuses to admit it to himself. The company can point out the obvious reason why Valter would want to know about the Beornings defenses, beg Oderic to see reason, or inspire Oderic to look within himself. If they do so, add a +1 modifier to the Final Audience Check.

Proposing Oderic returns

Oderic fears returning to the Beornings, as he believes that he will be put to death for killing Rathfic. The company could say they will speak for him at his trial, or convince Oderic that the honourable thing to do is take the consequences of his actions, Beorn might even exile him and he could become a wandering hero. If the companions convince Oderic add a +1 modifier to the Final Audience Check.

Success or Failure

If the heroes succeed at the Final Audience Check, they convince Oderic to admit to himself that the bandits are plotting to attack the Beornings, and that Oderic might still have a place among his kinfolk. Now, they must decide on their next course of action.

- They could bring Oderic with them back to Beorn, but that puts Stonyford in jeopardy.
- Oderic suggests that he could lead the outlaws into a trap by guiding them north, giving the Beornings time to rally an army. This tactic has the best chance of defeating the outlaws, but requires the company to trust Oderic to do his part.

If the company fail the audience, then Oderic violently opposes any proposition and attacks them. The company can still fight back and take him prisoner.

– Part Eight – Grim Tidings

The outlaw band must be stopped, and the company cannot do it alone! If Oderic remains allied with the bandits, or if the company have captured him, then they must flee and bring word to the Beornings as quickly as possible. However, if the company convinced Oderic to lead the outlaws into a trap, then the company must head to Beorn's stead as swiftly as they can to warn the chieftain so he can rally an army.

The Journey

The company is fifty miles away from Stonyford and more than a hundred miles away from Beorn's house.

- Both the trip to Stonyford and to Beorn's house are short Journeys according to the rules, with a Peril Rating of 2. Since time is of the essence, the rules on page 176 of the *Player's Guide* tell us that it would take four days to get to Stonyford, and from Stonyford it would take three days to get to the house of Beorn. Straight from the forest to Beorn requires six days.

Forced March

The company can also press themselves, and march for more hours each day than they would otherwise dare. If the company undertakes a forced march, they halve the duration of each leg of a journey (round fractions up). The same number of Journey events occur, but the heroes cannot benefit from any rests while in a forced march.

- For every day spent in a forced march past the first one each hero must make a **DC 15 Constitution** saving throw. On a failure, the hero gains a level of Exhaustion. The company can stop the forced march at any time, see Interrupting Journeys on page 59 of the *Loremaster's Guide*.

On a forced march, the trip to Stonyford would take the company two days to complete, and would require each companion to make one **DC 15 Constitution** *saving throw. The trek from Stonyford to the house of Beorn also takes two days and requires one saving throw as well. Going from the forest to the house of Beorn directly is three days, meaning each hero must make two* **DC 15 Constitution** *saving throws.*

Clouds Gather

When the company reaches his house, the shapeshifter is quick to react. Beorn may not have desired to be chieftain of a whole people, but when they are threatened, he does not stand idly by.

"These outlaws are a danger to me and my folk, and will be driven from Wilderland. Tonight, you shall sleep in my hall, for we leave for battle at dawn!"

His wondrous horses ride from Beorn's stead at great speed, and bring word of the danger to many Beorning settlements and outposts in the region. Sooner than the companions expected, he assembles a fighting force of Beorning warriors to battle the outlaws. He puts the host under the command of another one of his trusted lieutenants, then vanishes into the wilderness. The Beornings know he will return to them when battle is joined.

Oderic's Fate

If Oderic is in the company's custody, he begs to be allowed to participate in the coming battle. He swears that he will return to the company if they free him for the duration of the fighting. If the company convinced him to go with them willingly, then Oderic is as good as his word – after the battle, he returns to them to face his judgement at the

Carrock. If they took him prisoner by force, but treated him fairly and convinced him to stand trial honourably, then he will also return after the battle. However, if they captured him by force and treated him as an enemy, then he throws himself into the fray and dies heroically in battle.

The Battleground
The location of the battle depends on the previous actions of the company:

Oderic guides the outlaws against the Beornings
Oderic brings the outlaws to a stand of trees on the west bank of the Great River a few miles north of Stonyford. There, they make rafts and sail across the river by night; at a spot he shows them where the crossing is easy. They attack Stonyford the next morning. Beorn's army arrives too late to save the village, and battle is joined in the ruins of the settlement. See the map on the front end papers.

Oderic is a prisoner
Without Oderic to guide them, the outlaws must travel north to the one safe crossing spot they know – the Old Ford. There, on the banks of the Anduin, they meet Beorn's army and fight. See the map on the front end papers.

Oderic tricks the outlaws
If the companions convince Oderic to lead the bandits into a trap, then he brings them north in the direction of the Old Ford, but convinces them that the best way of travelling without being noticed is to follow him into a steep-sided valley called the Gloomy Fold, near the ford. Travelling through this stony valley puts the outlaws at a disadvantage – it slows them down and lets the Beornings trap them. See the map on the front end papers.

BATTLE IS JOINED!
The companions are not the commanders of the Beorning forces in the battle – their time to command will come in another adventure (see page 118). However, they do fight on the front lines. Depending on the circumstances, they face either a band of blood-thirsty outlaws flush with victory or a tired band of foes. The enemy is the same in either case, but the side that holds the upper hand varies by the field of battle.

- Battle at Stonyford: The outlaws have Advantage in the first d4 rounds of combat.
- Battle at the Old Ford: Neither side has Advantage.
- Battle at Gloomy Fold: The Beornings and their allies have Advantage in the first d4 rounds of combat.

In their section of the battle, the company faces one Outlaw Warrior and one Outlaw Archer per hero (see page 51)

In the Fray
The swirling melee of a large battle is confusing, and there are foes all around. Enemies lurch in and out of range; new foes join the fight and wounded enemies fall back. The ground underfoot becomes red-slick with blood.

If the companions defeat their foes, then they break through the outlaw lines and see Valter the Bloody, the outlaw captain. Valter leads his army from the rear, and when Beorn shows up (see below), he turns tail and runs.

The only way for the companions to catch or kill Valter in the battle is to break through the lines, and then engage him in combat until Beorn arrives.

If Oderic sided with the outlaws, then the company find him at Valter's side. However, when Beorn arrives and Valter flees the field, then Oderic remains and dies fighting either the companions or Beorn.

Beorn! Beorn!
At a key moment of the battle, just as the outlaws seem about to rally, the Beornings start beating their spear-butts on the ground and chanting 'Beorn! Beorn! Beorn!' over and over. As the chanting reaches a crescendo, a hulking shape appears at the flank of the Outlaw forces. Beorn has arrived, wearing the shape of a giant bear.

If the bandits were charged by a storm made flesh, the effect could not be more devastating. Some of the outlaws throw down their weapons and surrender; others are crushed or torn to pieces by the wrathful bear.

The battle is soon over.

AFTER THE BATTLE
With the outlaws defeated, the companions can bind their wounds and attend to the fallen, while they learn about the fate of the other combatants.

Oderic

If the company freed Oderic to fight in the battle, then he either returns to them as he promised, or else sells his life dearly in battle. If he sided with the Outlaws, then he is most likely dead unless the companions took him prisoner. If he tricked the Outlaws, then he survives the battle and is captured by the Beornings.

Valter The Bloody

The outlaw chief escaped death and vanished into the wild – unless the company were able to break through the enemy lines and catch him, in which case Beorn's wild attack kills him.

Brunhild & Helmgut

If the battle took place at Stonyford, then both of Oderic's relatives perished in the fighting. Otherwise, they attend the trial.

- Part Nine -
Judgement at the Carrock

The Beornings are a simple people, but they know their law. Cases are brought before a clan chieftain or before Beorn himself for judgement. Speakers on both sides may argue for their cause, trying to curry the favour of the listeners. But since Beorn is the source of all law, ultimately everything depends on the judge.

If he lives, Oderic is brought before Beorn for judgement to answer for his crimes. If he sided with the outlaws, then Beorn makes a summary judgement, and the companions need not be involved at all. However, if Oderic was brought back as a prisoner, or if he tricked the outlaws, then the case is not so clear-cut. He killed Rathfic – but how should he be punished for this crime?

The Trial

Beorn settles himself on a stone at the Carrock, overlooking the silver thread of the moonlit Anduin, and listens to his followers.

Motivation

Beorn wants justice. He is not a cruel man, not neither is he a kindly one. He will weigh the evidence given to him and see what the best thing to do is.

Expectations

-4: If any of the characters attempt to lie, they must pass a **DC 15 Charisma (Deception)** check. Regardless of success or failure, the so-called hero gains a point of Shadow.

Introduction

The companions do not need to introduce themselves here. Ava is the first to speak at the trial, and she introduces Oderic's case for all to hear. She describes how Oderic was always a strange, troublesome boy, how he was jealous of Rathfic, and how he broke into Rathfic's house and killed him. She then calls on Helmgut to describe what he saw, and Oderic's foster-father mumbles a few words about how he found his son with a knife in his hand standing over Rathfic's body.

Beorn then asks if anyone else wishes to speak. If the companions wish to intervene, or if they want to push Brunhild into speaking, now is the time.

Interaction

It is up to the heroes to speak for or against Oderic. They can use **Charisma (Persuasion)** to speak of his heroism. They can call Brunhild or Helmgut as witnesses and interrogate them with **Intelligence (Riddle)**. They can appeal to Beorn's mercy with either **Charisma (Persuasion)** or **Intelligence (Traditions)**. They can reflect that Oderic's aid turned the tide of battle using **Wisdom (Insight)**, if appropriate.

Each argument can be used once, each requires **DC 15** to succeed. Each successful argument adds +1 to the Final Audience Check, each failure applies -1.

Judgement

When everything is said and done, one character may make a final argument with an **Intelligence (Traditions)** check to resolve the audience. Regardless of the result, Beorn sighs and learns forward. "Kinslaying is the worst of crimes" he rumbles, "and this boy certainly murdered Rathfic."

Failure: "I am sorry, but the law is clear. Oderic is to be cast out of the lands of the Beornings, never to return east of the Great River, condemned to live as an outlaw, an Orc or a Warg, in the shadows of the Misty Mountains. Every free man is given the right to slay him, would he defy his exile and dare to return."

Success by 0-5: "Oderic fought bravely, but he is still guilty of a crime. He is condemned to pay a man's worth in gold to Brunhild and her father Helmgut, or serve as their thrall for life."

Success by 6 or more: "Your words have moved me. I think Oderic did not mean to kill Rathfic, and while he acted unwisely, he was not the only one to do so. We will be merciful."

Oderic accepts his fate stoically, no matter what happens.

Aftermath

Regardless of what happens at the trial, Beorn thanks the companions for recapturing the prisoner and warning him of the outlaws. He gifts them, if they ask for it or if it was previously agreed-upon, with 50 silver each. If they did especially well, he promises them the friendship of the Beornings for as long as there are honest men in these lands.

Fellowship Phase

This is an excellent opportunity for a member of the company to gain Beorn as a patron, or to open Beorn's house as a sanctuary.

- those who - tarry no longer

for heroes of level 3 or 4

- **When:** The company may undertake this quest at any time in any year from 2946 onwards. Thematically, it works best during the autumn of the year, when the leaves of Mirkwood turn yellow and red.
- **Where:** The adventure begins in the eaves of Mirkwood, anywhere along the forest's northern edge or along the western border as far south as Rhosgobel, but ideally near the Forest Gate.
- **What:** The company are called upon to escort an elven noblewoman from Mirkwood to the High Pass.
- **Why:** The Elf-woman asks the company to serve her, and offending so powerful an Elf would be unwise.
- **Who:** Irimë is a High Elf of the house of Gil-Galad. She has lived in Middle-earth since the days of the First Age, and now tires of the world. She is travelling West, to the Havens and from thence to the Undying Lands.

Adventuring Phase

This adventure is divided into seven parts.

Part One – The Borders of the Forest
While travelling, the companions meet a band of Elves, including Legolas, son of Thranduil and Galion. They are asked to escort Irimë to the High Pass, where she will be met by the sons of Elrond.

Part Two – Weary of the World
The company travels across Wilderland, and Irimë speaks of the history of the land and her sorrow. The companions suspect they are being followed by Orcs.

Part Three – The Hill of Woe
Waylaid by an Orc-host, the companions fight to survive until they are rescued by the Eagles.

Part Four – A Guest of Eagles
The company spends a night in the Eyrie, and Irimë speaks of the growing shadow over Middle-earth.

Part Five – The Ruins
The Eagles bring the company back to the High Pass, where they wait for the sons of Elrond. While the companions slumber, Irimë is attacked by an evil spirit, and the company are drawn into her struggle in their dreams.

Part Six – Dark Dreams
While trapped in the wraith-world, the dreaming companions are thrown into the pits of Dol Guldur. If they can sustain their hope, Irimë may prevail.

Part Seven – Dawn in the West
If Irimë survives the night, she bids the company farewell and offers her blessing for the dark days to come.

The Long Memory of the First-born

If there is an Elf among the companions, the first encounter with Legolas and Galion unfolds differently, and the Elf would already know or have heard of the lady Irimë. Before the game begins, take the player of the Elf aside and tell him what he knows about Irimë.

Irimë of the House of Gil-Galad is one of the most respected courtiers of King Thranduil's court. She is a Noldorin Elf, and was close kin to the rulers of the kingdom of Lindon. It is said that she wove the cloth of Gil-Galad's shining banner. She came east with Thranduil after the War of the Last Alliance, and brought light to the Elvenking's halls for many years. In recent centuries, it is said that Irimë grows weary of the mortal world, and more and more her heart turns towards Valinor in the Uttermost West, where most of her kin now dwell. When Irimë seeks the solace of the Grey Havens, Middle-earth will be forever diminished.

– Part One –
The Borders of the Forest

This encounter may happen at any time when the company are in or near Northern Mirkwood. They might even be on another errand when they meet the Elves.

You can foreshadow this encounter by having the company see signs of Orcs, such as footprints or young trees hacked down with swords for no reason other than destructive malice. The company might even run into Goblins as an Event on their Journey.

- Before the Audience begins, check for passive Perception from the company's Look-out or Scout. The DC for this test is 15 – only the truly wood-wise can detect the tread of Elves in the forest. If the check is successful – or if there is an Elf in the company, or someone with a Wisdom of 16 or more – then the Elves greet the companions openly. Otherwise, the first sign the company see of the Elves is when they suddenly find they are surrounded by archers in the trees.

A Chance Meeting

One of the Elves steps forward to parley with the company. If the companions have had dealings with him before, they recognise Galion, Thranduil's former cup-bearer. If there are Elves in the company (or again someone with a **Wisdom** of 16 or more), then Galion asks them to speak with the lady Irimë and Prince Legolas; skip onto *The Lady's Request*, below. Otherwise, Galion addresses them in a hostile tone.

"You trespass in the Woodland Realm, mortals. We thought you Orcs at first by your smell. Lucky for you we stayed our hands, or you would be dead now. Tell me, have you seen Orcs in your travels. A band of them is nearby. They are hunting us, and we are hunting them."

Galion

If the company dealt with him before, then he may be more friendly – or less! – depending on how that encounter went. Galion wants news of the Orcs and of conditions on the road west. Anyone making a successful **DC 10 Wisdom (Insight)** or **Intelligence (Lore)** realises that it is unusual for an Elf to take such an interest in the wider world, and that Galion must be planning a journey.

Asking questions of Galion is unwise, as he sees it as prying into elven affairs. However, if the company are courteous, he does reveal that a large number of Orcs – *"...powerful Mordor-Orcs, not Goblins from Hithaeglir!"* (the Misty Mountains) – came out of the Heart of Mirkwood some weeks ago and have harried his company ever since.

After a few minute's talking (or if the company impresses Galion), he brings them to meet the leaders of the Elves – see *The Lady's Request*, below. If they were especially polite, he gifts them with travelling supplies including waybread and fresh water before they leave (the company automatically gets a result of 7, *Feasts Fit for the Kings of Ancient Times*, on their next Embarkation roll.).

The Lady's Request

Two of the Elves stand apart from the rest, and both seem... brighter, perhaps? Or more solid than the rest? It is hard to put one's finger on it. A companion with **Wisdom 16** or more, or proficiency in **Lore** (or who is an Elf or Dunedain) recognises these as noble Elves.

One is dressed in green and brown, and carries a bow upon his back. He appears young, confident and brave, an Elf-lord in his prime. He is one of the nobility of the Woodland Realm. The other Elf wears a gown of shimmering white and cloud-grey silks, unmarked and untorn despite the thickness of the undergrowth in the forest. Her face is hidden by a grey veil, but her arms are adorned with silver bracelets, and upon her finger a ring glimmers with its own inner light. She must be one of the Noldor, of whom but a few remain in Middle-earth. The pair spend a few moments speaking to one another in the Ancient Tongue.

It is unlikely any of the company speak this language (save those with proficiency in **Lore**, see page 31 of the *Player's Guide*). After a moment, the young Elf-lord turns to the company and bows.

"Greetings. I am Legolas, son of Thranduil. This is the lady Irimë, of the House of Finwë. The lady is journeying west, to the High Pass. It was our errand to take her there, but these Orcs must be driven from our land." He pauses and glances at the veiled woman, then goes on. *"The lady has requested that you bring her the rest of the way."*

Expectations
(Legolas)
+2: Everyone understands the gravity of the charge. (The company swear to defend Irimë with their lives)
-1: A Plague on the Stiff Necks of the Dwarves! (If there are any dwarves in the company.)

(Irimë)
+1: Speak only beauty. (If the adventurers greet her in Elvish)
-1: I have the privacy of my thoughts. (No-one should ask questions of Irimë that she does not wish to answer.)

Introduction
Legolas does most of the talking; Irimë stands impassively, watching the companions as they speak. As they speak, though, her gaze falls upon each of them, one by one, as if reading the intentions of their hearts.

Interaction
The meeting is brief, and the companions will do better to play upon their major strengths if they want to make a good impression. As far as Legolas is concerned, Irimë has made a request of these mortals, and they should carry it out without delay, and be honoured that so great a noble has deigned to entrust her safety to them. The longer he dickers with the company, the greater the chance the Orcs will cause more mischief.

Legolas tells the company that the Lady is travelling to the hidden valley of Imladris, which is Rivendell in the Common Tongue. She has sent word ahead of her coming, and riders were sent out from the Last Homely House to meet her at the crossing of the mountains. The company are to bring her from the edge of Mirkwood to the High Pass.

If the company asks for a reward, the Legolas says that his father Thranduil will recompense them (this applies a -1 modifier to Final Audience Check). If they continue to press, he grows impatient with the mortals (this is a -2 modifier). If they ask about the Orcs, Legolas assures them that none will leave the forest alive. If the heroes thank him for this, grant a +1 modifier to the Final Audience Check.

If the company are courteous and respectful, then Irimë finishes the conversation by casting back her veil, revealing a beautiful and ageless face.

"I am Irimë of the House of Gil-Galad. Elen sila lumenn' omentielvo."

Conclusions
If the companions fail the Final Audience Check, Legolas looks as though he is about to change his mind and bring Irimë to the pass himself, but the lady touches his arm and whispers a rebuke in Elvish. Legolas frowns, but lets Irimë have her way.

If on the contrary, the companions have impressed the Lady, compare their individual actions with the entries below:

Negative Modifier(s): the Lady is not impressed by the adventurer. She will generally ignore the adventurer's presence and won't address them directly, favouring other heroes who achieved a better result during the encounter (if any).

This lack of consideration from such a beautiful and wise creature weighs heavily on the companion.

+1 Modifier: if one or more companions achieve such a result, Irimë is intrigued with their ingenuity. When she speaks, she makes sure she addresses them directly, curious about their reactions.

+2 Modifier or multiple +1 Modifiers: Irimë is impressed. Apply the results as above; additionally, at the end of the adventure the Lady will bestow her blessing on such companions, if they survive, see *Blessed by the First-born* on page 76.

Supper by the Forest Eaves

The Elves travel with the company until twilight falls, then invite them to dine with them. In a clearing, the company find a table covered in a white cloth, lamps that glow with a silver light hanging from low boughs, and a supper fit for Hobbits. The next morning, the Elves are gone, except for Irimë, and she has changed her shimmering gown for more practical travelling clothes, including a heavy hooded cloak that hides her features. Even more curiously, the company find that they are close to the western border of Mirkwood, near the road to the Old Ford, no matter where they thought they were in the forest. Presumably, the company's Guide was wrong about their whereabouts; the alternative is that the company were transported many miles while they slept, which is of course impossible.

– Part Two –
Weary of the World

The journey from the edge of the wood to the Old Ford is done along a well-travelled path. If the company have come this way before (as they may have done if they played through *Of Leaves & Stewed Hobbits*), they gain Advantage on the first skill check made on the journey.

- The journey from the eaves of Mirkwood to the Old Ford should take one or two days, while the trip from the Ford to the High Pass normally takes two days, but this time it might take a day more, as the Lady cautions the company about spending the whole journey on the Road. If there are Orcs abroad, they are likely watching the Road, and in any case, there may be prying eyes about, and Irimë would prefer not to reveal her presence in the Wild.

The Journey has a Peril Rating of 1 and provokes 1d2 Journey Events with **DC 13**.

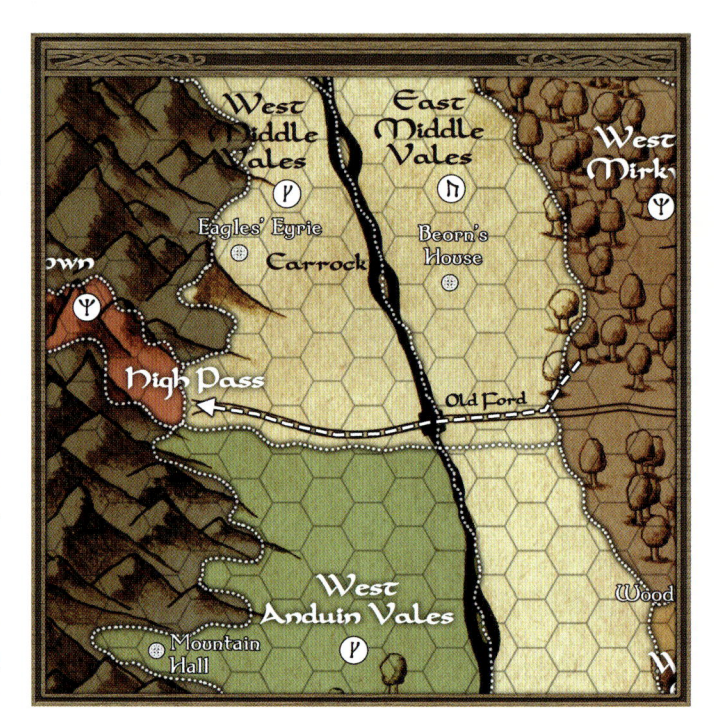

The Shadow of the Past

As the company travels, Irimë speaks only when some feature of the landscape reminds her of the past. Sometimes she sings songs of long-ago battles. While Irimë never directly betrays any emotion, her tales of the past are always tinged with sadness: she always describes how the glories of the past were destroyed or tarnished.

Intersperse the following memories with signs of the Orcs (see A Darkness in the Present below).

- At the Old Ford, she describes how a great bridge built by the Dwarves once spanned the river, and how it was made even greater by the men of lost Arnor. Great armies rode across that bridge, and she remembers the ice-spear of her kinsman Gil-Galad glittering in the sunlight. He rode away into shadow.

- Looking back at Mirkwood, she speaks of Eryn Galen, the Green Wood, for so the Elves used to call it before the Shadow came to Dol Guldur. The Wise may have driven the Necromancer from his fastness in Southern Mirkwood, but evil still lingers in its depths.

- Near the river, she describes how the Anduin flows south past the Golden Wood of *Laurelindórenan*. There is a strange note in her voice when she speaks of that land, and cautions the company against travelling there, lest they fall into the enchantment of the Lady of the Forest.

- East of *Laurelindórenan*, she says, the river once watered the Garden Lands, where the Enyd Bess dwelled until the Enemy hunted them all down. The burning of their gardens was one of the worst wounds the Enemy ever inflicted upon Middle-earth. All that is beautiful fades or is destroyed.

- At night, she sings of Beleriand, which is drowned beneath the ocean, and the days of heroes.

- The Men of Dale and Woodmen she refers to as 'Middle-Men' or 'Men of Twilight', to distinguish them from the Men of Númenor she knew of old, and the 'Men of Shadow' who dwell in the East. They once had great kingdoms, but now they are a scattered people who do not remember their own great works.

- She claims to have known men like Beorn in the Second Age. They were dear to Oromë, she says, he who the Northmen call Béma, and learned secrets from his servants.

- She rarely speaks to Dwarves, and then only when she must. She does speak of Moria's glorious halls, which she visited long ago. Her bracelets were made there, and are inlaid with *ithildin*, moon-silver. It was a beautiful city, but the Dwarves were too greedy…

- Hobbits fascinate her. She has not seen any of the *periando*, as they are named in the Ancient Tongue, in many long years. They once dwelt in these parts, digging their little holes in the banks of the Great River. She does not know what happened to them; no doubt the Enemy drove them away.

Most of the words spoken by Irimë about her past hardly mean anything to adventurers who are not long-lived Elves, as the old lore of mortals runs only skin-deep in comparison to the life of the elven Lady. But something in her voice seems to awaken ancestral recollections in all who listen.

- Every companion who spends any part of the journey listening to Irimë receives an Experience Award, as visions of the past are stirred within their minds.

Playing Irimë

Irimë is one of the oldest creatures the companions are ever likely to meet. The long years weigh heavily on her. When playing the Elf, speak quietly and sadly. Look off into the distance, as though you can see things others cannot. Never smile, unless it is tinged with melancholy.

A Darkness in the Present

After crossing the Old Ford and entering the wild lands west of the Anduin, the companions realise that they are being pursued by Orcs. Build this threat subtly. For example:

- The company's Scout spots a small band of Orcs ahead of the company.
- The company's Look-out spots cooking fires at night.
- Irimë extends her hand, and a sparrow lands on her finger. She whispers to it, and it tells her that Orcs are nearby.

A successful **DC 15 Dexterity (Stealth)** check lets the companions spy on their pursuers. They are being followed by a sizeable Orc warband, composed of at least two dozen Orcs, maybe more – certainly, too many for the company to fight with any hope of victory. These Orcs are not the same band that Legolas spoke of; more than one hunting party was sent out to find Irimë.

Once the company discover they are being chased, they may decide to turn back and head for a Sanctuary like

Beorn's house instead of risking the Road. If they do so, then the Orcs catch them before they reach safety (go to Part 3) – even if they stay ahead of their pursuers, there are more Orcs coming down from the Misty Mountains to catch them between hammer and anvil.

Flight to the Pass

These Orc warbands are not random misfortune – they are part of a greater design. The Gibbet King has sensed the presence of Irimë, and knows that her sorrow is her weakness. It sent the Orcs after her – and if they cannot capture her, the spirit will act directly...

The company's only chance is to press on and evade the enemy. For each of the three days of travel that separates them from the High Pass, the company's Scouts must make a **Wisdom (Survival)** check to find routes up the hillsides that are not being watched by Orcs.

- On a successful roll, the company seems to gain ground, as they advance steadily along well-hidden paths. However, the DC for the check rises each time – the first is at **DC 15**, the second at **DC 18**, and the third as **DC 21** as the orcs close in.

- If the characters make three successful checks in a row, they manage to sneak past the orcs and reach the High Pass. Skip onto *Part Five – The Ruins*.

- If they fail a check, run *Part Three – the Hill of Woe*.

- Alternatively, if the characters alert Irimë to the danger posed by the orcs, and pass a **DC 20 Charisma (Persuasion)** check, she is convinced to put forth her power and summon aid immediately, even though she fears it will draw the attention of darker foes than orcs.

– Part Three –
The Hill of Woe

As the darkness draws in, the Orcs come closer. The noose closes upon the adventurers. They know there are many Orcs on their trail, but then the company's look-outs spot more Goblins coming down from the hills. There is no escape – all that is left to do is to choose a place to make a last stand. A rocky outcrop is the most defensible spot in the area, see page 90 of the *Loremaster's Guide*. They may hold out for a short time, but there is little hope of escape. See the Hill of Woe map on the back end papers.

Ask what preparations the company intend to make. Fire is a necessity, as the light is dying; the company might also scout around to survey the terrain, finding boulders to use in their defense (see page 91 of the *Loremaster's Guide*). For her part, Irimë stands on the rock and sings in Elvish, a high-pitched keening chant that sounds like a funeral dirge.

The Orcs Assemble

Instead of attacking straight away, the Orcs gather a short distance away in the gloom (just out of bow-range), and start their own yowling and shouting to drown out Irimë's song.

- The sight of so many Orcs requires a **DC 10 Wisdom** saving throw from each member of the company: failure means the character is Frightened for the first d4 rounds of combat.

The Orc-captain shoves lesser goblins aside and strides forward to issue a challenge to the company: *"Give us the elf-woman, and the rest of you can go!"* The company can ignore the Orc, reject his (false) offer, or make their own response. A sufficiently brave response, coupled with a successful **DC 25 Charisma (Intimidation)** check can cow the Orcs, giving them Disadvantage in combat until the character who intimidated them is struck and takes damage.

The Assault

"Good! Tonight we eat man-flesh! Kill them all except the elf!" roars the Orc-captain, and he charges up the hill towards the company. A black tide of Orcs surges after him. The adventurers are outnumbered twenty to one, and all they can see is a wave of fangs and jagged swords and blood-shot eyes. But before battle is joined, something unexpected happens (read the following to the players):

Irimë raises her hand, and from the jewel of the ring she wears a bright light blooms, as if a star had uncloaked itself beside you. The blaze dismays the Orcs. Some turn and flee, and those in the lead must raise their shields to shade their eyes from the elf-light. The advantage is yours!

While the Orcs seem terrified by the light, the companions feel heartened by the blaze: any companion who is Frightened may immediately make another **DC 10 Wisdom** saving throw to remove the condition.

The Battle of the Hilltop

Irimë's blaze of light means the Orcs are Surprised, and gives the heroes Advantage in the first round of combat. But it does not stop the Orc attack. There is a host of Orcs here, far too many for the company to defeat. Each time an Orc falls, another takes its place. Appear merciless – evoke the feeling that the companions' doom is at hand. Use the following episodes as examples to set the pace:

- Three Black Uruks form a shield-wall and start marching up the hill, trying to force a wedge between members of the company and prevent the companions from fighting side by side. How do the adventurers break this shield-wall?

- One suicidally brave Goblin leaps over the front lines and attacks the rear guard (this Goblin has the **Great Leap** special ability). Who deals with this intruder?

- Another Orc Soldier carries a jar of some vile concoction; it looks like tar, but clings and burns without heat or fire. The Orc tries to hurl it into the face and eyes of one of the companions; if this attack hits, the companion is blinded and for the rest of the fight, and his vision is restored only with a successful **DC 13 Wisdom (Medicine)** check.

Keep up this relentless assault until at least six rounds of combat have passed, or until two members of the company are unconscious. Award XP for defeated foes as normal.

The Eagles

When it seems that all hope is lost and the company will soon be defeated, the defenders feel a wind rush by overhead, and they hear the beating of tremendous wings. The Orcs fall back in terror as a flight of gigantic birds swoops upon them from above! First Irimë, then any other wounded companions, and finally any who are still able to fight are picked up by the Great Eagles of the Misty Mountains. Other Eagles grab Orcs in their talons and fly off with them, then drop them from a great height to break on the rocks below. The Orc captain roars to rally his troops: *"Stand and fight, you maggots! They're only feathery cows!"* He grabs a huge black bow and looses an arrow at one of the departing Eagles. The arrow flights straight and true, piercing the Eagle's breast. The bird does not fall, but its flight becomes more laboured.

The Eagles fly the company into the mountains. The flight would be terrifying if the company could see their surroundings, but in the darkness, all they can feel is the rush of the wind and the beating of the Eagles' wings. The bird carrying the companion with the heaviest armour and other gear makes several cutting remarks about the adventurer's weight and choice of armour, but all the Eagles manage to escape the hail of Orc-arrows and fly off into the night.

After a short but exhilarating flight, the Eagles bring the company to their eyries.

> ### The Eagles are Coming!
> As Tolkien himself remarked in several instances, the Great Eagles are a dangerous storytelling device. An intervention on their part can be easily seen as stripping the players of their chance to influence the course of the adventure. To avoid this feeling on the players' part, you could try to personalize the reasons for the intervention of the Great Eagles, exploiting any suggestions coming from the players themselves. For example, is there a Dwarf in the company with a raven friend? The bird could have gone, or have been sent, in search of help, finding the Eagles. Or did a companion blow a horn before battle was joined, or made something that could be noticed? Did the heroes meet the Eagles before, or are they friends with Radagast? Even if Irimë's song could explain their arrival, adding a modicum of player-driven elements can only improve the result.

- Part Four -
A Guest of Eagles

Dawn finds the company on a narrow stony ledge, high in the mountains. Companions who know the mountains well (or who have studied maps in Dale, Erebor or Hobbiton that showed Thorin's journey) might deduce they are not at the main eyrie of the Eagles, but at some other outpost nearby.

The Lord of the Eagles arrives shortly after they wake. With a wingspan of more than 100 feet, his arrival is a sight to behold. He lands on the edge of the platform, his dwarf-wrought golden crown glittering in the morning light. He addresses Irimë first of all, and she thanks him for heeding her prayers.

"We heard your song on the wind, but it was the light that guided us to you. Long has there been friendship between your kind and mine, and we came when we were needed."

Next, the Lord of the Eagles turns to the companions.

"Gaerthor, one of my chieftains, was grievously wounded as he rescued you from the Orcs. Tell me, whose lives did he buy with his courage?"

Motivation
To discover the worthiness of the company.

Expectations
+2: Two-legged folk are of little merit to the Eagles. (If the characters offer – and succeed – in treating Gaerthor's wound.)
+1: All are enemies of the one Enemy (the characters defeated many orcs)
-1: Bows get in the way of hunting sheep (if the characters object to the eagles stealing sheep and goats from the farmsteads of the Anduin valley)
-2: The Lady Irimë is to be honoured (if the characters blame Irimë for their plight)

Interaction
Offering to help the wounded Eagle requires a **DC 15 Charisma (Persuasion)** check – the Lord of the Eagles is hesitant to trust outsiders (see *Healing Gaerthor*, below).

As far as the return of the adventurers to their journey is concerned, the Lord of the Eagles initially refuses to carry any companion wearing heavy armour, arguing that the weight is too great for his fellows to bear except in great need. He argues his point further, adding that he does not see why adventurers should walk around wearing all that iron ("how will you ever fly, weighed down as you are?"). Arguing with the King of All Birds imposes a -1 modifier to the Final Audience Check. Exchanging news gets the company an interesting perspective on recent events. The Eagle explains that something has stirred up the Orcs in recent weeks. Heroes with similar tales add a +1 modifier to the Final Audience Check.

The Lord of the Eagles considers Elves and Dwarves as Friendly, whilst all other cultures are Neutral, other than Beornings and Woodmen of which he is Mistrustful (due to their bows).

The Final Audience Check may yield the following results:

Failure: The Lord of the Eagles commands that the company be dropped off back on the main road. The adventurers face another day of march before they reach the pass.

Success by 0-2: The company convinces the Eagles to leave them higher up in the hills, closer to the pass (see *Part Five: The Ruins* below). He will not carry them over the mountains.

Success by 3-5: As above, but the Lord of the Eagles adds the following: on his more far-reaching flights, he has seen something in the West Nether Vales, a new fortress on the moors south of the River Gladden. He does not know what it is, but he dislikes it (see *A Darkness in the Marshes*, pg 77).

6 or more: As 3-5 above, and the Lord promises that if the companions call, he will come to their aid if they are within his reach: this lets the company call upon the Eagles once during the adventure while within fifty miles of the Eyrie.

Healing Gaerthor

If he agrees to let a companion attend Gaerthor, the adventurer faces a difficult challenge – removing the Orc-arrow requires a **DC 20 Wisdom (Medicine)** check. Succeeding at this feat gains the favour of Gaerthor: if called, the Great Eagle will come to the aid of the company once during the adventure (as for the "6 or more" entry above, but limited to Gaerthor only).

Departure

Once the company are ready to leave, Irimë bids farewell to the Lord of the Eagles, and the adventurers embark on a new flight. The journey down the mountain is more pleasant than the flight up, assuming one equates 'pleasant' with 'being able to see instead of flying blindly in the dark'. The company can see all of Wilderland laid out beneath them, like an astoundingly detailed map. In the distance, there is the shadow of Mirkwood, then there is the silver ribbon of the Anduin, its green vales, and then the towering wall of the Misty Mountains.

The Eagles drop the company off either on the road leading to the High Pass (one day away), or else half-way along, close to the spot where Irimë is to meet the riders from Rivendell (the mountain ruins, see *Part Five* below), depending on the outcome of the encounter.

– Part Five –
The Ruins

Sooner or later, the company arrives at the ruins of an old town. If the companions played through *Of Leaves & Stewed Hobbit*, they recognise the tumbled stones as the place where they fought the Night-Wight. Irimë also remembers this place, but hers is a different memory.

"I have been here before. This was Haycombe, the trader's town leading to the Cirith Forn en Andrath. It was built by Middle-Men with golden hair who traded over the Mountains. They were a kind folk. They held a market here, and my kin from Lindon would come sometimes, and we would dance in the snow. The Men would laugh to see us run."

"They are gone, now. Some went South, with a brave chieftain called Eorl. Others stayed, until the shadow in the forest reached out and destroyed them. Treachery brought the enemy into the town, his horrors took the people here as slaves, and then there was no more laughter in the pass."

Irimë explains that this is where she is to meet the emissaries from Rivendell. She suggests that the company make camp here and rest. If the companions are worried about Night-Wights, then they can instead camp in a less comfortable but more defensible position in the surrounding hillside.

Twilight

Again, the evening draws in. Irimë does not sleep; instead, she wanders the hillside, following the unseen path of streets that were buried centuries ago. She steps lightly over snowfalls, remembering her vanished kin, and the lights of the market. As the stars come out overhead, she raises her voice in a song to Elbereth Starkindler.

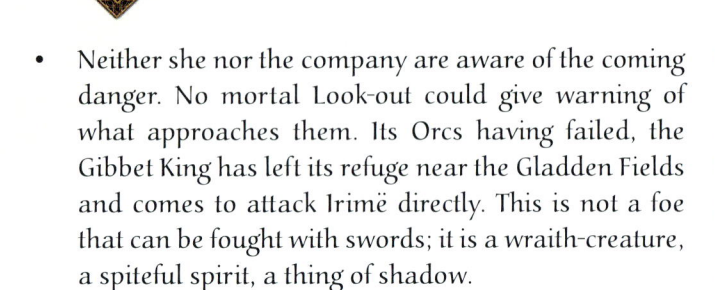

- Neither she nor the company are aware of the coming danger. No mortal Look-out could give warning of what approaches them. Its Orcs having failed, the Gibbet King has left its refuge near the Gladden Fields and comes to attack Irimë directly. This is not a foe that can be fought with swords; it is a wraith-creature, a spiteful spirit, a thing of shadow.

If the company have a Look-out, then the first sign of the spirit is a feeling of unnatural coldness. This is not the chill of the mountain air, but the clammy cold of sickness. A shadow slithers through the night. Off in the distance, the Look-out sees Irimë glimmering softly, as if surrounded by a moonlit radiance – and then the shadow is upon her, suffocating her light. Irimë casts a single desperate glance back towards the sleeping adventurers... and then utter darkness falls upon the whole company.

Irimë's Dream

The next part of this adventure takes place in a dream of sorts. On one level, Irimë is struggling with the Gibbet King as it tries to consume her spirit. She is not strong enough to resist alone, so she is drawing on the companions to aid her. The companions experience this spiritual struggle as a dream-like state as they are all drawn into the wraith-world. (A close comparison for what is happening to them would be the Hobbits' experiences in the Barrow-Downs, where Merry dreamt of being a Man of the North who perished in battle with the forces of Angmar).

Set between Worlds

In the physical world, the companions are all asleep (also the adventurers who were on look-out or still awake for any reason). In the wraith-world, Irimë battles the spirit. Being mortals[1], the companions cannot perceive the wraith-world directly, and so they dream.

Time flows differently in dreams. Events may seem to take weeks or months, but only a few minutes pass in the waking world. Expenditures of Inspiration within the dream are real, as are Shadow point gains, but hit point damage vanishes when a companion awakens. Similarly, any Exhaustion accrued in the dream disappears when the hero wakes up. Any companion who is killed in the dream does not immediately awaken, but is instead trapped in a terrifying darkness for some time and then awakens, having gained two levels of Exhaustion and 1d6 Shadow points (see also the *Slain Companions* sidebar on page 71). Telling other people in the dream that they are dreaming is futile, as is trying to wake up or to control the dream.

From time to time over the course of this dream, the Loremaster should describe how the companions sometimes glimpse the waking world. They stir in their sleep, and see Irimë wrestling with the spirit in the darkness, but then plunge back into the dream.

The Dream Begins

The companions awaken, exactly where they fell asleep, in the same positions on the mountainside. All their equipment and weapons are at hand. The mountainside, though, has changed. Where once there was an old and ill-maintained track, there is now a well-travelled road. Where once there were ruined walls and fallen stones, there is a town called Haycombe. While it is but a small town compared to the great cities of the South, it is a far larger settlement than any that exist in Wilderland today, save perhaps Esgaroth or Dale. It is protected by high walls of timber.

The company can hear the sound of laughter and the bustle of a market from inside the town, and it is clear that many travellers have gathered here. Entering the town, the companions are greeted by a crowd of tow-headed children, who swirl around them and start pestering them with questions: who are they? Where did they come from?

Exploring the town, the dreaming companions realise that every sight and sound feels familiar to them, as though they belong to this place and time. Should they address any villager they discover that they not only perfectly comprehend their language, but they speak it fluently too.

They are greeted warmly by the locals, who appear to be of the same stock as the Woodmen, although most seem to travel on horseback or else delight in feats of

---

[1] Elves of Mirkwood are not mortals, but are of lesser 'spiritual stature' compared to a Noldo like Galadriel, Irimë or Glorfindel. Any Elf companions, Dunedain with the *See the Unseen* Virtue, or scholars with the secrets of *Ancient Lore* or *Dark Knowledge*, may be able to recognise the dream for what it is, but cannot escape it.

horsemanship; they are clearly horse-tamers and riders, and even refer to themselves as the *Éothéod*, the horse people. In the centre of town is a large square, where the market is held. The square is crowded with merchants, traders and travellers from across the North.

The Alehouse

A building stands out from other houses for the signboard swinging over its door, showing a scrawny goat falling down a cliff. *The Falling Goat* is a alehouse and inn, and offers the companions a good place to rest and consider what is happening.

The place is not especially crowded when the companions arrive, as most people are at the market in the main square. There are four people in the alehouse who are of especial importance in the dream.

Aldor: The place has been run by Aldor since he started brewing ale for his neighbours many years before; today he is an old greybeard who has lived in the town all his life. He greets the companions as he hurries around the crowded alehouse. Aldor is a storehouse of tales, rumours and stories about Wilderland, both truthful and 'enriched' by his vivid imagination. He is an old man, the count of his years writ in wrinkles on his face.

"Welcome, welcome good folk. Here for the market, no doubt. Sit, have a drink, and rest here a while. Have you come from the south? Any word of the Master's return? I've heard tell he's on the road, but news is hard to come by of late."

Playing Aldor: Everything reminds you of something from your youth, or a story someone told you. Stroke your beard. Groan a little when you move; you're old.

Geb: Also in the alehouse is a wandering minstrel and trickster called Geb, a Woodman. He is a rogue and a charmer, and is drawn to any comely women among the company; failing that, he identifies the richest-looking companion and starts trying to wheedle money out of them.

"Noble travellers, you look like the sort who'd have a coin or two to spare. It's good luck to pay a minstrel, you know. Give me a coin and I'll sing you a song of Scatha the Worm, and brave Fram the Dragonslayer!"

Playing Geb: Never say what you actually feel; cloak everything in glib words. Let others take the risks; save your own skin if you have the chance. Smile and tell jokes; even when you are in grave danger, you can use morbid humour.

Haleth: One of the older children from the crowd outside keeps following the company wherever they go. This child of eleven years is named Haleth, and he dreams of being a warrior. He attaches himself to the most heroic-looking of the player characters.

"Have you a squire, sir? I could be your squire. I'd polish your armour and keep your sword sharp. My father is the captain of the Master's guards, and he's gone away South, but when he comes back I'm sure he'll tell you how brave I am."

Playing Haleth: Don't be an annoying kid. Hero-worship the companions, but don't play him as a fool. Bergil, son of Beregond (see *The Lord of the Rings*, V:1) is a good model to follow. Keep your eyes as wide as possible.

Rodwen: If the company seek out Elves (perhaps in the hope of finding a past version of Irimë), then they encounter Rodwen, an Elf from Mirkwood. She travelled west from the forest to visit the market as an emissary of King Thranduil. Unusually for her kind, she enjoys the company of mortals, and finds them entertaining.

"The shadow never truly departed our forest, and I do not know if the present trouble is but a passing darkness, or if some power has once again inhabited Dol Guldur."

Playing Rodwen: Be fascinated by anything that mortals do. Take a detached perspective on events. Pause before speaking.

The Inn

The Falling Goat was originally Aldor's family house. It has a large common-room on the ground floor, with a half-dozen tables, benches and a blazing log-fire. Next to the common-room is a kitchen; off to the side are two private parlours. Upstairs, there are small sleeping rooms for guests.

Rumours in the Inn

Asking around gets the company some sense of where – and when – they are:

- The lord of this people is named Heáfod; Woodmen and Beornings or Scholars with proficiency in Lore recognise this as a name out of Mannish legend, belonging to a time when a powerful Northman nation ruled the northernmost vales of the Great River.

- Many travellers have brought word of a new darkness in the great wood to the east. For many years, there had been a respite, and it was hoped that the shadow had departed Mirkwood. Recently, the tales claim, there has been smoke and foulness issuing from the Hill of Sorcery in Southern Mirkwood.

- Some months ago, the Alderman of Haycombe, one of Heáfod's most trusted followers, went on a journey south to survey the Hill of Sorcery, and to see for himself if there is any truth to these tales of a new shadow.

- Despite these rumours, the mood in the town is merry. While little trade comes over the mountains these years, the town still attracts merchants from the South.

From these stories, and from the manner of the people, the company can work out that they are witnessing events that transpired some five hundred years ago. It is a good idea to have one of the companions stir in their sleep at this point, see Irimë and the spirit, and realise that not all is as it seems.

Return of the Alderman

Once the companions have had a chance to gather some information, and have met some of the other characters in the inn, they hear the sound of a commotion outside. From the shouts and excited conversation, they hear that the Alderman of Haycombe has returned from his journey south! The crowd outside is too thick to easily push through, so Haleth suggests the company watch the procession from the upper level of the inn, which overlooks the main square.

If the company do not already know, Haleth tells them that the Alderman of the town went away south some weeks ago, and is now returning. If the company shove through the crowd, or if they watch with Haleth from upstairs, they see the Alderman's caravan approach. At the head of the procession is the Alderman's golden wagon, accompanied by the guards he took South with him. He is followed then by a large number of men in strange red armour.

- As the procession grows closer, call for **DC 10 Wisdom (Insight)** checks from the company. Those who succeed have a growing sense of danger, as if disaster is about to strike. A total of 20 or higher lets a companion catch a weak breath of foul air coming from the caravan, the smell of things long-dead, along with the realisation that all the Alderman's guards have pallid skin, blank white eyes, and shamble rather than march.

The procession stops in the middle of the market square. The crowd draws in close to hear the Alderman of the town. The Alderman – a tall man, wearing an exceptionally fine torc of gold and well-made armour – stands and raises his hands. *"People of Haycombe! People of the North!"* he announces. *"Your true lord has returned!"*

And then the killing begins.

Fate of the Alderman

The Alderman of Haycombe was a victim of the Necromancer, who reclaimed Dol Guldur around the year 2460. When he travelled south with his retinue he was captured by the Necromancer and driven insane. His guards were tormented and murdered, and then raised again as undead warriors. Then, the Alderman was sent back with a contingent of Men from the East to destroy his town. The Necromancer had a deeper plan than mere malice – the destruction of the town would leave the High Pass unguarded and unprotected. With one hand, he removed Haycombe; with the other, he summoned Orcs out of Mount Gundabad to block the pass, and thus divide the North.

Siege of the Inn

The men in red armour are Easterling warriors. They are the first to strike: they attack with shocking speed, targeting any warriors within reach of their weapons. The guards of the Alderman are revealed for what they are: walking corpses, animated by dread sorcery. They attack the crowd, spreading panic like wildfire. Over the carnage, the companions can hear the insane laughter of the Alderman of the town.

Undead warriors stumble towards the inn; now is the time for swords! The companions are probably inside the alehouse, with Aldor, Geb, Haleth and others they might have met so far. Refer to the Inn Map on the back end papers.

- **Barricading the Inn:** Companions who think to fortify the inn by blocking windows and locking doors gain Advantage as long as they hold the inn; the building's walls are strong and this is a good place to hold out.

- **Battling the Undead & Easterlings:** There is a host of foes, too many to overcome. The first wave of attackers consists of undead warriors that lumber clumsily towards the company. The undead are ungainly, but are possessed of fearsome strength. Worse, wounding them is not always enough – they keep coming even after taking blows that would kill a mortal man.

If the company kill the undead (there are two undead warriors per companion), then the Easterlings join the fray. These savage men fight with great axes, and speak in a foreign tongue that sounds like a harsh bark to Northmen ears. If the company defeat some of the Easterlings, the others fall back and set the inn's roof alight. The company are then forced to choose between surrender and burning to death – no victory is possible here – the town is doomed. But who knows what opportunities will come later...

If a companion is reduced to 0 hit points in this struggle, he momentarily wakes up and sees Irimë struggling with the spirit on the mountainside. Keep dropping references to the waking world into the dream when possible, to remind the players of their true situation.

> ### Slain Companions
>
> If a companion dies here, or later in Dol Guldur, the Loremaster has several options to keep the player in the game. The player could temporarily take on another character, like Geb, Rodwen, Aldor or Haleth. There is no need for game statistics for these temporary characters. The character could awaken in the present day, and find his companions locked in a trance while Irimë battles the spirit. Optionally, you could present challenges for that companion, like keeping the entranced companions alive and warm when it begins to snow, or having goblins creep out of the hills and menace the helpless dreamers.

Undead Warriors

Once young and valorous men, the guards of the Alderman have been stripped of their lives and will by the Necromancer's dark arts. Their shrivelled bodies are all that is left of them.

Undead Warriors
Medium undead

STR	DEX	CON	INT	WIS	CHA
13 (+1)	8 (-1)	12 (+1)	3 (-4)	7 (-1)	3 (-4)

Armour Class 9
Hit Points 27 (5d8+5)
Speed 20 ft

Damage Immunities poison
Condition Immunities Charmed, Exhaustion, Poisoned
Senses passive Perception 9
Languages None
Challenge 1/2 (100 XP)

Fell Spirit (Recharge 5-6). When the Undead Warrior would be reduced to 0 hit points, it may use its reaction to add 7 (2d6) temporary hit points.

Actions

Bony Claws. *Melee Weapon Attack:* +3 to hit, reach 5 ft, one target. *Hit:* 8 (2d6+1) slashing damage.

Easterlings

These men are mercenaries from the plains to the distant East, drawn to Dol Guldur with promises of bloodshed and fortune.

Easterling Warriors
Medium human (Evil Men)

STR	DEX	CON	INT	WIS	CHA
14 (+2)	13 (+1)	12 (+1)	11 (+0)	12 (+1)	8 (-1)

Armour Class 14 (corslet of mail)
Hit Points 22 (4d8+4)
Speed 30 ft

Skills Perception +3, Survival +3
Senses passive Perception 13
Languages Westron, Easterling
Challenge 1/2 (100 XP)

Actions
Great Axe: *Melee Weapon Attack:* +4 to hit, reach 5 ft., one target. *Hit:* 8 (1d12+2) slashing damage.

The Journey South

The dreaming companions are sharing the fate that befell the villagers of Haycombe almost five centuries ago: they are made prisoners by the Easterlings, and they find themselves chained together with the others – Aldor, Geb, Haleth and the Elf Rodwen – and forced to march south for many long days.

Along the hard march, those slaves who cannot keep up are whipped; those who fall are left to die when where they lie. More than a thousand prisoners were taken in the sack of Haycombe, but less than five hundred survived the grim march south. The Easterlings drive the slaves quickly, and use long horse-leather whips when necessary, but they are not needlessly cruel. They do not torture their prisoners, nor make sport of them.

The days pass swiftly in the dream, like one moment of horror drawn out endlessly. Before the company know it, they have passed the Gladden Fields and are being driven south towards Dol Guldur. As the slave caravan passes the Narrows of the Forest, though, the Easterlings are met by a column of Orcs. The Easterlings leave the slaves in the tender care of the Orcs; the Men march east into the forest, while the Orcs whip the slaves south.

By the time Dol Guldur, the Hill of Sorcery, is in sight, all the companions will have multiple levels of Exhaustion, and the other prisoners are equally weary. Aldor, in particular, suffers from a terrible fever and wracking cough. The prisoners are driven into a dark tunnel that runs under the forest into the dungeons beneath the hill. They vanish into darkness.

A Glimpse of Irimë

An Elf, or else the companion with the highest **Wisdom**, wakes for a moment and sees Irimë contending with the spirit. Irimë has the strength to whisper a warning to the character. *"A spirit of despair – it has entrapped us all in sorcery! It will consume us if we cannot defeat it!"*

- Part Six -
Dark Dreams

The company are thrown into a lightless, noisome pit, their weapons and gear taken from them, together with Aldor, Geb, Haleth and Rodwen. They must be deep beneath Dol Guldur, the dreaded fortress of the Necromancer. The cell is cold and partially flooded with foul water that stings the skin. There is a single door, locked from the far side, and opened only when the Orc-guards throw in a few lumps of mouldy bread or bowls of some grey gruel. In the distance, the companions can hear screams and the sounds of lamentation.

At times, from far below, the companions hear noises, as of some tremendous machinery. At other times, they feel unreasoning, unrelenting terror, a feeling of fear so overwhelming that they can do nothing but cower. The air is tainted, choked with smoke, or with caustic fumes. The companions now face foes that cannot be fought with force of arms, but are none the less deadly: sickness, fear and suffering.

- Call for Corruption checks now and after each of the following scenes. The DC for these **Wisdom** saving throws starts at **DC 8.** If the companions are unable to keep their spirits up, then the DC for the Corruption tests rises by 2 with each test. Ask the players how their characters endure this endless darkness, and how they intend to stave off despair and madness. This is a time for skills like **Performance**, as well as the invocation of suitable backgrounds and good roleplaying. The players should also include the other four prisoners – if the other prisoners succumb to despair, then it gets even harder to avoid Corruption.

For example, a company of adventurers are trapped in the dream. The players decide that, as nothing here is real, they will just wait until they wake up. As they are doing nothing to keep their spirits up, the DC for the next corruption test rises to **DC 10**. Next, the Loremaster describes how Aldor is dying of a fever. The company manage to keep Aldor alive by getting the old man to remember happier days in lost Haycombe. The Loremaster decides that this counts as keeping their spirits up, so the third Corruption check stays at **DC 10**.

Escape?

Escaping the dungeons of the Necromancer is impossible in the dream: all the prisoners from Haycombe found their fate in Dol Guldur. The companions can try if they wish, and the first attempt counts towards keeping their spirits up. However, there is no way to succeed – even if they were to somehow overpower the Orc-guards, there are far worse things in these dungeons.

Aldor's Sickness

Old Aldor fell sick on the journey south, and barely made it to Dol Guldur alive. The old man is dying of a fever. If the company point his illness out to the guards, then the Orcs march into the cell and pour a vile brown-orange liquid down his throat that makes him convulse and vomit, but does not break the fever.

The only way to save Aldor is with **Wisdom (Medicine)** checks. A prolonged series of rolls are needed to keep him alive. The DC for these tests is the same as the DC for the Corruption checks. Remind the healer that he must spend hours every day nursing a dying man. Aldor is going to perish anyway – why waste time on him?

Geb's Betrayal

The door to the cell opens, and a Woodman walks in bearing a tray of food. This is good food, not the gruel and Orc-bread the company has eaten for many weeks – meat and roasted vegetables and good ale. The Woodman is a tall and handsome young man who introduces himself as Annatar, and offers food to the company.

"There's no need for you to suffer down here. The Master of this place has many Men in his service – aye, and Dwarves too, and other folk. Kneel to him, accept him as your lord, and you shall be given a place of honour in his service. Think on this offer, friends – it is better to live than to die, is it not?"

Annatar leaves the food for the company, then departs, saying:

"I shall return tomorrow – give me your answers then."

Let the company debate the wisdom of serving the Necromancer. Of the other prisoners, Aldor is too weak to serve, Haleth refuses, and the Necromancer would never permit an Elf – even a Wood-elf – to live. However, the minstrel Geb is tempted by the offer.

"I don't want to die here in the dark, simple as that. What difference does it make who I kneel to, or what oaths I swear. Can you eat honour? Will valour keep you warm in this dungeon?"

The company can try to argue him out of serving, or suggest that he put his talent for deception to good use and pretend to serve the Necromancer. Again, the DC for any tests is equal to the DC for the ongoing Corruption checks.

Those Who Kneel

If a player character agrees to serve the Necromancer, that character gains 5 Shadow points immediately. The companion is taken from the dungeon cell – and remembers nothing more until the dream ends, except a dim memory of horrors and the feeling of being watched.

Geb the Servant

If Geb chooses to serve the Necromancer honestly, then the next time the companions see him in the dream, he is dressed in fine armour and is in the company of a band of other cruel guards. He never acknowledges his former cell-mates, and the light has gone from his eyes.

Geb the Trickster

If Geb chooses to serve the Necromancer, but is secretly planning to help the characters, then he can help them with a single task, like smuggling in medicine for Aldor. However, he is caught and executed shortly afterwards.

Haleth's Death

Orcs burst into the cell and point at the companion with the highest **Strength**.

"The lads want some sport. You're coming with us, slave!"

The companion is dragged out of the cell and a sack is pulled over his head. The Orcs pull him through endless corridors and forge-hot chambers until he is thrown down onto a sandy floor. The bag is removed, and the companion finds himself on lying in the middle of an arena. A crowd of Orcs jeers at him from a ring of stone benches around the arena. On the far side of the ring is a portcullis. There is something behind it, something that snorts like a bull and moves like a lumbering mountain – a Hill-troll!

One of the Orcs throws down a sword or other weapon to the companion. The portcullis cranks open, and the Troll emerges blinking into the firelight. When it scents the companion, it roars a challenge and slams its mighty fists into the ground.

The chances of a lone, unarmoured warrior defeating a Hill-troll in single combat are remote, but let the companion try nonetheless. If the companion is knocked out in the fight, he is thrown back into the cell; if he dies here, he awakens from the dream (see *Awakening*, below). On the incredible chance that the companion beats the Hill-troll, then the Orcs return the prisoner to the cell – skip right onto *The Spirit*. In this case, Haleth was slain by the orcs while the hero fought the troll.

After the fight, the Orcs return to the cell (possibly dragging the unconscious companion with them), and announce that it was so much fun, they are going to do it again tomorrow. One of the Orcs jabs a finger at the young boy, Haleth. *"You're next, boy! We'll be back tomorrow night!"*

Saving Haleth

The young man wanted to be a warrior, but he has never held a sword. The companions could spend the next few hours trying to prepare Haleth for what awaits him in the arena and teaching him the basics of combat. Alternatively, one of the other companions could volunteer to stand in for Haleth, if they can find a way of convincing the Orcs that the replacement offers more amusement than the sight of a boy being torn to pieces by a Troll.

- If the companions choose to train Haleth, the teacher should roll either an **Intelligence** or **Strength** saving throw against the same DC as the ongoing Corruption checks. If successful, then the boy acquits himself well, and wounds the Troll in battle. Haleth dies, but he dies fighting bravely. If the saving throw succeeds by 10 or more, he slays the Troll but is returned to the cell broken and dying. The Orcs return after the battle regardless of the outcome and throw the boy's body into the cell.

Awakening

By this time, any companions who have awoken see the first rosy fingers of dawn to the East. Irimë stands as she has stood all night long, locked in magical conflict with the spirit, but the frozen features of her face are flushed pink by the first light of the rising sun. The final phase of the struggle is at hand.

The Spirit

Back in the dream, the cell is suddenly filled with an eerie presence. An unearthly greenish light fills the chamber, and the companions see a thing of shadow looming over them. The spirit is vaguely man-shaped, like a shadow cast on a wall, but its outline shifts and warps as it moves. The spirit lashes out with fingers of darkness and seizes the Elf Rodwen. It holds her up by the throat, and shakes her. Her features change – one moment, she is Rodwen, the next, Irimë.

The spirit speaks through the dead body of Haleth. The boy's broken, bloodied lips and smashed jaw move, and a sepulchral voice echoes from his dead mouth, addressing the adventurers.

"Do you know what the Noldor-witch has done? She dared not face me alone, so she dragged you into this dream to

defend her. This has ever been the way of the High Elves – to use others as their pawns! They despise the race of Men, fearing your growing strength. They hate the Dwarves, and are jealous of your craft. Even their own kin they do not trust. I am more merciful than she. Leave her to her fate. Deny her, here and now, and you may awaken."

Any companions who deny Irimë instantly awaken from the dream, but gain 3 Shadow points.

The Final Challenge

Those who do not deny Irimë remain in the dream. *"Share her fate then!"* hisses the spirit through Haleth's corpse. Utter darkness crashes down upon them: *"Despair!"* commands the spirit.

The following test is rolled to determine whether Irimë prevails over the Gibbet King or is conquered by desperation. The difficulty of the roll depends on how well the companions have managed to endure the torments of the dream; the starting DC for the test is the same as the Corruption check DC, and is modified as follows:

- Add +2 to the DC if Aldor is dead.
- Add +2 to the DC if Geb betrayed the company.
- Add +2 to the DC if Haleth did not die bravely.

This is a group check; at least half the companions must pass a **Wisdom** saving throw for Irimë to succeed.

If Irimë fails

The companions find themselves back in the waking world. A cloud passes in front of the rising sun, casting a shadow over the Mountains. Irimë collapses to the ground, unconscious. Her skin becomes pale and wan, and her eyes are blank and lifeless. All her power is gone. The spirit was victorious. It flees the High Pass before the sons of Elrond arrive, carrying its prize back south to its hidden fortress.

If Irimë succeeds

The companions find themselves back in the waking world. They see Irimë standing before the rising sun. A shadowy horror hangs in the air, lashing her with fingers of darkness, but she is unafraid. She lifts her hand, and it is as though the dawn shines through her fingers. The spirit wails and vanishes as the morning breaks over Wilderland.

- Part Seven - Dawn in the West

At the breaking of dawn, a company of travellers approaches from the west, led by two Elf-Lords who are alike in appearance and garb, dark-haired, grey-eyed, their faces elven-fair, clad in bright mail beneath cloaks of silver-grey. These are Elladan and Elrohir, the sons of Elrond.

Irimë failed

If the spirit defeated Irimë, then Elladan races to her side. He presses the cold steel of his vambrace to her lips, to see if she still draws breath.

"What has happened here?" he asks. *"She still lives, but all her strength is gone from her."*

When the company explain the events of the dream, he nods in understanding.

"An evil spirit assailed her, and she was unable to defeat it. Her body is here, but her mind wanders a dark labyrinth and may never return. We shall take her to my father's house, where she may find healing."

The two brothers place Irimë's unconscious form on a horse, and turn back for Rivendell. One of the other Elves stays to bid farewell to the company, and to offer them help and healing if they need it.

Irimë succeeded

Elladan and Elrohir rush up to Irimë's side. They explain that they sensed a dark presence, and came as quickly as they could. Irimë assures them she is safe.

"A spirit attacked us in the night. Some ghost out of Dol Guldur, perhaps. It tried to destroy us..." She smiles at the companions for the first time. *"But it seems there is still strength and fire in the hearts of the Free Peoples. These companions aided me in my struggle, preserving hope when all hope seemed lost. I spoke truly when I said our meeting was ordained by the stars."*

She tells the company that she will continue on to Rivendell, and urges them to bring word to the wizard Radagast of their experiences.

"The spirit was driven off, not destroyed. I did not think such evil things were abroad in this age of the world, but I was wrong. Darkness is coming, I fear, and I have not the strength to fight again. I go into the West, but I leave you with my blessing, for what it is worth."

The Lady bestows her blessing upon all the companions who impressed her during their first meeting (see page 62) and upon those who distinguished themselves in the wraith-world: from now on they will be recognised as Elf-friends (see page 102 of the *Player's Guide*) and gain a new ability.

Blessed by the First-born
...I see you are an Elf-friend; the light in your eyes and the ring in your voice tells it.

Once per adventuring phase, you may invoke the name of Elbereth and gain Inspiration. You may only do this at night when you can see the stars coming out, or when you are in a dark place and in need of hope.

The Journey Home

The path down the mountainside is eerily familiar – the company travelled this way before, when they were chained prisoners in the dream. When they pass the ruins of the market town, they remember the buildings as they once were, and can almost hear the laughter of the children in the streets.

Whether it was defeated or victorious, there is no sign of the spirit or its Orc servants. They have fled away south – and finding them is another tale. For now, the company's path lies east, to Rhosgobel or some other destination. The Road leads ever on...

Fellowship Phase

Although it is many leagues away, the company may travel to the halls of the Elvenking and claim a more mundane reward there. Galion promised that Thranduil would recompense the adventurers for their efforts in protecting Irimë.

- If Irimë survived the journey, then Thranduil gives them a pouch of white gemstones (worth 500 sp) as a reward, and they may stay in his halls during the Fellowship Phase. If Irimë perished, then they get a paltry reward, and the Elvenking's hall is not a welcoming place for them.

If allowed to remain, the company can use Open Sanctuary at Thranduil's Halls, or try to gain Thranduil as a patron. This is also an excellent place to Heal Corruption.

– A Darkness – in the Marshes

For heroes of level 4 or 5

- **When:** The company may undertake this quest at any time in any year from 2946 onwards. However, it works best as a sequel to *Those Who Tarry No Longer*.
- **Where:** The adventure begins at Rhosgobel. The wizard Radagast has learned of a strange threat in the west; he sends the companions to Mountain Hall, hoping that the Woodmen know more. From there, the company travels into the marshes of the Gladden Fields.
- **What:** News has come to Radagast of a growing danger somewhere west of the Great River. The Orcs who attacked the Lady Irimë were in league with this mysterious threat, as were the outlaws who attacked the land of the Beornings in *Kinstrife & Grim Tidings*.
- **Why:** Radagast fears – correctly – that some evil driven out of Dol Guldur has taken root across the Great River. If this threat is allowed to fester, the Shadow over Mirkwood could spread to encompass all of Wilderland.
- **Who:** The wizard Ragadast is the primary patron for this adventure; the company also meet the head of the House of Mountain Hall, Hartfast son of Hartmut.

Adventuring Phase

This adventure is divided into eight parts.

Part One – Wizard's Counsel
The company meet with Ragadast in his home at Rhosgobel, where the wizard explains his concerns and asks the companions to investigate.

Part Two – Across the River
The company travel from Rhosgobel to Mountain Hall. Along the way, they spy traces of the enemy's movements.

Part Three – The Harrowed Hall
The company arrive at Mountain Hall, and meet with Hartfast, the chieftain. He has his own troubles with Goblin attacks, and can spare little time for the company's questions. He does point the company towards the Gladden Fields, saying that some of his hunters have spoken of strange sights in that unpleasant land.

Part Four – The Passage of the Marshes
The company travel through the noisome swampy terrain of the Gladden Fields. After several days of arduous travel, they find eerie ruins atop a stony hill.

Part Five – Slave & Hunters
The company meet an escaped slave and battle the Orcs who hunt him. He relates his tale, and reveals the location of a secret route into the fort.

Part Six – By Secret Ways
The company enter the fort by a secret passage and spy on the enemy. They learn that the enemy's plans involve a powerful and ancient relic.

Part Seven – Fly, You Fools!
The company are discovered and must fight their way out of the fort. They are pursued across the Gladden Fields and the vales of Anduin to Mountain Hall. The company must stay ahead of the Orcs for as long as they can.

Epilogue – The Shadow of the Future
Returning to the fort, the company discover that the enemy has withdrawn from its fastness. The company must have discovered the enemy before he was ready to reveal himself...

Following On...

If your company played through *Those Who Tarry No Longer*, then they are the ones to bring the news to Radagast. Otherwise, Ragadast learns of the potential threat through his own spies, and summons the companions to help him.

– Part One –
Wizard's Counsel

The adventure begins at Rhosgobel, the small village of the Woodmen that has grown up around the house of Radagast on the edge of the wood. The wizard's cottage lies a short distance away through the trees, but it can only be reached when the wizard wants visitors. For some days, the company has rested here in the great long hall of the Woodmen, waiting for the wizard's summons. The Woodmen are slightly concerned – Radagast has admitted no visitors in several weeks, and while long periods of isolation are not uncommon for the wizard, it has been some years since he was so secretive.

The summons comes one evening, as the dusk draws in. A bushy-tailed red squirrel leaps from tree to tree, then lands on the roof of the hall and scurries along the supporting pillars before it drops down in front of the company. It bows in the manner of a courtier, and beckons the company to follow it. The company notice it has a golden chain around its neck.

Following the squirrel brings the company along a path of crushed white stones that the companions tried to follow previously and didn't seem to lead anywhere. The path winds its way through the woods, travelling alongside the sharp-thorned brown hedge that protects Rhosgobel from the wild woods beyond, and brings the company to a small cottage in a little clearing. The lights of the cottage are warm and welcoming as the night draws in. A horse eats grass contentedly in the field beside the house. The squirrel runs ahead of the company, climbs up the wall, and rings a little bell by the door. The door swings open of its own accord. *"Come in, come in,"* says the voice of Radagast.

The Wizard
The cottage is crammed with all sorts of stuff - the gifts of generations of grateful visitors and villagers, from painted earthenware to travelling gear, to jars of herbs and spices. There are cages containing sick or wounded animals, casks of wine, moth-eaten blankets, framed woodcarvings piled against one wall, a teetering pile of scrolls, a writing-desk that overflows with parchment, letters and notes, and any number of birds hopping in and out of the window or roosting in the thatched roof.

Inside, Radagast sits in a comfortable-looking chair, wearing a ratty brown robe. He looks exhausted and weatherbeaten, but an energetic spark still animates his dark eyes. A simple supper of bread, cheese, jams and fruits is spread out on the table – there is enough for the whole company. Radagast insists that the company eat first, before he moves onto the reason he called them here. There is no need for formal introductions, the Wizard already knows them.

Motivation
Radagast seeks a band of worthy adventurers to run an errand for him.

Expectations
+1: Travellers bring tidings (if the characters bring news of the Dwimmerhorn or other word from afar)
-1: Greed is a flaw in the hearts of men (if the players ask for too many rewards or boons)
-2: "A habit of the old; they choose the wisest person present to speak to" (if the characters interrupt or question Radagast's wisdom)

Interaction
Radagast begins by explaining what he needs from the company.

"News – well, rumour and wild stories - has reached me of late. There is talk of Orcs moving across Wilderland, of evil things stirring up, of disquiet and sorrow and all manner of unpleasant things. This news comes from all quarters, but mostly from the west."

"I was so concerned that I sent word south to the head of my order, Saruman the White, who is wise beyond all others. He said that the best thing to do would be to act quickly and quietly, and with caution. My intent is to send you in search of the root of these stories. Your mission is to gather information and report back – learn all you can, but do not reveal your presence to the enemy! I think the best place to start is Mountain Hall, the main settlement of the Woodsfolk west of the Great River. Hartfast is head of the council of Elders there – he is a good man, very sensible, and little happens in the vale of Anduin that does not escape his notice. Ask him for news."

Likely questions from the company are listed below, together with the wizard's response. Each question gains the company a +1 modifier to the Final Audience Check, as long as they are respectful of Radagast's answer.

What are we looking for?
"As you may know, some years ago, the Necromancer was driven from Dol Guldur. He could be back – and if it is him, then you must be very careful indeed. He is a foe beyond any of you, and beyond me too for that matter. More likely, though, the withdrawal of the Necromancer means that some evil thing, perhaps one of his servants, is trying to fill the void he left. We forced the Necromancer to leave, but there are any number of Orcs, spirits and mean-spirited men in the lands around Dol Guldur who would obey a new overlord."

"So, you are looking for... well, I don't know. Something evil. With luck, it is just some bandit, with less luck, a new Great Goblin. If I knew what it was, I wouldn't be sending you, would I?"

What is our reward?
"Reward? What, like gold and treasure and magic swords? Don't be absurd. You shall have the gratitude of all living beings in Wilderland, and that is worth more than silver or precious stones."

If it is the Necromancer, wouldn't he come back to Dol Guldur?
"The Hill of Sorcery is watched by many eyes. No, he will not return to that fortress until he is secure in his power. I think whatever this enemy is, it has yet to build its full strength. We must root out this weed of evil before it grows!"

Why Mountain Hall?
"Most of the recent troubles that have plagued the land happened west of the Great River. The hall is the only safe haven in that area and east of the Mountains for many leagues."

What help can you give us?
"There are any number of things I might work on you, but I'm not sure if they would help you or hinder you. Say I put a spell of concealment upon you – that will help you hide from Orcs and men and beasts, but it would make it easier for... other things to sense you. If I put a spell or two on you, then I am writing 'these are friends of Radagast' across your faces in letters of sunlight that can be read by anyone with the wit to read them. Still, I will leave it up to you – if you'd prefer to risk a little magic, in the hopes that whatever you find is just a dumb brute and not one of the Necromancer's horrors, then you shall have it."

If the companions ask for a spell, then Radagast offers them a choice of magical boons. Compare the margin of success for the Final Audience Check with the entries given below.

Failure: Radagast has changed his mind, he won't risk any magic on the company: in his opinion these adventurers should try not to catch the attention of anyone who might take notice...

0-2: Radagast promises he will work his magic: he will give them one magical boon.

3-5: As 0-2 above, but he may be convinced to give up to two magical boons.

6 or more: As above, but he may be convinced to give up to three magical boons.

Radagast's Magical Boons

The following list contains some examples of the type of magic that Radagast may employ to assist the company in their quest. While the number of boons depends on how the encounter turned out, the precise choice depends on the Loremaster, even if the adventurers might have attempted to influence Radagast advancing specific requests (for example, "Can you hide us from the eyes of our enemies?" or "Can you help us to endure the journey?").

Beast Protection

The wizard promises he will tell his animal friends to assist the company. When the company leaves, every animal will keep an eye on their progress until the end of the adventure.

- For the length of the adventure, all companions benefit from Advantage on all **Wisdom (Animal Handling or Perception)** checks.

The bonus is granted as animals send warnings to the companions whenever danger is near: birds sing wildly or stop singing all of a sudden, a thrush starts flying about the companions' heads to catch their attention, a hart jumps in the middle of their encampment turning its head in the direction of the enemy, etc.

Spell of Concealment

When the company leaves his presence, Radagast places a spell of concealment upon them.

- For the duration of the adventure, all companions benefit from Advantage on all **Dexterity (Stealth)** rolls.

Travel Blessing

Radagast casts a spell on the company's boots (or Hobbit feet!).

- For the length of the adventure, all companions have Advantage on **Wisdom (Survival)** checks.

Storm Bag

Radagast digs up a battered leather pouch with a waxed black drawstring. The pouch is oddly warm to the touch.

- If the pouch is opened, it seems empty and the warmth disperses, but within minutes a tremendous thunderstorm appears. The storm brings dark clouds, high winds and torrential rain (or snow, if opened in winter or in the mountains). The bag only works once.

Mirkwood Cordial

Radagast gives the company a flask of a powerful alcoholic beverage, enough for six sips of the thick liquid. He accompanies the offer with a warning: *"Beware, as this liquor has been distilled from rare herbs I picked deep in the forest of Mirkwood. Remember, one sip at a time."*

- Sipping from the flask once a day restores 1d4 Hit Dice. Drinking two sips or more in the same day restores Hit Dice proportionally but induces a stupor making a character Miserable for 24 hours for each sip after the first (this means that the drinker may now fall prey of a *Bout of Madness*, see page 183 of the *Adventures in Middle-earth Player's Guide*).

LEAVING RHOSGOBEL

Once Radagast tires of the conversation, he announces that it is time for bed. The companions can sleep in the spare rooms of his cottage – and although the cottage looked like it could only contain one or two rooms from the outside, the company find there are just enough bedrooms for all of them. Radagast does not sleep that night, as he has been away from home for several weeks and needs to catch up on news from the animals who watch Dol Guldur. The company see him walk away into the forest and vanish.

The wizard does not return the next morning. The company are woken by the dawn chorus of birds in the thatch, and can break their fast on the leftovers before departing.

– PART TWO –
ACROSS THE RIVER

A Woodwoman named Banna greets the company on the edge of the forest. She is tall and gangly, and while her features could not be called pretty, there is a merry glint in her eye. She says that Radagast asked her to accompany the companions to the River, where they can take boats upriver and then travel west to Mountain Hall.

Banna

Banna is one of Radagast's aides and messengers. She is eternally optimistic and positive, and loves tramping through the forest and the vales of Anduin more than anything else. She is curious about other folk, but has no desire to leave the lands she knows and loves – maybe one day, when she has seen all the forest and walked every valley from the Forest Gate to the Mountain Pass, but not yet. While she is a good shot with a bow and can handle a knife, she only fights in defence of her homeland. She knows little about the outside world, but knows everything about the lands of the Woodmen, down to the smallest piece of gossip or the best-hidden path through the woods of the Western Eaves.

Playing Banna: Be cheery and upbeat. Ask questions of any companions who are not Woodmen or Beornings; Banna has never seen a Dwarf or a Hobbit, or even a house that was made out of anything other than wood. Tilt your head as if listening to the wind every few minutes. Address animals as 'Master Rabbit, Mistress Cow, Lord Bear' and so on – treat them as people.

Banna will not accompany the party west of the Anduin, but can show up in future adventures as a guide or messenger.

The Journey

The first part of the journey will see the company travel from the western eaves of Mirkwood to the Great River. The second has the companions paddle against the current along the River Anduin to a landing spot chosen by Banna. The third leg brings the company from the Great River to Woodland Hall.

The Journey has a peril rating of 2.

- The sixty miles trip from Rhosgobel to the River Anduin is done across open terrain in Border lands, taking no more than three days and provokes 1 Journey Event at **DC 14**. Refer to the **Wilderland Adventures Journey Table** starting on page 143.

- The journey upriver is long, some forty miles by boat, taking between four and eight days depending on the weather and how hard they row (see below). The Anduin is especially fierce during the early spring and summer, when meltwater from the mountains feeds the streams, but late summer and early autumn are more pleasant. The company will experience 1d3 Journey Events on this section, at **DC 14**. Refer to the **Wilderland Adventures Journey Table** on page 143.

- The journey from the Great River to Woodland Hall is more than eighty miles across pathless areas and hills in Border lands, taking six days. This section of the journey will also provoke 1 Journey Event at **DC 14**. Refer to the **Wilderland Adventures Journey Table** starting on page 143.

Planning the Route

As usual, the companions will plan their route, under the auspices of their chosen Guide. Banna knows most of the way, though, so the company may choose to listen to her. Listening to Banna's directions lets the Guide roll 1d8+4 on their Embarkation roll.

> ### Alternative Routes
> Banna's suggested route is the easiest, but not the only option. The company might choose to cross the Great River by boat to the west of Rhosgobel, then head north-west across the Nether Vales or even through the Gladden Fields. Alternatively, they could take the boats up the Gladden River. Both routes are much harder, but bring them closer to the Dwimmerhorn; optionally, you could skip Part Three and jump right to Part Four or Five if the company choose the harder road.

From Rhosgobel to the Great River

Banna leads the company northwest, to reach the river north of the Gladden Fields. The travelling is pleasant, and they swiftly leave the forest behind to march across the green fields that slope down towards the River. Banna brings the company to where the Woodmen have cleverly hidden some boats in a little coppice overlooking the River.

Up the Anduin

Assuming the companions follow Banna's planned route, then the next part of the journey involves paddling upriver, to the point where Banna will bid the company farewell after dropping them on the western shore.

The companions must all make a **DC 10 Strength (Athletics)** check (raise the DC by 2 in spring): if more than half their number pass the test, the journey upriver takes four days, and provokes 1 Journey Event. Otherwise, they struggle against the current and spend six days paddling northwards and experience 2 Journey Events. If all the companions fail the test, the journey takes eight days, and provokes 3 Journey Events. Any Journey Events arising in this time occur as the company make camp for the night, scout the local area around their campsite, and seek to replenish their food supplies.

The Gladden Fields

The first day of the boat journey is the worst, as the company begin quite close to the Gladden Fields. There, the river is cloaked in a thick mist, and the company are beset by buzzing flies and mosquitoes. Banna insists that the going is easier later on, and she is proved right, as the mist gives way to clear skies.

If there are any Hobbits in the party, she points to lines of small hills by the river-banks. Her grandmother told her stories of a fairy folk who lived in holes under those hills, long ago, and who could vanish from the sight of men at will.

From the Great River to Mountain Hall

The third part of the journey is the longest and most perilous. Before she departs, Banna suggests that they travel due west, skirting the woods, and to follow the mountain stream until they reach the Hall. The terrain on the west bank is tougher to navigate, with fewer known trails. In places, the company must struggle up rocky slopes, or navigate tangles of gorse and thorny plants. Around half-way through the journey, the company may be lucky enough to find a well-worn path, used by travellers coming from the Old Ford who are going to Mountain Hall.

– Part Three –
The Harrowed Hall

The fast-flowing river waters that protect Mountain Hall (see the *Loremaster's Guide*, page 16) are icy cold as they tumble down from the snowy heights of the Misty Mountains. The waters churn and cascade around the hall, surging down a gully that was shaped and widened by many years of craft. The hall has no protective hedge or walls – it needs only the river and the cliffs. A narrow bridge crosses the river, leading to the knot of outbuildings and storerooms at the front of the hall. Behind the long hall itself, a watchtower rises as if in imitation of the towering peaks around.

When the company approaches the bridge, they are challenged from the other side by the doorkeeper of Mountain Hall, old Beranald.

"Stay where you are, strangers. Your journey has led you here to seek our hall. I see you are warriors. I must ask who you are, in the name of Hartfast, head of the House of Mountain Hall."

A pair of guards cross the bridge to hear the company's answers. If there are any Woodmen who will vouch for the rest of the company, they can cross freely. Otherwise, the company must make a **DC 10 Intelligence (Traditions)** check to be allowed entrance to the hall, and must give up their weapons to the keeping of Beranald (see below). If they fail, they are kept waiting outside until Beranald summons more guards to keep an eye on the strangers.

The company are given a simple meal of bread, cold water and grey mutton. If they ask to see Hartfast, they are escorted up the hill past the watchtower to a cave entrance.

Mountain Hall

1. Narrow Bridge: This bridge is the only easy crossing over the fast-flowing river. North and west of Mountain Hall, the river cuts through a steep gorge; east of the hall, the river clings to the sheer slopes of the mountains on one side, and is too swift and cold to ford. The Woodmen have fortified this river over the years by placing sharpened stones along the west bank to further dissuade trespassers. There is a hidden boathouse several miles east that marks the uppermost point at which the river is navigable.

2. Approach Road: This ramp is the only way into the hall. It cuts back and forth across the mountainside, and at its narrowest is wide enough only for a single cart. The ramp is lined with carved stones to ward off evil spirits.

3. Doorkeeper's House: Here dwells Beranald, doorkeeper of Mountain Hall. Woodmen of good standing may be allowed to keep their weapons, but all other visitors must leave their weapons here in Beranald's care. Doing so gains a +1 modifier for the coming Audience.

One square equals 10 ft

mountain hall

4. Great House: This high-ceilinged building is the heart of the settlement. It has walls of timber and is kept warm by three huge fire-pits. One fire is kept burning at all times of the year, and the Woodmen believe that if this fire ever goes out, doom will befall their hall.

5. Trading Post: This is a trading post where furriers, hunters and farmers may barter for the work of the forges and the mines. Adventurers may also acquire supplies here.

6. Mine Entrance: At the back of the village is the entrance to one of the mines worked by the mountain folk. There are three other mines farther up the gorge, and another two mines over the mountains.

7. The Burg: This tall tower was raised by a great chieftain of the Mountain Folk. His daughter, said to be the most beautiful maiden ever seen in Wilderland, cast herself from the top of the tower when her lover was slain in battle with Dwarves. Her body was never found; one story claims that the remorseful Dwarves found her and placed her drowned, half-dead body in a crystal coffin, where she sleeps until her lover returns from beyond the land of the dead.

8. Hartfast's House: This large house is the home to Hartfast son of Hartmut, head of the House of Mountain Hall. It is always busy and full of life; Hartfast sired five sons and seven daughters, and has more grandchildren than he can remember or bother to count.

The Mine

The entrance leads into one of the mines that worm their way into the Mountain's roots. By the standards of the Woodmen, these are extensive excavations – to a Dwarf, they are a child's idle scratchings. The Woodmen kindle torches made from rushes, and bring the company down into the mine. The walls and floor are slick with water, and icy drops fall from above. The torchlight makes the walls glitter.

These mines mostly dig useful metals out of the ground – copper and tin and iron primarily, but they have found some gold here too. It has long been the dream of the mountain-folk to strike *Mithril*, the fabled Moria-silver, but they have yet to do so.

The tunnels wind on and on, and the company descend several flights of stairs until they come to a larger cave. There, four burly mountain-folk stand with their ears pressed against the far wall. One of these folk turns to greet the company. This is Hartfast, the chieftain of Mountain Hall.

Meeting Hartfast son of Hartmut

Hartfast looks like the Misty Mountains; craggy features, absurdly tall, and a wild shock of white hair. Golden amulets are braided into his grey beard. He has seen more than fifty winters here in the mountains, but he is yet unbowed. He does lean on a stout walking stave more than he used to, but he can still swing an axe or draw a bow with the best of his grandsons.

He is a proud man, and has little time for outsiders – not even the other Woodman tribes are truly welcome here. It is a long way across the River to Woodland Hall, and Hartfast considers them distant cousins at best. Behind his back, the other Woodmen call him the 'tallest dwarf' for his stubborn pride and standoffishness.

Playing Hartfast: Stand and look down on the players. Demand respect. Have no patience. Use silence as a weapon. Don't talk unless you have something to say, and let foolish statements hang in the air.

When the companions first meet him, Hartfast scowls at them, and brusquely demands that they explain their presence in his mountain fortress.

Motivation

To protect his people and his position

Expectations

+2: To be shown the respect I deserve. To be treated as a Woodman, despite living far from Mirkwood
+1: To be given gifts by supplicants. If the name of Radagast is invoked
-1: If Hartfast suspects the player characters will stir up evil with their actions

Interaction

Providing news from afar gains a +1 modifier, as Hartfast is always hungry for tidings from the outside. But begging for favours with little preamble earns the heroes a -1 modifier instead. If the company hints about any threat from the lands to the west of the River Anduin, then Hartfast shrugs.

"Aye, there's something afoot down south, in the Gladden Fields. There's always trouble in those parts, around Dwimmerhorn. I pay it little heed – I've worries closer to home."

Dwimmerhorn, he explains, is an old fort made by 'evil folk' that sits on a stony hillock in the marshes. At least, it usually does – Dwimmerhorn moves of its own accord, they say, and is never in the same place twice. It is said by the mountain-folk that the fort was built by servants of the Necromancer many years ago. It was abandoned by the enemy several times in the past, but it draws dark things to itself, and is never empty for long. From what he knows, it was somewhere in the western part of the Gladden Fields. Local hunters may know more. That puffed-up trapper Magric, for example, knows the marshes very well, even if he is too big for his britches.

If asked for more tales of Dwimmerhorn, Hartfast calls over another one of the greybeards, who says that the marsh fortress is atop a 'great black rock' and that there is only one way up, a narrow path that is watched by many eyes. The fort was always well protected. Orcs and worse things dwelt there, and it was reputed to be haunted. Tales speak of dungeons and treasures delved deep into the black rock below. Some say the rock fell from the sky.

Some of the hunters who come to Mountain Hall to trade have not been seen in several weeks. Maybe something happened to them in the marsh. If he had time and men to spare, then he would look into the matter, but he doesn't right now.

If asked about his 'worries closer to home', Hartfast beckons the company over and bids them put their heads against the stone wall. In the distance, echoing through the stone, they hear the tap-tap-tap of a hammer in the depths.

"Goblins", says Hartfast. "They dig in search of our mineshafts and tunnels. They want to find a secret way in to my hall. We've killed many on the surface, but they are more dangerous down here in the dark."

A Dwarf can suggest useful strategies for dealing with underground combat; Hartfast welcomes such advice (this wins a +2 modifer for the Final Audience Check), and would in fact pay to have a few Dwarves come to his hall for a few years to expand the mine and teach his followers the secrets of dwarven stone-craft.

If the companions ask for aid, make a Final Audience Check, and compare the margin of success to the entries below:

Failure: Harfast has no time, provisions nor men to spare. The companions are left to their own devices. They will be required to leave as soon as possible, and won't be offered provisions for the journey: they will have to hunt to provide their own food.

0-3: Hartfast offers the company hospitality for several nights and supplies for the journey south.

4+: Hartfast sees wisdom in the company's quest, and offers to find them a guide, in addition to the boons above. If the company accepts, then will introduce them to a hunter named Magric (see Magric the Trapper on page 87).

Hartfast & the Dwarves

One potential follow-on from this adventure is for the company to act as intermediaries, bringing Hartfast's request to King Dáin of Erebor. The veins of ore beneath the Misty Mountains are very rich, and while the Dwarrowdelf is lost to Durin's folk, there are other mines to work.

However, both Hartfast and the Dwarves have stiff necks and do not share wealth easily. If the company pursue this quest, then they must later sort out disputes between Hartfast and the Dwarves who come to live in his hall, for both sides believe the other is cheating them of their rightful wealth. Treasure is ever the downfall of friendship between Dwarves and Men.

Night at Mountain Hall

After their encounter with Hartfast, the company can stay in the hall. Depending on how well-disposed Hartfast is to the company, they may get more grey mutton and stale bread in the common hall, or a hot meal and a real bed in the Great Hall.

A Rude Awakening

During the night, the companions are awoken by shouts from outside. If they rush outside, call for **DC 18 Wisdom (Perception)** checks. Those who succeed spot a trio of Goblins (see the *Loremaster's Guide*, page 102) scrambling up the steep mountain slope to the east of the hall!

The Goblins crept up into Mountain Hall from the mines at night and tried to set fire to the storehouse. They were discovered by two watchmen: they stabbed one, but could not prevent the other from sounding the alarm.

- The Goblins are deftly climbing the sheer mountain side and have too much of a lead to be caught, but an archer might attempt to pick them out with an astonishingly good shot — it must be made at Disadvantage and the Goblin receives a +5 bonus to AC for the conditions!

Every archer can make only one attempt before the Goblins will be out of range. If the shot is successful, the Goblin is too surprised to react and falls to its death regardless of the damage inflicted.

- If the companions pause to ask the surviving watchman about what happened, they discover that his companion was stabbed but is now nowhere to be seen.

Companions who didn't lose time in shooting the Goblins and who succeed in a **DC 15 Intelligence (Investigation)** check find bloody tracks and discover that the wounded Woodman stumbled in the dark and fell over the cliff into the river to the north of the trading post: they are just in time to rescue him as he can be spied below as he clings with his remaining strength to the stony shore.

- If the companions do not search for the missing watchman, or tarry too long to shoot at the escaping Goblins, the watchman's corpse is found the day after, stuck among the rocks where the bridge crosses the river.

A Bitter Morning

The morning after, Hartfast visits the company and thanks them for their help, or asks them to leave at once, depending on what happened during the night.

- If the companions didn't inquire about the missing watchman, Hartfast shows them his body and asks them to leave at once, regardless of whether they killed any fleeing Goblins or not.

- If they ignored the fleeing Goblins and rescued, or at least searched for the watchman, Hartfast thanks them for their help and the concern shown for his folk. He provides food for the coming journey, even if he didn't offer to do so the night before.

- If they killed at least one Goblin and rescued the watchman, they are met with Hartfast's approval and gratitude. He offers food and a guide for the coming journey (again, Magric, see below), and invites the companions to accompany him as he climbs the steps leading to the burg to behold the Horn of Warning before they take their leave (see the box, below). With this informal ceremony, Hartfast has recognised the companions as friends of the House of Mountain Hall.

> ### The Horn of Warning
> Inside the burg, the stone tower overlooking the narrow dale, the Woodmen of Woodland Hall keep their greatest treasure: the great Horn of Warning. Carved from the tusk of a Cold-drake, it is a huge blowing horn, wrought with images carved by the hands of many skilled craftsmen. It hangs from the beams of the roof of the tower by means of two gilded chains. Legends say that whoever beholds the Horn of Warning will be able to hear its sound if they are within sight of the Misty Mountains.

The company may depart the day after they arrive, or stay a while if Hartfast offered them hospitality.

Magric the Trapper
Tall, handsome and well-spoken for one of the Woodmen, it is said there is Elvish blood in Magric's family. He lives alone, hunting and trapping in the vales of the Gladden River. He comes to Mountain Hall each month or so to trade. He talks easily, laughs easily, and has an interest in all the doings of the wider world. Over the campfire, he is always curious about the homelands and the cultures of the people he travels with. He is an exceptionally skilled guide, and knows many travel songs to make the miles go quicker.

Secretly, though, Magric is a servant of the enemy. He was caught by Orc patrols in the marshes of the Gladden Fields and brought in chains to the Dwimmerhorn. There, he was threatened with torture, and he bought his freedom by agreeing to act as the enemy's spy. He justifies this betrayal to himself by claiming that he had no choice, and that he did what he had to do to survive.

Playing Magric: Joke and talk with the companions, but never mean it. Try to say exactly what you think the players want to hear. Subtly encourage the company not to worry and to trust in your guidance. Rub your wrists every so often, as if remembering the marks left by chains.

Travelling with Magric
When the company is travelling south with Magric, if any companion is curious about Magric's motivations and talks with or observes the guide for some time, allow a **DC 15 Wisdom (Insight)** check. If successful, the character realises that there is something strange about Magric's behaviour, and that while he knows exactly where he is going, he is pretending to be unsure about their course.

Unless the company challenge Magric before this happens, he turns on the company in Part Five.

– Part Four –
The Passage of the Marshes

The journey south from Mountain Hall to the Dwimmerhorn is a difficult one, as the company do not know exactly where the fortress is located. The journey is easier if the company have Magric guiding them.

The Journey
The first part of the journey has the companions travel from Mountain Hall to where the Gladden River flows out of the Misty Mountains. On the second section of their journey, the adventurers enter the marshes of the Gladden Fields, searching for the Dwimmerhorn.

- On the first leg of the journey, the company skirts the foothills of the mountains for nearly forty miles to the south, then heads east for another thirty along the Gladden River. It takes them five days

- Once inside the Gladden Fields, the company trudges along for twenty miles of marshy terrain. The uncomfortable trip takes three days.

The Journey has a peril rating of 2 and provokes 1d2 Journey Events split between the two sections.

Planning the Route

If the companions let Magric assist their Guide, they may roll 1d8+4 on their Embarkation Roll.

From Mountain Hall to the Gladden River

Travelling along the wolds and valleys of this district is easy enough, although the foreboding peaks cast long shadows over the land. In the warmer months of the year, great beds of iris and flowering reeds crowd the banks of the Gladden River.

Into the Gladden Fields

The Gladden Fields are not the worst swamp in Middle-earth – these are not the Dead Marshes or the Long Marshes south of the Long Lake. But its tangled terrain can be confusing, as the company blunders from one watery hillock to the next, and the thick fogs that rise from the marsh may turn travellers from their path, but there are few mortal perils here... at least, outside the region around the Dwimmerhorn.

Searching for the Dwimmerhorn

To reach their destination, the company must search the marshes. If they are on their own, their hunters and scouts are allowed to make two skill rolls each per day (making a successful **DC 13 Wisdom (Perception** or **Survival)** or **DC 15 Intelligence (Investigation)** check: when the companions have accumulated at least six successful rolls, they can be considered to have reached the Dwimmerhorn.

To enliven the search, a particularly good roll can yield a significant clue and assure the company that they are on the right track. Possible clues include:

- **A well-trod path:** A trail winds its way among the great rushes and tangled reeds of the marshy terrain. It seems to have been used recently.

- **An ominous sight:** The companions catch a glimpse of a distant dark rocky hillock. They succeed in heading towards it for a while, and then lose it in the rising fog; this happens multiple times, giving the companions the uneasy feeling that the stories about the moving Dwimmerhorn might be true.

- **Orc-camp:** the adventurers uncover signs that Orcs have recently camped in the area; chewed bones and discarded remnants of food litter the area, the tall grass has been savagely trampled and small trees and plants hacked to pieces for no apparent reason.

If the company is guided by Magric, he leads them straight towards the fortress. Another possibility is to have the companions stumble upon a slave escaping its captors… (see the next chapter: *Slave & Hunters*).

– Part Five –
Slave & Hunters

As the company make their way through the marshes, check the Look-out's passive Perception score against **DC 10**. If successful, the company hear the sound of several foes crashing through the marsh, and the savage howling of hunting Wargs. A band of Orcs is bearing down on the company!

If the company are travelling with Magric, then any companion who succeeded may also make a **DC 15 Wisdom (Insight)** check; if successful, he notices that Magric paled when he heard the Orc-noise, and that their guide has fallen back to the rear of the company.

The Orcs will be here in moments – if the companion wish to prepare to ambush the enemy, they can hide with a **DC 10 Dexterity (Stealth)** check.

The Fight in the Marshes

A single figure stumbles into view through the willow trees. It's a Man, a Northman by his looks, dressed in rags and obviously in great distress. His hands are manacled together. His face is drawn and gaunt with months of starvation, and he is scarred from whippings and beatings. Close on his heels are the Orcs and their Wolves.

- As soon as the Northman appears, if Magric is with the company, he jumps in the open and runs towards the Orcs crying out "Ambush! Ambush!" His betrayal removes any chance for the company to Surprise the enemy.

The Enemy

There is one Orc Soldier per companion, plus a Black Uruk and a pair of Wild Wolves. If Magric is present, then the company must also deal with their treacherous companion. The Orcs were expecting to be dealing with a lone escaped slave, not a party of doughty adventurers, so they are taken aback when battle is joined. The Uruk roars commands to the soldiers, ordering them to capture the company and not to fear *'a pack of farmers and elf-maggots!'* Refer to the Marsh Map on the back end papers.

Complications

The Gladden Fields count as a Bog (see page 90 of the *Loremaster's Guide*). There are solid patches of ground (see the map) but heroes must make a **DC 10 Wisdom** saving throw to find one before the battle begins.

Fight Events

The Loremaster should read and consider the application of the following battle events at appropriate moments.

Call for Aid: The Orc-Horn

If the Uruk or half of the Orc Soldiers are slain, one of the Orcs takes an action to seek assistance from nearby allies by wildly blowing his orc horn. 1d4 more Orc Soldiers arrive in 1d6+1 rounds. If all the original opponents are slain, the other Orcs are unable to find them and do not appear.

Act of Desperation

The escaped slave leaps to his feet and wraps his manacles around the neck of one of the Orc Soldiers. The throttled Orc slumps to the muddy ground, dead.

Magric's Cowardice

If the Orcs are losing, then Magric flees the battle, running north. He knows the marshes well, and will have advantage on attempts to evade pursuit, while pursuers will suffer disadvantage. He shall return in *Part Eight* of this adventure.

After the Fight

Once the Orcs are defeated, the company can tend to their wounds and the wounds of the escaped prisoner. The slave introduces himself as Walar, a Woodman. He tells his tale desperately, the words spilling out of him, as though trying to make up for months of isolation in a minute of companionship.

He recognised Magric the moment he saw him, for it was Magric who brought about his thralldom – the trapper told Walar that he had found a cache of treasure in the marsh, and that he needed Walar's help to recover it. The pair went into the Gladden Fields, and Magric handed him over to the Orcs. For long months, now, he has suffered as a slave on the Dwimmerhorn. The fortress is not far away.

Likely questions for Walar are listed below, together with his responses.

What were you doing there?
"They made us repair the walls of the fort, and to work in the smithy, making weapons for the Orcs. They whipped us without reason, tortured us... they made us suffer for sport!"

How many orcs were there? What else lives there?
"I don't know how many Orcs there were. A great many. There were Men, too, not as many. And in the temple... there was something else, something horrible. It... was a watchful shadow. It hated us. It delighted in our torment."

Temple?
"On the north side of the rock, there is a stone building. They never let us see beyond its doors, but I heard whispers from within. The dead dwell there, I am sure of it! I do not know what evil they wreak there, but... please, no, don't make me remember!"

How did you escape?
"When I was repairing one of the side walls, I saw that there was a goat path down the side of the rock, on the far side from the main road. I waited for weeks until I had my chance. Two of the Orcs began quarrelling over typical Orcish things, and while they brawled, I jumped over the wall and climbed down the cliff. I nearly fell, but luck was with me, and I reached the bottom alive. A sentry spotted me, and I fled, and they have been on my heels ever since."

Walar is too weak and exhausted to accompany the characters to the Dwimmerhorn. If they free him from his chains, then he will wait for them in the marshes and return with them to Mountain Hall.

- Part Six -
By Secret Ways

Following Walar's directions, the company travel across the marshes until the black rock of the Dwimmerhorn looms out of the mist. The rock rises more than one hundred and fifty feet above the marshy plain. Tufts of

the dwimmerhorn

One square equals 5 feet

green grass grow from small ledges and cracks in the black cliffside, but the rock is almost sheer in places. Climbing it will be exceedingly difficult. Atop the rock, the company can make out a low curtain wall encircling several buildings, a ghastly temple of black stone among them: a sickly greenish light flares from time to time from its narrow windows.

The Dwimmerhorn

More than two thousand years ago, Isildur was ambushed by Orcs and slain in the Gladden Fields. The One Ring – Isildur's Bane – slipped from his finger and was lost in the waters of the Great River. When the Enemy came to Dol Guldur, he sent out his slaves to search the marshes and the river for signs of the Ring. The Dwimmerhorn housed but one of their outposts and watchtowers.

When Gandalf entered Dol Guldur for the first time in the year 2063, the Enemy fled before him, and his servants dispersed. The Dwimmerhorn was abandoned and laid empty for many long years. It was repaired and reoccupied centuries later, when the search for the One Ring resumed. When the White Council attacked Dol Guldur and the Necromancer was again forced to retreat, a minion of the Enemy, the spirit known as the Gibbet King (see page 5), fled to the Dwimmerhorn and now dwells there.

The Gibbet King commands more than two hundred Orcs, and can demand service from the Orcs of the Misty Mountains when necessary. Evil men who lived in Dol Guldur and worshipped the darkness have followed the spirit into exile. And other horrors may sleep beneath the Dwimmerhorn, awaiting their true master's call.

The Dwimmerhorn

1. The Road: The easiest approach to the fort atop the Dwimmerhorn is this narrow path that winds across the south face of the rock. In places, the path is so narrow that only a single traveller can pass, and it is impossible to climb it without being seen from the gatehouse above.

2. Gatehouse: This crumbling fortification controls the main approach to the fort. The road ends at an iron portcullis that is controlled from the gatehouse. Arrow-slits and murder-holes allow those within to rain death down on attackers. There are a dozen Orc Guards in the gatehouse.

3. Curtain Walls: The low walls are no more than eight feet tall at their highest, but they run right up against the edge of the cliff, to dissuade those who might try to climb the rock.

4. Orc Barracks: This long building is a den for the Orc warriors who dwell here. The building stinks like a midden and is lit only by foul-smelling candles. At any time, there are more than a score of Orcs here or in the courtyard outside. Their taskmasters keep the Orcs hard at work, whipping the slaves or drilling for battle.

5. Storehouses: These contain supplies looted from the surrounding countryside. The storehouses are simple buildings of wood, not stone.

6. Smithy: This smithy is at work night and day, churning out weapons for the Orcs.

7. Warg Den: The blood-thirsty wolves are kept here, tended by slaves and fed with slaves.

8. Keep: The keep is only partially intact, and the whole upper floor is crumbling and uninhabitable. The lower floor is used to house the human servants of the spirit, as well as the Orc-captain Ghor (see sidebar).

9. Temple: See *The Shadow in the Temple*, below.

10. Pits: Slaves are kept in this underground prison, dug into the upper surface of the rock. They have little shelter from the weather – instead of a ceiling, they have only an iron grating.

11. Catacomb Entrance: This foreboding crypt leads down into tunnels beneath the rock. What lurks there is a mystery.

12. Secret Path: This is the secret path discovered by Walar. Using the path allows members of the company to scale the rock and enter the fort by secret.

Ghor the Despoiler

...a huge Orc-chieftain, almost man-high, clad in black mail from head to foot, leaped into the chamber...

Ghor was bred in the Mountains of Shadow, the western fence of Mordor in the distant south. He came north to serve the Necromancer in his woodland fastness. When Dol Guldur fell, he gathered a band of strong Orcs and went reaving through Mirkwood, hunting and killing until the Elves ambushed them, and only Ghor survived. Alone, he wandered aimlessly, hunting Woodmen for meat. In the last year, he heard a call and found his way to the Dwimmerhorn. Here, he quickly rose to become captain of the fort (the previous captain he threw from the top of the wall). He is a strong, proud Orc, at the height of his strength, with a fearful iron helm bearing the sign of the Red Eye. None rival him, and now that Bolg son of Azog is dead, it shall be Ghor son of Ghâsh who rules the North!

Ghor the Despoiler
Medium humanoid (Orc-kind)

STR	DEX	CON	INT	WIS	CHA
18 (+4)	12 (+1)	18 (+4)	11 (+0)	11 (+0)	16 (+3)

Armour Class 15 (cobbled-together Orc armour)
Hit Points 93 (11d8+44)
Speed 30 ft

Saving Throws Str +7, Con +7, Wis +3
Skills Intimidation +6
Senses passive Perception 10
Languages Orkish, Black Speech, Westron
Challenge 5 (1,800 XP)

Leadership. As a bonus action, Ghor can command a single orc within 30 ft orc other than himself. That orc takes its turn immediately after Ghor.
Horrible Strength. If Ghor makes a successful melee attack, he may use his bonus action to cause 4 additional damage of the same type as the original type.

Actions
Multiattack. Ghor makes two axe attacks.
Heavy Orc-axe. *Melee Weapon Attack:* +7 to hit, reach 5 ft, one target. *Hit:* 11 (2d6+4) slashing damage.
Battle Cry (1/day). Each orc within 30 feet other than Ghor gains Advantage on attack rolls until the start of the war chief's next turn. Ghor may then make one attack as a bonus action.

Burglary

Not even one of the Elf-lords of old could storm the Dwimmerhorn single-handedly and live to tell the tale, and the companions are not yet legendary heroes. They need stealth and secrecy, not force. Radagast gave them the quest of finding out what evil lurked in the Gladden Fields, and the answer to that question is within the dark temple atop the rock. Ideally, the company make it into the Temple and eavesdrop on the spirit. However, it is possible that their spying is spotted earlier. When the company is discovered, they must flee or perish – move onto *Fly, You Fools!*

Crossing the Marshes

The first step is to cross the marshland at the foot of the rock without being seen. This requires a **DC 15 Dexterity (Stealth)** check; if the check fails then the hero is permitted a **DC 10 Wisdom** saving throw to spot the danger and dive into cover in the nick of time.

Climbing the Cliffs

Climbing the cliffs requires a **Strength (Athletics)** check. Most of the cliff face is a daunting climb (**DC 20**), but the secret path described by Walar is simply hard (**DC 15**). Companions who choose to take their time must succeed at one **DC 10 Dexterity (Stealth)** check and two **DC 10 Strength (Athletics)** checks.

Falling

Failing a roll while climbing means the companion slips and falls. Fortunately, the cliff – while steep – is not sheer. A falling hero slides for 1d6 x 10 feet, taking bludgeoning damage as normal.

Sneaking Around the Fortress

Once the burglar reaches the top of the cliff and clambers over the wall, he can explore the Dwimmerhorn. Moving from building to building requires a **Dexterity (Stealth)** check, with the DC varying from 10 to 20 depending on distance and circumstances.

The Shadow in the Temple

The fortress of the Dwimmerhorn is crudely built, raised by Orcs and their slaves. It is functional, but the wind whistles through gaps in the stones, and the buildings lean and totter. The temple, though, was built by servants of the Enemy out of the East. They cut the black stone of the Dwimmerhorn with wicked cunning and raised up a grim basilica in the manner of their homelands.

The black walls are devoid of decorations or statues, but their surface is polished like a mirror, and reflects back twisted images. Many narrow windows open high along the walls, letting out a greenish luminescence.

Entering the Temple

The heavy doors of the temple are tall and forged of green bronze, but they open easily when pushed inward. As soon as they cross the threshold, the companions are nearly frozen on the spot in fear, and can enter only with great effort: if the company obtained any magical boons from Radagast at the beginning of the adventure (see page 79), there is a chance that what is inside the temple takes notice of the power bestowed upon them and attempts to dispel it.

Lockmand

A trader and dealer in strange artefacts and curiosities, Lockmand hails originally from Esgaroth, where he was one of the previous Master's closest associates. When the old Master fled, Lockmand decided that his affairs in the south suddenly needed urgent attention, and he left Lake-town in haste. He has not been seen in the north in several years.

He fancies himself to be witty, urbane and sophisticated, and in his riddle-talk he has quite convinced himself that morality is a thing for simple men. He speaks of 'alliances of convenience', of 'contracts and treaties and understandings', and believes that by helping the Enemy he will bring a great new order to the North. Lockmand plays little part in this adventure, but the company will meet him again in *The Crossing of Celduin* (page 99). It is very important that the heroes get but a glimpse of his appearance, lest they recognise him when they meet the trader in Dale.

- One companion (the one with the highest Wisdom) must make a **DC 15 Wisdom** saving throw for every spell laid upon the company (the Beast Protection, the Spell of Concealment, the Travel Blessing, even the Storm bag, but not the Mirkwood Cordial).

For example, if the company was adventuring under a Spell of Concealment, the Travel Blessing and carrying the Mirkwood Cordial, then two rolls would be required.

- If a saving throw is successful, the spell resists and the power in it remains concealed.

- If the saving throw is failed, the spell is broken and the company feels the wizard's benevolence leave them: all character gain a point of Shadow and the company's presence has been noticed.

- Finally, if the roll fails with a natural 1, not only the spell is broken and the company gain Shadow points, but all companions are daunted and are Frightened for as long as they remain inside the temple.

The Sanctum

Inside the temple, many pillars of black stone support its tall roof. Upon entering, the companions see that the unseemly light originates from the far end, where a heavily sculpted casket with an open side lies against the wall of a small shrine. Coffin-sized and apparently made of gilded wood reinforced with iron bands, the casket displays an oversized length of chain, each black metal link the size of a human head. The luminescence seems to radiate from the chain itself.

Bathed in the green glow stand two figures – one is a human (Lockmand), the other is the Orc-captain Ghor. They are deep in conversation, but even the hoarse voice of the Orc is kept at a whisper. Between them, lying on the floor, is an ancient withered corpse, with pale skin drawn tight over bones. It is dressed in a black robe, its unmoving head featureless but for a gleam in its eye-sockets. A harsh and chilling voice emerges from the corpse's lips as the spirit speaks through them.

- The companions are too far away to hear the conversation, so they must sneak closer if they are to listen. This requires a **DC 15 Dexterity (Stealth)** check. If successful, they catch a few words of the conversation between the three.

The Conversation

The man, the Orc and the spirit are planning their future moves.

The Orc urges that they need to move sooner rather than later. *"The mountain-maggots want plunder and war. They say they didn't come south to sit and wait in their holes. They want to kill!"*

The human argues that they are not ready. *"We need more time. The Chain is useless to us, unless we master its secrets. We must bide our time, until we can strike with the greatest weapon in all of Middle-earth."*

The corpse stirs and whispers, every word a shiver along the companions' spines. *"Send word to the mountain tribes. They will wait, or they will die with the rest of the North. Double your patrols. If we are discovered, all may be lost."*

The Orc and the man kneel before the corpse, then depart. Stealth tests are again needed to avoid being spotted.

Exploring the Temple

Once Lockmand and the Orc have left, the companions may want to have a look around. The temple is empty, except for the gilded casket containing the chain and the dried corpse sprawled in front of it. Even from a distance, the companions notice that the gleam that previously animated the eye-sockets of the corpse seems to have been extinguished. No voice emerges from its lips, and now it appears as nothing more than the desiccated remains of a man. Looking at the casket and its content from any distance is uncomfortable, and makes the observer feel a tightness in his chest, as if invisible bonds were closing around him.

- If anyone gets close enough to touch the chain, they gain 1 Shadow point. The chain is too big and heavy to be stolen.

Discovered!

If by some great fortune the company have managed to avoid detection thus far, then the spirit senses the intruders and raises the alarm. The burglars are surprised when a shadowy figure slithers towards them. Any of the company who saw the spirit in *Those Who Tarry No Longer* recognises it as the same horror.

The spirit hisses a word in the Black Speech of Mordor, then vanishes. A moment later, the Orc-horns blow.

> ### The Chain of Thangorodrim
>
> The chain inside the temple is a relic of great power. It was forged in the Elder Days by the dark powers of the world, and was used to enslave proud, rebellious dragons. When placed around a creature, the chain robs the creature of all free will and forces them to serve the master of the chain. It was carried out of the far north by evil men in the second age, and rested in the tunnels under Mount Gram for many centuries.
>
> When the Necromancer claimed Dol Guldur as his new sanctum, the chain was brought there and given into the keeping of the Gibbet King, although the Necromancer retained mastery of the artefact. Particularly troublesome slaves were subjected to the iron mercy of the Chain.
>
> When Dol Guldur was assaulted by the White Council, the Gibbet King had the Chain moved to the Dwimmerhorn, so that he might study it and master it fully.

– PART SEVEN – FLY, YOU FOOLS!

Once the company is discovered, they must escape. The flight from the Dwimmerhorn itself is perilous – the company must climb down the rockface again, or else fight their way across the courtyard and out past the gatehouse. If the company stop or try to hold their ground, they will be overcome. Their only hope lies in stealth and swiftness.

Climbing down the Rock

It is easier to climb down than up, requiring only a **DC 10 Strength (Athletics)** check. The Orcs fire arrows at the escaping intruders, so the longer the company cling to the wall, the more attacks they are subjected to (they are subject to one arrow shot each if they do not tarry unnecessarily).

As the company escape the shadow of Dwimmerhorn, they hear Orcs shouting commands from above. "Find them! Kill them! No escape!" The portcullis grinds open, and brigades of Orcs march forth. The company are the quarry in a bloody hunt.

The Journey

The company is ninety miles away from Mountain Hall, across the marshes and bogs of the Gladden Fields and the foothills of the Misty Mountains.

The Journey has a Peril Rating of 2 and provokes 1d2 Journey Events.

- Based on the usual journey rules, the trip back to Woodland Hall requires eight days of march.

As first presented in the adventure *Kinstrife & Dark Tidings* the companions can also press themselves with a Forced march (see page 55).

- If they undertake a forced march, the return trip will take four days, but it requires two **DC 15 Constitution** saving throws.

- As far as the pursuit is concerned, attempting a Forced march raises the company's Lead by 2 points. See *Hunted!* below.

Wilderland Adventures

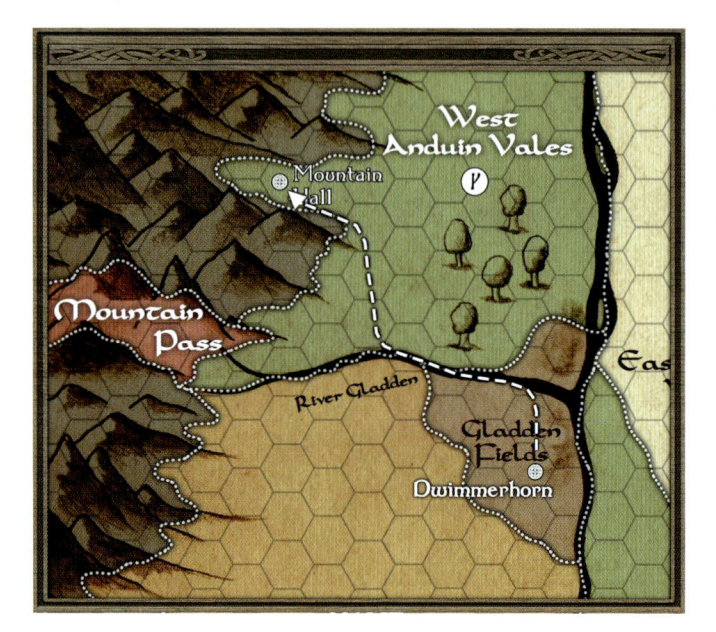

Other Routes?

While Mountain Hall is the closest haven to the Gladden Fields, the company may decide to head to Rhosgobel or some other destination, or try to lead the Orcs away from Mountain Hall. If the players choose this, then adapt the journey to the company's new destination.

Hunted!

The company is pursued by Orcs out of the Dwimmerhorn. To handle the hunt, the Loremaster must keep track of the company's Lead, which measures how close the Orcs are on their trail.

At the start of the hunt, the Lead begins at a value determined by how the chase began.

- The characters were caught inside the Dwimmerhorn: Lead of 2
- The characters were spotted outside the Dwimmerhorn: Lead of 3
- The characters escaped the Dwimmerhorn without being seen: Lead of 5

This rating diminishes whenever the companions fail at a roll made to resolve the journey.

If the Lead rating is reduced to zero, then the company has been overtaken by its pursuers (see *Overtaken!* below). If the company reach their destination before this happens, then they are safe from the Orcs.

Distance of the Pursuers

At the beginning of the pursuit, the distance between the company and its pursuers is rather small. The company can increase their Lead by attempting the following:

- **Hiding their tracks (Hunters):** This requires a **DC 15 Wisdom (Peception)** check. Each Hunter in the company may only make one check for the entire journey. On a success, Lead increases by 1; on a natural 20, by 2.

- **Taking unexpected paths (Scouts):** This requires a DC 15 Wisdom (Survival) check. Each Scout in the company may make only one check for the entire journey. On a success, Lead increases by 1; on a natural 20, by 2.

If any of the rolls described above fail, the Loremaster reduces the Lead of the company by one for each failed roll. If any one of the tests fails on a natural 1, the company has left a trail or lost ground: roll 1d6 and deduct that much Lead.

Overtaken!

If the Lead is ever reduced to zero (or less), then the company has been overtaken by outriders and scouts. They have a last chance to either hide from these pursuers (requiring a **DC 15 Dexterity (Stealth)** check), or ambush them (their foes are Surprised and the heroes have 2d4 rounds to defeat them before the main host arrives). The scouts consist of one Messenger of Lugbúrz and one Orc Soldier per hero.

- If they succeed, their Lead rating is restored to a value of 1. If they fail, an enemy scout spots the company and reports back to the main body of the pursuers (see Caught in the Open, below).

Caught in the Open

If the company are overtaken by Ghor's hunters, they have several options, most of them unappealing.

96

Stand and Fight
The company are massively outnumbered, but they could try fighting. They face some fifty Orcs, mostly Orc Soldiers and Snaga Trackers, led by Ghor himself. The company must find a place like a narrow gorge or rocky outcrop (see page 90 of the *Loremaster's Guide*) that they can defend without taking on all the Orcs at once.

I'll Hold Them Off
One or two members of the company could make a heroic last stand, sacrificing their own lives by fighting the entire Orc-host while the rest flee. The survivor's Lead is increased to 3, plus one per Orc slain by the defenders.

Unlikely Aid
The companions may be able to call upon unlikely allies to help them escape, such as the Lord of the Eagles, if they won his favour in *Those Who Tarry No Longer*. Allies may either increase the company's Lead, or end the chase prematurely.

Arrival at the Hall
When the company return to Mountain Hall, they find a dozen archers levelling bows at them across the narrow bridge. They are under the command of Beranald, the doorkeeper.

A moment later, Hartfast arrives to speak to the company. The traitorous guide Magric is at Hartfast's side.

The chieftain challenges the company: *"You are not welcome here. Magric has told us about how you tried to murder him in the marshes. You are outlaws and Orc-friends! If I see you again, I shall have you put to death. Leave now and never return!"*

The company must plead their case. This requires a **Charisma** check (probably **Persuasion**, although **Intimidation** or **Intelligence** (**Traditions**) can also work). The DC for this test starts at **DC 16**, modified as follows:

-**2**: if Walar is with the company
-**2**: if the company left on good terms with Hartfast, or -**4** if they left as friends of Mountain Hall (they have been shown the Horn of Warning)
-**2**: if the company are clearly injured after battles with Orcs

-**1**: if there is at least one Woodman in the company
+**2**: if there are no Woodmen or Beornings in the company

Treachery!
If the company succeeds in the test and instills some doubts in the mind of Hartfast, then a blade flashes in Magric's hand and he attempts to swiftly stab the chieftain: if the companions didn't expect anything like that, then Magric is able to wound Hartfast grievously, before he dives into the river. If no companion gets him with a spear or bow, he rapidly disappears as the bows of the Woodmen send arrows into the raging waters.

If Magric's attempt to assassinate Hartfast is foiled and the turncoat is still alive, the chieftain of Mountain Hall turns on him with cold fury.

"How many of my people have you led to slavery? How long have you plotted with my enemies? Damn you! If it is gold that you want, then gold you shall have! Take him to the deepest part of the gold mine and wall him up in a side tunnel. Let the traitor live in the same darkness as his Orc-friends!"

If the company fails in winning back Hartfast's trust, the companions are refused entry into Mountain Hall, and must face the Orcs alone – see *Caught in the Open* on page 96 for guidelines on how to deal with the unfortunate result.

Assassins in the Hall
The company finds safety in Mountain Hall. The settlement is well fortified, and Ghor's force lacks the strength to besiege it. Woodmen Look-outs spot Ghor's host approach the hall, and the Orcs even send some scouts up the valley, but the Orcs turn back and seem to retreat south towards the Marshes rather than risk an attack on the hall. Hartfast is pleased by this, and invites the company to stay for some days so they can rest and recover from the long chase. He assigns them places to sleep in a house near the trading post, and allows them to keep their weapons instead of leaving them at the doorkeeper's house.

Unbeknownst to the company, Ghor travels only a few miles south before turning west. He meets with Goblins of the Misty Mountains, who show him secret underground passages that connect with the mines of Mountain Hall. These passages are too narrow for Ghor's entire host, but are perfectly suited to sneaking a small number of assassins into Mountain Hall. Ghor himself leads this secret attack. His intent is to sneak into the Hall, find the company, and kill them before they can tell the Wizard or others what they have discovered.

Waking in the Night

One night, check passive Perception against **DC 12** unless the company keep a Look-out even when sleeping in the hall. If any hero succeeds, then they are woken by the sound of guttural voices outside their house, and have time to grab weapons and don armour. If they fail, then the first warning they get is when the Orcs smash down their door, and the company begins the fight without armour.

The Assassins

The assassins are led by Ghor himself; he is accompanied by two Orc Soldiers and two Snaga Trackers (whose snuffling nostrils have located the abode of the companions). All are armed with poisoned blades (each enemy has the Venomous special ability, see page 117 of the *Loremaster's Guide*).

- The company must survive for six rounds before help arrives. Afterwards, the Woodmen come with Hartfast in the lead, and the Orcs are surrounded and slaughtered.

– Epilogue –
The Shadow of the Future

Surviving Ghor's assault brings this adventure to an end. After resting at Mountain Hall, the company can bring word to Radagast at Rhosgobel of what they saw in the marshes. The wizard is deeply troubled by the company's description of the spirit and the Chain.

Strangely, when more scouts are sent to keep watch on the Dwimmerhorn, they find the hilltop fort to be completely deserted. The Gibbet King and his servants have vanished into the marsh as though they never existed.

Radagast speculates that the enemy did not expect to be discovered so soon, and has retreated to some other place of safety. He fears that the enemy is still plotting against the Free Peoples, and that the stroke will fall where they least expect it...

Fellowship Phase

Either Rhosgobel or Mountain Hall may be made into a sanctuary through the *Open Sanctuary* undertaking. The characters could also use Research Lore to investigate the Chain of Thangorodrim, and how it is said to be able to enslave the wills of others.

– The Crossings – of Celduin

For Heroes of Level 5 or 6

- **When:** The company may undertake this quest in any year from 2946 onwards. The adventure *A Darkness in the Marshes* should be played first. The adventure starts in the last days of November, when the city of Dale is preparing for the Gathering of Five Armies. If the adventure is set in 2946, then this is the first Gathering, held five years after the battle that gives the celebration its name, otherwise it is the ongoing annual celebration.
- **Where:** The adventure takes place east of Mirkwood, in Dale and the regions south of Lake-town.
- **What:** A raven brings word of an army approaching the Crossings of the River Running (the Celduin in Elvish), and the company are sent south to hold off the attackers until King Bard can rally an army.
- **Why:** Treachery has struck in the heart of Dale, and a villain has poisoned many of King Bard's best warriors during the Gathering of the Five Armies.
- **Who:** The company meets and interacts with King Bard the Dragonslayer, and face in battle the spirit whose machinations have plagued Wilderland.

Adventuring Phase

This adventure is divided into eight parts, taking the heroes from frolic in Dale to a desperate battle at the crossings.

Part One – The Gathering of Five Armies
Adventurers, warriors, travellers and heroes from across the North gather for the great feast celebrating the victory at the Battle of Five Armies. The companions arrive in Dale for the festivities, as does a certain Grey Pilgrim…

Part Two – A Golden Prize
A merchant from Esgaroth offers a prize for the best warrior and best archer in Dale, and almost every fighting man in the town enters the contest. The merchant also promises that every entrant, regardless of how well they perform, will be part of a great feast. The companions may or may not choose to enter the contest.

Part Three – An Ill-Made Party
The feast is poisoned, and most of Dale's soldiers are stricken with illness! The merchant attempts to flee – the company may be able to capture him before he escapes in a boat.

Part Four – Raven's Tidings
A raven of the Mountain arrives, bringing word of an army that marches against the North. Soon it will cross the River Running. To buy time for the Kingdom and Lake-town to mount a defence, King Bard calls all those who can still travel and fight to serve in this hour of need.

Part Five – South to the Crossings
The company travel south to the Crossings of Celduin, rallying the countryside as they go.

Part Six – The Calm Before The Storm
The company arrive at a small village, and prepare for the battle to come.

Part Seven – The Battle Begins
The enemy attack the village, trying to force their way across the river. Battle is joined!

Part Eight – The Last Day
Having repulsed the first attackers, the company have only a few more hours to hold out – but are they clinging to a fool's hope?

– Part One – The Gathering of Five Armies

Word has spread throughout the North about the magnificence of the festivities held in Dale at the end of the month of November. For weeks now, travellers and traders have made their way to the town. The roads are crowded with all manner of folk, both locals and strange foreigners. Farmers who never travelled farther than Esgaroth rub shoulders with Elves of Mirkwood and Dwarves who came all the way from the Iron Hills or even from the distant Blue Mountains; some visitors have come north from as far away as Dorwinion.

If the company were separated during the most recent Fellowship Phase, they may have agreed to meet at Dale. Half the Free Folk in Wilderland will be here. Characters whose patron is not attending, or who are of exceptionally high standing in their communities, may be sent as official emissaries to represent their folk.

Arrival in Dale

The town is filled to overflowing when the company arrives. A sea of pitched tents has sprung up around the Traders Gate, and the Merchant Way (the road leading to Esgaroth) is positively crowded. There is a carnival atmosphere in the town, an abundant joy that mixes the excitement of the feast with the glorious end of the harvest season. Pedlars offer the company trinkets and sweets as they push through the crowded streets. Jugglers, fire-eaters and other entertainers caper and dance. Every inn is full, and every voice is lifted in song.

If any of the companions are from Dale, then they can stay with their kin or in their own homes. Visitors have trouble finding lodgings; rooms at inns like the Drunkenstone cost several gold pieces, and everyone else must camp outside the town. Dale-folk with a good reputation may be offered a bed at the Royal Palace.

> ### The Drunkenstone
> This was one of the first inns built in Dale, and was originally called the New Inn. A man named Skelid recently purchased it and changed the name. The sign hanging outside depicts the fabled Arkenstone above a mug of beer. Many of the older Dwarves of the Mountain consider this to be disrespectful to the gemstone, but that has not stopped younger, wilder Dwarves from wetting their beards with the inn's ale. Skelid is young and ambitious, with his fingers in many pies in Dale, and he sometimes has need of discreet adventurers who are not afraid of a little underhanded work or burglary.

The Market

Traders have come from far and wide to the great market, the biggest in the North in many years. Dale is a young kingdom, and one with coin to spend. The former Desolation of Smaug has bloomed and brought forth rich harvest after rich harvest. The Dwarves of the Lonely Mountain get most of the benefit of this new wealth, as the Bardings hire stonecutters and builders and artisans. The market brings many other treasures and wonders to Dale – clothing and jewellery from Lake-town, leather and woodcraft from as far as Mirkwood, wine from Dorwinion, smithcraft from the Iron Hills.

Many of the stalls offer toys, games or curiosities. Candied apples and figs, meat on sticks, ale, wine, dwarf-spirits, mead from the Elvenking's halls and all manner of delights are to be had. There are carvings and banners celebrating the victory at the Battle of Five Armies. Some stalls offer stranger things – books of lore, ancient scrolls, magical talismans, charms, love potions and enchanted philtres, rings that ward off evil, scales and claws from Smaug (they may look like bear claws or lizard scales, but the merchant insists they were plucked from the dragon's corpse). The company pass two traders brawling, both accusing the other of selling a fake Black Arrow when they swear they have the original.

Masks

Several stalls are selling painted wooden or leather masks, and they are doing a lot of business. If the companions ask, they learn that it is a fashion imported from Dorwinion, and that almost everyone will wear one tonight, after the ceremonial opening of the festivities.

Amusements & Contests

In the streets around the market, there are games and diversions where a lucky companion could win a few coins.

Riddle-games

One of the most popular contests among the folk of Dale, the Riddle-game is held on a stage. Wit and charm are just as important as cunning here – if you can't make the crowd laugh with your riddles, they are likely to boo you off the stage in the early round of the contest. By the end of the contest, though, the few surviving contestants are those whose minds are a storehouse of riddles and puzzles.

- If a companion participates in the Riddle-game, he must make a series of three **Intelligence (Riddle)** checks. The first is at **DC 10**, the second at **DC 15**, and the third at **DC 20**. If he succeeds at all three, he wins the Riddle-game and gains an Experience Award.

Sample Riddles:

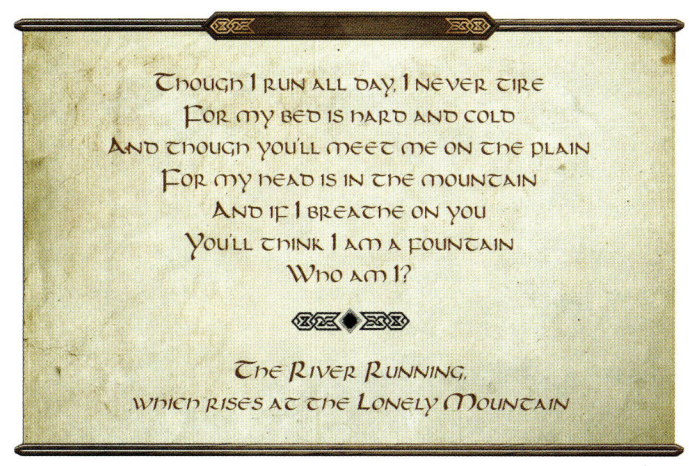

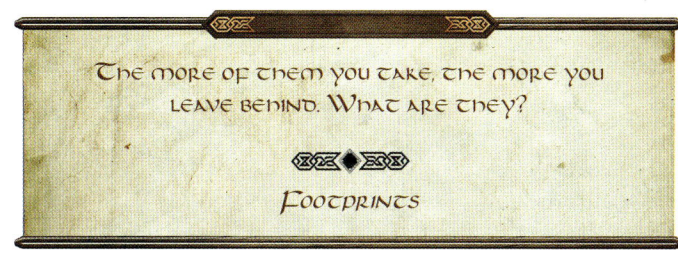

> Though I run all day, I never tire
> For my bed is hard and cold
> And though you'll meet me on the plain
> For my head is in the mountain
> And if I breathe on you
> You'll think I am a fountain
> Who am I?
>
> The River Running, which rises at the Lonely Mountain

> The more of them you take, the more you leave behind. What are they?
>
> Footprints

> You bury me when I'm alive, and dig me up when I die. What am I?
>
> A plant

Song-contests

To enter the singing contest, a character must have proficiency in **Performance**. The DC to beat is 15. A companion who succeeds acquits himself well; a companion who passes by 5 or more is invited to sing at the Royal Palace on some future day, and a companion who passes by 10 or more is given a purse of silver pennies (20s) and asked to sing at the masked ball this evening. Any success is worth an Experience Award.

Games of Chance

The most popular forms of gambling in Dale revolve around dice and a popular Dwarf game that is basically dominoes played with runes. There are stranger games however, like betting on which rat will make it out of the maze first or wagering sums of money on the colour of the hood of the next stranger to come around the corner.

THE OPENING CEREMONY

At twilight, a crowd gathers around the fountain commemorating the Fall of Smaug, in front of the Royal Palace. A procession of nobles and courtiers emerges from its great front gate, and is welcomed by cheers and shouts from all bystanders. The group is led by Dáin, King under the Mountain, and a trio of elven emissaries clad in green and gold; they are followed by the Master of Lake-town. Last, King Bard makes his appearance, followed by his most trusted counsellors, all archers who formerly served in his company when he was but a Captain in Esgaroth.

King Bard steps forward to address the crowd. His dwarf-wrought crown glitters in the light of many lanterns. His frame is as lean and hard as it was when he brought down the Dragon, but this night his grey eyes are alight with joy.

"People of Wilderland!' he shouts. "Years ago we were strangers to each other, as we hid in shadows. We were afraid of a world where Dragons ruled and Orcs were free to plunder. Then, one day our worst fears came upon us, and threatened to bury us forever, together with our weaknesses and worries."

The crowd grows silent, as an old man wrapped in cloak and hood emerges from among the king's counsellors and takes place by Bard's side. Bard continues his speech:

"But then the clouds that darkened our days were torn by the wind, and a red sunset slashed the West. We fought together at the Battle of Five Armies, and we prevailed together. And today we are here to testify that since that day we stand united!"

As the crowd erupts, the old man casts aside his hood and cloak, raising a tall staff: Gandalf the Grey has come to Dale! Sudddenly, the staff of the wizard blazes forth with a flash, and behind the Royal Palace, the sky over Dale erupts with the most magical fireworks, bright enough to illuminate the flanks of the Mountain. Flowers and trees and candelabras and shooting stars, and then a flock of great golden eagles that burst like the dawn.

The Grey Pilgrim

The Gathering of Five Armies might be the first occasion for the company to encounter the wandering wizard. If this is not the first Gathering, then perhaps Gandalf is visiting Dale to evaluate the current political climate surrounding the courts of Men, Elves and Dwarves. Regardless of the precise cause for his presence, Gandalf is busy making private meetings with the various rulers of the area (especially if the year is 2948 or later) and won't take part in the celebrations (he will leave before the masked ball begins). As a consequence, only companions with access to the court of King Bard can hope to get to talk to him: it requires a Barding character with the King's Men virtue to be invited to the Council, or a private meeting if King Bard is a patron of the company. If the companions have played through the A Darkness in the Marshes adventure, then it is Gandalf who seeks them out. The grey wizard has conferred with Radagast, and is now worried about the true nature of the spirit that the company last saw on the Dwimmerhorn. Regardless of the nature of the encounter, the meeting is brief - Gandalf is busy with many concerns - and starts with the wizard questioning the companions about what they know about the spirit. Then, it is his time to talk, and his is an interesting tale...

> ### The Dungeons of Dol Guldur
>
> "Many years ago I myself dared to pass the doors of the Necromancer in Dol Guldur for the second time, to secretly explore his ways. What I discovered in that occasion is not a matter that I will discuss here, but suffice it to say that I found the place to be even darker and oppressive than before. It seemed to me that a new power had allied itself with the Necromancer, and ruled the deeper pits of Dol Guldur."
>
> "It was there that I found Thráin, the father of Thorin Oakenshield, wandering witless and near death in the blackest dungeons. I came too late, and he died before I could help him, but with his last words he uttered the name of his gaoler and tormentor: the Gibbet King."
>
> "I fled that accursed place before the Necromancer could spy my presence, but I knew that my visit didn't go unnoticed. I felt the eyes of that dreadful lord of prisons upon me. The Gibbet King saw me, but seemed content to let me go."

The Masked Ball

As the fireworks die down, everyone in the crowd puts on a mask and starts to mingle. Musicians put hand to harp and mouth to flute, and the warm night is filled with song and dancing. There are several sets of musicians, notably a band of thirteen Dwarves (including Bombur himself) who get into a sort of musical battle with a group of Elves. While the two sides have very different styles (dwarven bombast contrasted with elvish harmonies), they are equally enthusiastic, and end up joining together to produce the strangest music ever heard in the North – but at least you can dance to it!

- If a companion won the singing contest, he is invited to sing. A successful **DC 20 Charisma (Performance)** check here wins the hero even greater renown and an invitation to play at the courts of the Elvenking and the King under the Mountain.

Folk at the Gathering

There are several characters that might be met at the ball:

Bombur the Fat: As one of the thirteen dwarven companions of Thorin Oakshield on the Quest of Erebor, Bombur certainly qualifies as 'great'. Since his adventure he has adjusted to his new uneventful life, and he is rapidly becoming the fattest Dwarf under the Mountain. He is here as part of King Dáin's court, and to sample the Barding's food. Dwelling mostly in dining halls and kitchens, Bombur knows all the gossip and secrets in Dale and the Lonely Mountain, and can be a useful source of information for the company if they befriend him. At the masked ball, he wears a Dragon mask – although no mask could hide his weight.

Elstan: When Bard became king of Dale, Elstan was among the first to swear loyalty to him. The tall grey-eyed, gaunt northerner is called the First Captain of Dale, and commands the Royal Barracks. He is famed for his skill with the sword, his dwarf-forged spear, and his gleaming suit of armour. Whenever the kingdom is threatened, he is there to defend it. The people love him, and he is the favourite in the melee to be held tomorrow. If any of the company is a member of the King's Men, or are known for their service to Dale, then Elstan greets them. Others can try to fight their way through his crowd of admirers. Elstan wears his visored steel helm in lieu of a mask.

Gerold: Said by some to be kin to Beorn, Gerold is a fierce mercenary. A veritable giant of a man, his size belies his speed and reflexes. He can bury his axe in an Orc's head with a serpent-quick flick of the wrist. If he calls any place other than the battlefield home, it is nearby Esgaroth. He is here for whatever prize can be found in fighting contests held during the gathering. Gerold wears no mask – he's here for the free drink.

Galia: This young Elf-maid carries a bow that seems much too large for her slender frame, but her skill at archery is legendary even among her woodland kin. Of late, she has succumbed to wanderlust, and this visit to Dale is the start of her wanderings in the north. She wears a delicate wooden mask that resembles the moon.

Lockmand: The merchant Lockmand is everywhere tonight. He is a merchant from Esgaroth who left after the previous Master fled the town. He has recently returned to the north, having made his fortune trading in 'antiquities and curios', and is eager to share his wealth. Secretly,

Lockmand is in league with the spirit. He wears a great golden mask that looks like a beaming sun.

- A successful **DC 13 Intelligence (Riddle)** check reveals rumours that he has a questionable past. He was closely associated with the old Master of Lake-town, and is now trying to curry favour with King Bard.

Observant characters may spot Lockmand speaking to Harrod the Fool in a corner about half-way through the evening.

Harrod the Fool: A jester in green-and-red motley, Harrod prances through the crowd, making fun of everyone of note. He fixates on the proudest members of the company and mocks and mimicks them mercilessly.

Harrod is not as young as he once was, and he hopes to win a place in King Bard's court to provide for him in his old age, so he no longer has to wander from village to village, making peasants laugh for a warm meal and a place to sleep beside the fire.

- Towards the end of the evening, Harrod's spirits suddenly improve, and he capers with renewed vigour. Secretly, he was just hired by Lockmand to play a prank at the feast tomorrow night...

The Challenge

Towards the end of the evening, Lockmand the merchant clambers onto the stage to address the crowd.

"People of Dale! Tomorrow, there will be a great contest of arms! Swords! Spears! Archery! Let us gather all the defenders of the North, and see which of them is the greatest! In honour of this fine Gathering of Five Armies I shall give a prize to the victor! Behold!"

He gestures to two of his servants, who drag a huge iron-bound chest onto the stage. Lockmand throws the lid back. Gold and gems spill from the chest, which is crammed with treasure. *"For Wilderland!"* shouts Lockmand. *"For the Free Folk of the North!"*

– Part Two –
A Golden Prize

Lockmand's servants must have worked all night long, for Dale awakens to find that a field has been cleared outside the town, between Ravensgate and the river. The company spot posters nailed to walls, calling for warriors to sign up for the tournament, which begins at noon.

> in honour of this day
> # A CONTEST
> archery   strength   horsemanship
>
> a purse of silver for each
> and a *grand melee*
> a chest of gold for the winner!
>
> all participants shall be feasted and honoured
> entrants should present themselves
> at the contest field before noon

Entering the Contest

If the company choose to enter the contest, they can do so, and they are not alone – it seems that every warrior of note in Dale, as well as half the fighting Dwarves of the Mountain and most of the wandering heroes and adventurers in the North have signed up. A small army of clerks handles the entrants. The characters are asked where they hail from, which events they wish to enter, and are reminded that all entrants, regardless of how well or poorly they do, are invited to a feast at Lockmand's expense.

The Contests

Each of the three lesser contests - Archery, Strength, and Horse riding - works in the same way. There are three rounds – two qualification rounds, and a final round against a named opponent.

Qualification Rounds

Each companion makes two rolls for every qualification round. The first test is to gauge the situation and prepare (evaluation test) and the second to resolve the contest itself. The DC used is the same for both rolls in a round and is indicated in the Contests table below.

- Succeeding in the evaluation test grants Advantage in the contest itself.

For example, in his first qualification round of an Archery contest a companion would first roll **Wisdom (Perception)** *to aim and compensate for wind and distance (thus gaining Advantage) and then a ranged attack roll to hit the target (both rolls* **DC 15***); then, in the second qualification round he would roll the same skills to the same effect but against* **DC 20***.*

If a companion succeeds in both rounds of qualification, he proceeds to the final round. If multiple companions participate in the same contest, then any number of them can pass through the qualification rounds, but only the character who gets the highest result during the second round of qualification moves through to the final round.

For example, Caranthiel, Beli and Beran of the Mountains enter the Strength contest. Caranthiel fails in round one and is out, while Beli and Beran succeed and both proceed to the second round of qualification. This time, they both pass their **Strength (Athletics)** *checks, but Beli only scrapes past with an 18, whereas Beran gets a 21. As they are competing in the same contest, Beran is the one who goes through to the last round, where he will wrestle Gerold.*

Final Round

The final round is resolved with two tests, as in the previous rounds of qualification. The DC for the first test (evaluation) is **DC 20** for all contests, and success gains Advantage as before. The second roll is resolved as a contest against the Loremaster character.

For example, when Beran goes to the final round, he will have to first roll **Charisma (Intimidation)** *against* **DC 20** *to impress Gerold and build his confidence up (gaining Advantage) and then will have to make an opposed roll putting his* **Strength** *directly against that of Gerold; this means that Beran's player and the Loremaster will both roll the dice and directly compare their results.*

Archery

Each round involves firing at a wreath nailed to a wide wooden board. Contestants must put their arrows inside the circle inscribed within the wreath, or at least hit the wreath itself. In each round, the targets are moved further away (the DC increases as shown on the Contests table). The Wisdom check at the start of each round is to judge the wind whipping off the Lonely Mountain and to estimate the distance.

- If a companion does not win then it is Galia the Elf who cooly puts three arrows through the bulls-eye and takes the prize out from under the noses of the Royal Archers of Dale and the archers from the Bowmen's Guild of Esgaroth.

Horse riding

The contestants must ride by a set of straw targets at high speed, and thrust or hurl a spear into the targets as they pass. The **Wisdom (Animal Handling)** check is to control the horse, while the attack roll is to drive the weapon home.

Contests					
Contest	Skills Used	First Qualification Round DC	Second Qualification Round DC	Final Round DC	Final Opponent
Archery	**Wisdom (Perception)** and best ranged attack bonus	15	20	20	Galia (Short Bow +6)
Strength	**Charisma (Intimidation)** and **Strength (Athletics)**	15	20	-	Gerold (**Strength (Athletics)** +6)
Horse riding	Wisdom (animal handling), melee attack roll	15	20	20	Elstan (Dwarf-forged Spear +7)

- If a companion does not take the prize then it is Elstan, the First Captain of Dale, who is declared the winner.

Strength

These are wrestling contests, held in a fighting ring of sand by the riverbank. The Charisma check is to demoralise the opposition and get the support of the crowd, while the Strength test is the grappling contest itself.

- If a companion does not reach the final round, then the brutal Gerold is victorious. His final opponent is a strapping young Dwarf from the Mountain. Gerold uses his greater reach to outmanoeuvre the Dwarf, then lifts his foe by the beard and tosses him out of the ring and into the river.

Prizes

Lockmand promises that each winner will be presented with a purse of silver at the feast tonight.

- Each companion who is declared the winner in one of the challenges gains Inspiration.

The Melee

The final event – and the one that draws the most attention – is the grand melee. This is a big mock battle. Theoretically, it is every man for himself, but in practise different factions stick together. So, the largest force on the field are the warriors of Dale under their captain, Elstan, closely followed by the Dwarves of the Lonely Mountain and the warriors of Lake-town. The Elves do not enter the melee.

Early Rounds

The early rounds of the melee see the participating companions fight against a host of lesser foes. To determine how the adventurers fare in the chaotic mess have each companion in the melee make two checks.

- First, each player describes how their character intends to approach the melee. Is their tactic to sneak around and wait for opportunities to take down weak or distracted foes? Will they charge into the middle of the fray, scattering their opponents with forceful blows? Do they intend to work with the rest of the adventurers, or make common cause with the other participants from their home cultures ("*Men of Gondor, flock to my banner!*")

If a character has a suitable Virtue or class ability that matches their preferred tactic (*Reckless Attack* for charging into the fray, *Sneak Attack* for picking off weaker foes, *Captain of Gondor* for rallying their kinsfolk), they automatically succeed at this first check. If there is not a clear justification for the characters' edge in battle, the character must make a **DC 15** saving throw chosen by the LM – Strength, Dexterity or Charisma to avoid the worst of the scrum. If successful, the companion gains Advantage in the first phase of the battle.

Next, each character makes a melee attack roll against **AC 15** that determines how well the companion survives the first part of the melee. Check the result obtained on the table below.

Early Rounds	
Weapon Skill Result	**Conduct**
Failed with a natural 1	The companion is eliminated, losing two-thirds of remaining hit points.
Failed	The companion is eliminated, losing half his remaining hit points.
Success by 0-2	The companion survives, but loses half of his remaining hit points.
Success by 3-5	The companion survives, but loses one quarter of his remaining hit points.
Success by 6 or more	The companion is uninjured in the melee!

Following Rounds

Companions who survive the early rounds of the melee must make the same two rolls once again, only this time against a difficulty of **DC/AC 20**. If any survive this second part of the tourney, then they are among the last few warriors to survive and move onto the final round.

The Last Few Heroes

After an hour of heavy fighting, only a few warriors remain standing on the muddy field by the river. There is Gerold, the wild mercenary. Despite using blunt axes, he has maimed one foe and smashed the dwarf-forged shield of another. In the middle of the field, atop a little hillock, are a company of Dwarves from the Lonely Mountain, who fight with the tenacity of Durin's folk but are clearly exhausted. Finally, Elstan and a troupe of his best warriors (one for each companion) command the ground near the river, and have won the love of the crowd with their heroics.

- If the companions still stand, then they must choose whether to fight against Gerold or Elstan and his followers (the Dwarves are too distant). Whichever group they do not fight battles the Dwarves. If they win this fight, then they must finally defeat whichever foe is left (among Elstan or Gerold).

- Traditionally, only one warrior may claim the prize. However, if the company are the only combatants left on the field, they may either fight amongst themselves or else come to some agreement about who is considered the champion.

Gerold the Beorning
Medium Human

STR	DEX	CON	INT	WIS	CHA
18 (+4)	15 (+2)	16 (+3)	11 (+0)	12 (+1)	15 (+2)

Armour Class 15 (Unarmoured Defence)
Hit Points 90 (12d8+36)
Speed 30 ft

Damage Resistance non-magical piercing
Saving Throws Strength +7, Dexterity +5, Wisdom +4
Skills Athletics +7, Intimidation +5
Senses passive Perception 11
Languages Westron
Challenge 5 (1,800 XP)

Horrible Strength. If Gerold makes a successful melee attack, he may use his bonus action to cause 4 additional damage of the same type as the original type.
Skin Coat. Gerold has resistance to non-magical piercing damage (see above).

Actions
Multiattack. Gerold makes three axe attacks.
Great Axe. *Melee Weapon Attack:* +7 to hit, reach 5 ft, one target. *Hit:* 10 (1d12+4) slashing damage.

Reaction
Retaliate. If Gerold suffers a critical hit from a foe, he may use his reaction to make a single melee weapon attack against that foe.

Elstan, First Captain of Dale
Medium Human

STR	DEX	CON	INT	WIS	CHA
16 (+3)	11 (+0)	14 (+2)	11 (+0)	11 (+0)	15 (+2)

Armour Class 18 (heavy mail and shield)
Hit Points 65 (10d8 + 20)
Speed 30 ft

Saving Throws Constitution +4, Wisdom +2
Senses passive Perception 10
Languages Westron
Challenge 4 (1,100 XP)

Actions
Multiattack. Elstan makes two longsword attacks.
Longsword. *Melee Weapon Attack:* +5 to hit, reach 5 ft, one target. *Hit:* 7 (1d8+3) slashing damage or 8 (1d10+3) slashing damage if used with both hands.

Reaction
Commanding Voice. Elstan may use his reaction to utter a command when a non-hostile creature, visible to him within 30 feet, is about to make an attack roll or a saving throw. The target adds a d6 Command Die to that roll, provided it can understand the message. A creature can benefit from only one Command Die at a time, and creatures that possess Commanding Voice cannot benefit.
Parry. Elstan adds 2 to his AC against one melee attack that would hit him. He must be aware of the incoming attack in order to parry.

Elstan Followers
Medium Human

STR	DEX	CON	INT	WIS	CHA
15 (+2)	12 (+1)	12 (+1)	11 (+0)	11 (+0)	10 (+0)

Armour Class 16 (corselet of mail, shield)
Hit Points 16 (3d8+3)
Speed 30 ft

Senses passive Perception 10
Languages Westron
Challenge 1/2 (100 XP)

Battle Brothers. If three or more followers are fighting the same enemy, and that enemy has no allies engaged with the followers, the followers have Advantage on their attacks.

Actions
Longsword. *Melee Weapon Attack:* +4 to hit, reach 5 ft or range 20/60 ft, one target. *Hit:* 6 (1d8+2) slashing damage or 7 (1d10+2) slashing damage if used with both hands.

The End of the Contest

The victor of the contest is lifted from the battlefield by a crowd of cheering spectators and carried shoulder-high through the streets of Dale to the feast-hall prepared by Lockmand. Other warriors pick themselves out of the mud and stagger after the crowd, eager to get to the feast and drown their sorrows.

- If a player-hero won, he receives Experience Points for this outstanding deed (as if he defeated his foe in regular combat), and gains Inspiration.

If the companions were all defeated, then a battered and bruised Elstan stands victorious over Gerold.

- Part Three -
An Ill-Made Party

The company – along with virtually every warrior in Dale – is welcome at Lockman's feast. The merchant has raised a party tent in the market square. This is a feast even by Hobbit-standards, where it snows food and rains drink, especially the latter.

By the time the companions arrive, the sun has disappeared behind the stony arms of the Mountain and the barrels of wine and casks of ale have already been opened. After all, tourney fighting is thirsty work! King Bard is not present, nor is Dáin Ironfoot; Gandalf the Grey has already left the city. Bombur, of course, would never miss free food, so he is in a place of honour at the high table, next to the winners of the various contests.

In front of the high table is a plinth that bears the chest of gold promised to the winner of the melee and the three small bags of treasure for the best archer, wrestler and rider in Dale. Oddly, there is no sign of Lockmand, the merchant who organised the whole dinner. If the companions ask, then the servants assume that their employer is busy dealing with the cooks. The truth is much more sinister, although the company are unlikely to discover this immediately.

Treachery in the Dark

Last night, the merchant hired the jester Harrod to play a 'joke' on the winners. Harrod is to disguise himself as Lockmand; he will wear Lockmand's robes and mask from the ball the previous night, and pretend to have lost his voice cheering at the tournament. He will present what he believes to be a chest with naught but copper coins to the winner, open it theatrically, and then pull of his mask and reveal that he is in fact a jester. Lockmand will then enter with the real chest, or so he told Harrod.

- In fact, the 'fake' chest contains a nest of poisonous serpents and, by the time it is opened, Lockmand intends to be half a league down the River Running in a fast boat. The wine at the feast is poisoned, too. The poison is very diluted, to disguise its taste, but any warrior who drinks enough of it will be Incapacitated for several days.

Intrigue at the Feast

Suspicious companions may wish to pause their carousing to find Lockmand.

- If they do so, call for a **DC 15 Intelligence (Investigation)** check. Succeeding by 0-2 means the character finds 'Lockmand' – the disguised Harrod – arriving at the back of the tent; succeeding by 3-5 means the character surprises 'Lockmand' getting changed, and spots that it is the jester Harrod wearing the merchant's clothes and mask; succeeding by 6 or more means the character sees Lockmand and several of his surly guards loading a large heavy chest onto a boat and fleeing Dale under cover of darkness – see *Tracking Down Lockmand*, below.

Other companions may prefer to just enjoy the feast, trading tales of heroism on the battlefield and enjoying themselves. The food is excellent, and while there is a slightly bitter aftertaste to the wine and beer, there is plenty of it. Make sure to roleplay the servants offering food and drink to the companions, so you can determine whether or not a particular character takes part in the feast. This feast counts as a Short Rest, so characters may expend Hit Dice to regain lost hit points.

The Ungracious Host

Once the feast is in full swing, 'Lockmand' arrives. He climbs theatrically up to the high table, then points to his throat, shrugs and shakes his head. *"He's lost his voice!"* shouts someone at the back of the hall. 'Lockmand' nods, then picks up one of the three purses of treasure. He mimes drawing a bow, then gives the purse to the winner of the archery contest. The pouch contains 100 silver pieces. He then flexes his muscles and gives the second purse to the winner of the wrestling contest. Finally, he leaps onto the back of a passing servant and rides him around the stage like a horse, grabbing the third pouch as he passes and tossing it to the winner of the horse riding event. The crowd laughs. Bombur lets loose a great guffaw and rocks back on his couch, breaking it. He topples over backwards, and the crowd laughs even more.

Finally, 'Lockmand' goes to the chest and beckons everyone to come closer. He throws open the chest, digs his hands in and flings a shower of what was supposed to be copper coins into the crowd. He screams as he does so – the chest is full of snakes, not coins, and several just slithered down his sleeves and bit deep into his flesh. He falls to the ground, knocking his mask off, revealing the face of the jester Harrod.

- The snakes swarm everywhere, attacking in a panic. The companions can avoid being bitten by making a **DC 10 Dexterity** saving throw to dodge or kill any snakes that come nearby.

Poisoned!

The snakes are not the only calamity that strikes the feast. As warriors surge to their feet to avoid the swarming snakes, they suddenly feel dizzy and ill. Some collapse, others stumble. Any heroes who ate or drink at feast must make a **DC 10 Constitution** saving throw. On a success, they stay standing but count as being Poisoned for the rest of the adventure, or until they can treated. On a failure, they collapse, recovering after a short rest but are Poisoned until the adventure ends. Few of the victims of the poison drank a lethal dose, but most are Incapacitated and cannot fight.

Curing the Poison

The poison in the wine can be cured with purgative herbs, but such herbs are rare in the north. A **DC 15 Wisdom (Medicine)** check can restore a Poisoned character to full health in a matter of hours, but there are only enough herbs in Dale to cure a handful of warriors. More can be obtained in Mirkwood, but that will take several weeks. A Scholar might use their skills to cure her companions, but to heal all the warriors would take many days.

Questioning Harrod

If the company manage to save Harrod from the snakes, they can question him. He is confused and terrified, and his story is jumbled.

"He, he said, it was just a joke! He's supposed to be here with the gold, and everyone should be laughing! Where is he? What's he done to me? Oh mercy, what has he done?"

Tracking Down Lockmand

After sending the jester in disguise, Lockmand fled to a small boat that waited on the Running River. The companions are unlikely to be able to catch him, unless their suspicions were aroused earlier and they either got an extraordinary (6 or better) margin of success while searching for him (see *Intrigue at the Feast*, above), or specifically headed for the river docks.

- If the players' actions put them on the right track well in advance, they reach the merchant as his boat casts off from the dock and heads down the river.

In the darkness, the company can see four figures on the deck. One is clearly Lockmand; the other three are nasty-looking warriors from the South. When they spot the characters, two warriors pick up bows from the deck and start firing arrows to dissuade pursuit.

Chasing Lockmand

The characters can either race along the riverbank, swim after the boat, or take other boats and row after it.

- If the companions race along the river, Lockmand's boat distances them easily and disappears in the dark.

- Swimming after Lockmand is actually not a good idea, as the waters of the River Running are very cold in November. The Loremaster should only allow companions with proficiency in **Athletics** to actually try. Catching up with the boat is a contest between the swimmer and Lochmand's rowers, who have a +4 bonus to their rolls. The swimmer needs three successive victories to catch the boat. Should a swimmer fail a roll, he loses 1d6 hit points as he is briefly overcome by the freezing waters.

- If the companions can borrow a boat, they find that the river is fast-flowing and only barely navigable as its waters tumble from the Lonely Mountain; luckily, Lockmand's boat is weighed down by the heavy chest of gold, so the characters can catch up with the boat if they hurry. Chasing Lockmand on a boat is, again, a contest against Lochmand's rowers, but they have Advantage on their rolls because they know the river better than the adventurers.

Shot in the Dark
Two of the southerners aboard Lockmand's boat shoot arrows in the direction of any pursuer. It is dark, and the boat is moving, so their shots are mainly aimed to discourage, not to kill.

- If a companion gets a natural 1 on any roll while pursuing Lockmand, he is hit by an arrow for a loss of 1d6 hit points.

Fighting Lockmand's Guards
The guards keep firing their bows until the company board the boat, whereupon they draw swords and start hewing. The merchant is a craven coward and will not fight back; if his guards are overcome then he grabs the chest, throws it overboard and dives after it. The chest disappears quickly under the troubled waters, while Lockmand can be fished out of the waters at little or no effort.

Interrogating Lockmand
If captured, Lockmand reveals that he was sent to gather the best warriors in Dale in one place and poison them. An army is marching on Dale from the south. Doom is at hand – if King Bard surrenders and yields up his crown, then maybe his folk will be spared the suffering. Lockmand claims that his master commands *"...all the host of Dol Guldur – Orcs without number, men from the East, and a great host of Wights and Wargs"*. A **DC 10 Wisdom (Insight)** check reveals reveals that Lockmand is lying about the size of the enemy army, and that he is simply trying to sap the morale of Dale.

Lockmand's Chest
The chest that the black traitor sent to the bottom of the river can become the object of a recovery mission, probably a very adventurous one, especially because the gold it contains came out of Dol Guldur. Unbeknonst to the companions, the treasure is tainted by the touch of the Necromancer, and its malevolence it is sure to attract the attention of some of the most evil denizens of the Long Marshes, or even of the Mountains of Mirkwood...

- If recovered from the cold bed of the river, Lockmand's chest can be opened to reveal a fortune in gold. Anyone who takes a share of this treasure gains 1 point of Shadow automatically, and must pass a **DC 20 Wisdom** saving throw or gain 3 additional points of Shadow.

– Part Four – Raven's Tidings

By the next morning, Dale is afire with wild rumour. Tales of invasions, curses and poison are on everyone's lips. Some stories claim that everyone who was at the feast is dying. Others claim that it is the curse of the Dragon taking hold, or that it was the doing of the wicked Elvenking or those troublesome Dwarves or some other foe.

The Coming Foe
The next morning, a raven arrives in Dale. If any Dwarf companions in the group have the Ravens of the Mountain virtue, or a Barding has the Woeful Foresight virtue, then the raven comes to them. Otherwise, the raven alights on the roof of a bell tower and utters its doom to the townsfolk directly.

"Harken, men of Dale! Harken, folk of the Mountain! A terrible army approaches. Orcs and Goblins, with Wild Wolves to ride upon, coming with great speed up from the south. They ride for Dale!"

A Royal Council
The companions are among those least affected by Lockmand's poison – many warriors are Incapacitated or too weak to stand. Considering this, it is possible that they voluntarily propose to offer their help to King Bard. If they do not, they are summoned to his presence by one of his men. The king can be encountered at the Royal Palace.

When they go there, they pass through the vaulted stone portal into the lamp-lit hall, and find Bard sitting grim-faced on his throne, with a map of his kingdom spread out in front of him. Normally, this hall would be attended by many heroes and warriors of Dale, but only a few managed to struggle from their sick-beds to attend council. There are, however, plenty of merchants and townsfolk here, demanding that the king acts to safeguard Dale against its enemies.

The companions are received with a welcoming nod from the king, who at this juncture is more than glad to see a group of armed adventurers join his council. The crowd of onlookers is less discreet, and the companions are greeted with a cheer as soon as they pass the gates of the palace. If the company are unable to convince the fearful townsfolk that they can save the kingdom, then panic and fear may bring Dale down before the enemy even arrives. Dale calls for aid – will the company answer?

Motivation
King Bard needs heroes to defend his young kingdom. Anyone who can still fight is needed.

Expectations
+**2**: Heroes are first into the fray (the characters demonstrate their eagerness to defend the kingdom)
+**2**: Dale calls for aid (the characters can promise aid from a nearby land, like the Dwarves under the mountain, the Elves of Mirkwood, or the Men of Laketown)
+**2**: Wise counsel is always welcome
+**1**: Heroes are hale and hearty (the characters are clearly unpoisoned and healthy)
-**1**: This is no time for quibblers (the characters delay or haggle over rewards)
-**1**: No time for fools (the characters suggest foolish plans to defend Dale, or don't offer any plans beyond fortifying the Crossings of Celduin)
-**2**: And no time for cowards (the characters openly worry that the task is hopeless and Dale is lost)

Interaction
King Bard addresses the council with a sober assessment of the situation.

"Lockmand's treachery has blunted the spear of the forces of Dale. The greater portion of our strength is lost until the poisoned warriors recover. And when they do, it will be too late."

"The power of the Orcs of the North was broken at the Battle of Five Armies, but Wilderland is still stiff with Wolves, Orcs, and creatures of the worst description. It must be assumed that we face a powerful army."

"The enemy's outriders will be here soon. Dale has the strength to resist a siege, but if we retreat behind its stone walls, then the farmlands and outlying villages – not to mention Lake-town – will be vulnerable to attack."

"We must resolve what to do with the remaining time. There are two concerns at hand – stopping the enemy, and preparing Dale for war, even in the lack of its best defenders."

When the king is done with his speech, Reinald, the chief of his advisors, asks those assembled for counsel. Various concerns and strategies are addressed below; if the companions do not suggest them, then Reinald himself or one of the other counsellors present does so. Heroes that suggest strategies or agree to reasonable ones earn a +1 modifier for the Final Audience Check.

Stopping the Enemy

Looking at the maps identifies the likely route of the enemy. They are coming out of the south and the River Running lies between them and Dale. To reach the town, the enemy must either pass through Mirkwood (unlikely, as they would get lost and could not ride their horses through the woods), or through the Long Marshes (impossible for an army). Only the empty lands east of the marshes remain. However, there are few places to cross the River Running to the east: the enemy must be making for the Crossings of Celduin. Marked on the maps of King Bard along the blue ribbon of the river, two hundred miles south of Dale and almost one hundred miles east of Mirkwood, in the region known as the Nether Marches, a bridge crosses the Celduin.

- A character with proficiency in **History** or **Lore** automatically identifies the tower drawn near the crossing markings as an outpost of the old kingdom of Dale, a tollgate perhaps. The map dates the settlement back to the time of Girion, son of King Bladorthin of Dale.

The Town of Celduin

The companions might desire to find out more about what lies at the Crossings of Celduin. Any Northman knows that there are settlements along the River Running, living relics out of a past when a powerful kingdom ruled those lands. Some might be abandoned, and some others might still be populated to this day. Sometimes merchants from the south bring news and snippets of information, but usually everyone is too busy with their own lives to no interest in these matters. Traders from Lake-town might know more, and making a DC 15 Intelligence (Riddle) check while conversing with one might bear interesting fruits (see Part Six for details).

Seeking Help from Allies

While many of the best warriors of the Lonely Mountain are similarly afflicted by Lockmand's poison, Dáin will send help if asked. So too will the Elves of Mirkwood. However, the heroes will need to be passionate to convince the mistrustful townsfolk of this course of action – many fear that their allies will abandon them in their hour of need.

Preparing Dale

One of the merchants suggests that King Bard order all his subjects to take refuge behind the city walls, or to seek shelter within the Lonely Mountain. Another counsellor, a farmer, says that if they abandon the countryside to the enemy, the fields and orchards will burn and the harvest will be lost. Which course of action do the companions advocate? Whichever they choose, as long as they defend their answer, they receive a +1 modifier to the Final Audience Check.

Stormcrows

Some wild rumours trouble the council, and should be put to rest. Who sent Lockmand? Everyone knows that he was close to the old Master of Laketown; maybe Lake-town is jealous of Dale's newfound prosperity? Some of Bard's counsellors suggest that the folk of Esgaroth may be behind the impending attack. Unless a companion convinces the Bardings to trust their neighbours, then they argue against King Bard's decision to call on Lake-town for aid. Many fear that the poisoned warriors will continue to worsen until they die. A companion proficient in **Medicine** can assure the court that the poison is not necessarily fatal, and describe the course of herbs needed to cure the afflicted.

Conclusions

Make the Final Audience Check using whatever skills deemed appropriate, especially **History, Persuasion** or **Shadow-lore**. Heroes that used skill proficiencies to provide valuable insight earn a +1 modifier to the Final Audience check.

Failure: While Bard is determined to defend the kingdom, many people believe that all is lost and the city must be abandoned. Dale will be sorely wounded by this panic, and the city beset by looters and fearful rumours in days to come. The companions will have to hold out for an added day in *Part Seven – The Battle of the Crossings*.

0-1: Bard politely thanks the companions for their intervention, but privately dismisses any course of action they proposed as meaningless. This will teach him about admitting adventurers to his war council!

2-3: The king is worried, but sees an opportunity in these adventurers: he addresses them and the few others who are strong enough to travel and presents them with a plan (see the King Bard's Command box).

4-5: King Bard is greatly relieved, as the words of the companions plainly show him that not everything is yet lost! He proposes his plan as for 2-3 above, but gladly accepts suggestions and reasonable changes. Finally, he promises the companions a reward should they return victorious.

6 or more: King Bard is very impressed. Apply the results of 4-5 above; additionally, the king will consider the companions' admission to his restricted council of advisors should they return alive and victorious.

> ### King Bard's Command
> The king knows that it will take days for him to assemble a host mustering what forces are available from the lands surrounding Dale and the Mountain, and even weeks before reinforcements arrive from the Iron Hills and from Mirkwood, if they come at all. The enemy will probably arrive in less than two weeks, substantially less if they press on under the light of day. He needs time, so he intends to send the few healthy soldiers he has to rally the countryside around Dale and Esgaroth, and the company of adventurers to hold the crossings of the River Running against the enemy. A bridge is a very defensible place, one that can be held by a handful of valorous individuals. With luck, they will reach the river before the enemy can cross, and so give him time to muster a force large enough to meet the enemy in open battle.
>
> Bard does not expect the companions to hold out indefinitely – he just needs as much time as they can give him. He will not command them to go (unless they are sworn subjects of Dale), but he asks for their help in this time of need.

> ### Greedy Adventurers
> Haggling over payment in times such as these can hardly be considered behaviour worthy of a hero, so any companion who does so is considered to have committed a Misdeed and gains automatically a Shadow point.

– Part Five –
The Journey South

King Bard provides the company with swift horses for the journey south. They are to ride with all speed to the Crossings of Celduin, and to hold the river against the enemy as best they can. Meanwhile, messengers are dispatched to the surrounding countryside, to the Iron Hills, the Woodland Realm and Esgaroth. Ravens too are sent bearing letters to the allies of Dale.

The Journey

The companions are to travel south to the Long-lake. Then, the company's path moves into less travelled regions. The wild lands between Esgaroth and the river are not uninhabited, but are home to little isolated farmsteads and herds of sheep and cows, and there are few villages of note. They head south-east, skirting the edge of the Long Marshes, and then strike across the countryside east of Mirkwood towards the region known as the Nether Marches, beyond where the Old Forest Road exits Mirkwood.

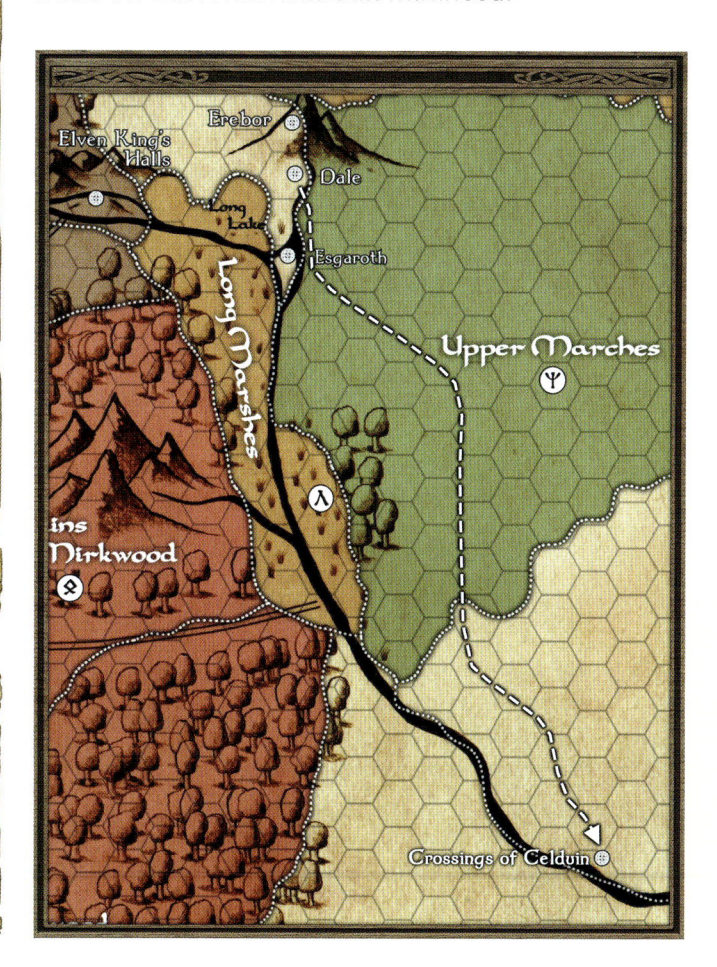

The first section of the journey will see them ride from Dale to the southern borders of the Upper Marches. The second part brings them first to the River Running and then to the Crossings of Celduin.

- The forty-league trip to where the River Running exits Mirkwood to turn east follows broken trails used by merchants.

- Once they reach the river, the companions ride for eighty miles over easy terrain, for two more days of travel.

The journey takes five days if completed on horseback. It has a Peril Rating of 2 and provokes 1d2 Journey Events at **DC 14**.

Planning the Route

Because they are using mounts, the company ignore the first level of Exhaustion they receive on the journey.

From Dale to the Upper Marches

The journey from Dale to the Long Lake is easy and uneventful. The companions ride through the vales of the upper river, formerly the Desolation of the Dragon. In the years since Smaug's death, this land has become a bountiful garden, bringing forth vast harvests of fruit and grain. They charge past many small hamlets, all of which are newly-built and have no defences worth mentioning. If the enemy makes it this far north, it will be disastrous.

The Upper Marches

From the Long Lake, the companions head across open countryside. The River Running becomes a silver ribbon off to their right, before it is lost behind trees and the mists of the marsh-fens. The land here is almost empty save for flocks of sheep and their herdsmen. The inhabitants of these lands are Northmen, kin to the Lake-men and Bardings; the king has dispatched messengers to bring words of warning to the areas surrounding Dale and Esgaroth, but it might take days for them to reach these places. The company could take time to seek out the herdsmen and warn them of the approaching army, but this would delay them. The herdsmen have some permanent villages, but they are not on the company's route. The company could search for a herdsman camp instead, but finding one is not a certainty.

Sounding the Alarm

If the company choose to seek out the herdsmen, call for a **DC 12 Wisdom (Survival)** check. Success means the company find a recently-travelled path and can follow it to a campsite where a dozen herders watch over their flocks. The herders are loyal to Dale, but only come to the valley for market every few months. They have heard nothing of the impending danger.

- Any appropriate skill check made at **DC 10** can be used to convince the herdsmen that Dale needs their strength, too. If successful, the herdsmen agree to contact their kinsfolk and send help to Dale's muster. They are excellent archers and fighters, so their help

A Thief In The Night

If the company failed to capture Lockmand earlier, the company passes a boat on the river that is travelling south from Dale to Lake-town. The boat crew pass on a strange story. A few hours previously, they spotted another boat docked at the river bank. There were four men on board, three of whom were surly river-folk, but the third was a merchant dressed in rich clothes. They seemed to be arguing over a chest.

If the company investigate by making a successful DC 10 Wisdom (Perception) check, then they find Lockmand's boat abandoned by the riverbank. Lying in the reeds nearby is the corpse of one of the guards. His throat has been cut. A successful DC 12 Wisdom (Survival) check reveals tracks heading off east. If the company is determined to find the traitor they can pursue Lockmand and his two remaining guards. Chasing down the treacherous merchant adds a day to the company's journey. The company overtake Lockmand as he tries to drag his pony out of the mud east of the river; the poor animal is weighed down by the chest of gold. See page 109 for more details on Lockmand and his guards.

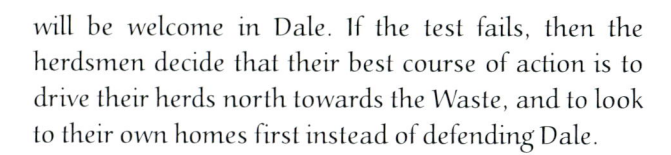

will be welcome in Dale. If the test fails, then the herdsmen decide that their best course of action is to drive their herds north towards the Waste, and to look to their own homes first instead of defending Dale.

Scripted Journey Event: A Flock of Crows

A huge flock of crows flies overhead. It suddenly changes direction and closes in to circle once around the company. Then, the flock scatters, with big black birds flapping in every direction. A successful **DC 12 Wisdom (Perception)** check (or bringing one down with a bow-shot) lets the company see that these are nasty gore-crows out of Mirkwood.

A companion with the Survival or other applicable skill or virtue can say that such behaviour in birds is very suspicious: it was as though the crows were sent to spy or scout the area. In the distance, the company see other flocks of such crows.

From the Upper Marches to the Bridge

Upon encountering the Running River again as it exits Mirkwood, the company turns east. The final part of the journey winds its path around rolling hills and river vales. These lands are empty indeed, although the company pass barrows and fallen stones that once marked the dwelling places of long-dead chieftains in time immemorial.

Scripted Journey Event: The Raiders

The company are not alone in this land. While the approaching army is still south of the river, a few bands of Orcs and Wolves from the Mountains of Mirkwood have left the forest to meet the coming host. One such band (one Orc Guard, two Wild Wolves and as many Orc Soldiers as heroes) comes across the company as they make camp.

- Call for a **DC 10 Wisdom (Perception)** check from the Look-outs to spot the enemy well in advance: Orcs and Wargs are a loud lot, and they are thrilled by the prospect of joining the invading host!

If the company is aware of their presence, the companions can try to ambush the Orcs. If the Look-outs fail, then they may be the ones ambushed!

Eavesdropping

If the company has time to eavesdrop on the Orcs, or take one of the brutes prisoner, they can learn something about their enemy from their excited comments (unfortunately, the Wargs speak among themselves only using their dreadful language and nothing can be gleaned from their growls and howls...):

- They have left their dens under the Mountains of Mirkwood because the 'gibbet boss' has sent word to leave the forest at once and meet the army at the crossings of the river. He is claiming that the time for revenge has come for all those who suffered by the hands of Elves, Men and Dwarves!

- Most of the army is still well south of the river, and some of the Orcs grumble that by the look of it there won't be enough of them to beat the Bardings and the Dwarves and the Elves all at the same time. The 'gibbet boss' has been able to draw all those who found refuge in Mirkwood out of the holes they had hidden in since the Battle of Five Armies, but, as one of the Orcs points out, they've less than a third of the troops that were there at the time. And for all the promises of the 'gibbet boss' about his dark magic, what counts is still goblin-feet on the battlefield.

- The 'gibbet boss' is a ghost or a wraith out of Dol Guldur, who speaks through the dead. Other Orcs are cheered by this, and are convinced that they'll be joined on the battlefield by an 'army of wights'. Others cynically argue that the gibbet boss will leave them in the lurch.

- There is only one place where the army can cross safely – the bridge at the crossings. The waters of the River Running are too cold and fast for an army to swim across.

- Part Six -
The Calm Before The Storm

As the company approaches the Crossings of Celduin, even from a distance they can make out its narrow stone bridge arching across the river. Somewhat unexpectedly, they see a town sitting on its northern bank, with houses clustered around a fortified tollgate built at the end of the bridge.

The Town

There has been a small village here by the bridge across the River Running for as long as men have travelled this path. Celduin takes its name from the Elven name for the river. It is currently home to around one hundred people, including some twenty men of fighting age. Its inhabitants are a proud and independent folk of Northmen who collect tolls from anyone who wants to cross the bridge.

Most buildings in Celduin resemble those of the town of Dale, at least those that have been rebuilt following the style of the old days. The bridge is different though, as it was built by Men from the South centuries ago, when a steady traffic of traders and merchants used to cross it on their way north, and it is only maintained by the inhabitants of Celduin.

Celduin

1. The Bridge: The bridge across the Celduin is made of white stone. It is kept in good repair, although the craft of the Men of the South cannot be replicated. The bridge is wide enough for two riders to go abreast, or for a single cart. Three warriors on foot could hold the bridge against many.

2. Tollgate: This two-storey fortification blocks unwanted travellers from crossing the bridge with a great iron portcullis. The upper level contains the wheels for raising

One square equals 10 ft

celduin

and lowering the portcullis, and also has a number of arrow-slits and murder-holes to attack those who would threaten the bridge. A narrow ladder leads up to the roof of the building.

3. The Inn at the Crossings: A large, stone-walled inn built to shelter travellers on the road. This is the second strongest building in town, and would make an excellent fall-back position or command post for the company.

4. Master's House: This is where the Master of Celduin lives. His house is bigger than any of the others in town.

5. Docks: More merchants pass through Celduin by the river than by the road, and the number of boats has increased steadily in the last five years.

6. The River Running: The fast-flowing River Running is not easily fordable here; crossing the river is a prolonged action, requiring six **DC 12 Strength (Athletics)** checks. Each failure causes 1d6 cold damage.

The Master of Celduin

When the company arrives in town, they are welcomed by a crotchety, half-blind old man named Erik, son of Erland. He is led by two young maidens of about twelve years of age, Erik's twin granddaughters Eydis and Erna.

> ### Playing the Master
> You're old, proud and cranky. Young people these days are always rushing around, talking about doom and dire portents and things being in thrall to other things and dragons and necromancers. Pay no attention to their nonsense. The only important thing is keeping the bridge open, the tolls collected, and Celduin under your thumb.

Erik is the current Master of Celduin, as was his father Erland before him, and his grandfather Egil before that. While the holder of the office of Master is chosen by the villagers, it has been in Erik's family for many generations. Since the death of Smaug, news of the crowning of King Bard have reached the town, to the dismay of old Erik: he worries that the influence of Dale will diminish his own power, and that in time the people of Celduin will look towards the new king in the north and not towards his household for leadership. Therefore, he strongly objects to any interference from the adventurers.

The Enemy is Coming!

The Master of Celduin takes the news about an approaching army with surprising calm.

"So? I am no vassal of Dale. If whoever leads this army is willing to pay the toll, why should I deny them the use of the bridge?"

The Master is no fool, and has no reasons to doubt the words of the adventurers: if they are saying that it is Orcs who are coming, then it's probably true. However, his duty is to protect the people of his village, and if the best way to do that is to let the Orcs past without a fight, then so be it! The village has only a handful of armed guards, and he fears that Celduin will be wiped out if they resist. The characters may argue that if Dale falls, so too will Celduin; the Master agrees, but says that if they offer him a choice between seeing Celduin falling after Dale and Celduin falling first, then he must pick the option that preserves the town for as long as possible. The companions can try to convince the Master to aid them as they see fit. Here are some examples:

- If they try to convince Erik that there is a hope of holding off the enemy, they can try, needing a **DC 20 Charisma (Intimidation)** check, as the old man resents the empty boasts of warriors.

- Arguing that Celduin is lost no matter what – but if they fight back, then they buy time for the people of Celduin to flee and for Bard to gather his forces, is a plea that falls on deaf ears and automatically fails.

- They may try to move him with promises of wealth with a **DC 15 Charisma (Persuasion)** check. If the Master helps them protect Dale, then King Bard will reward him, possibly even adding Celduin to the Kingdom of Dale and making Erik the first Lord of Celduin.

- Alternatively, they can bypass the master entirely and appeal to the people of Celduin with a song. This requires a **DC 18 Charisma (Performance)** check.

Whatever skills the heroes use, check their highest margin of success:

0-1: Erik is not really convinced by the words of the companions. He feigns acceptance, and secretly starts preparing a plan: he intends to sell the companions to the enemy, possibly sending his two young granddaughters as messengers, sure that no one will dare to raise a hand against such innocent creatures...

2-3: The Master agrees to help, albeit very grudgingly. He puts the defence of Celduin in the hands of the company, but will continually interfere with what the companions are trying to do: the DC of all rolls made to prepare the village for the coming battle is raised by +2.

4+: The Master resigns the control of Celduin, trusting the companions with its defence. He keeps busy preparing all non-combatants to evacuate the town.

I am the Master here!

If the companions fail, then the Master stubbornly refuses to help defend Dale. When the first wave of attackers arrives at nightfall, the Master sends one of his sons to greet the Orcs and declare that Celduin remains neutral in their war on Dale. The Orcs laugh and one of them skewers the Master's son on his spear, then kicks the body off the bridge into the River Running. *"We take what we want,"* shouts the Orc. *"You will be our slaves!"*

Preparations for Battle

The companions can now prepare for the battle to come. They can study the battleground and prepare the available defences. The paragraphs below list some rolls that can be attempted by the companions to successfully set up the fight. For each successful preparation, the characters gain one Preparation die (d6). During the battle, any player character can take and roll a Preparation die and add the result to any one attack roll, damage roll, saving throw, skill check, or add the result to their AC in reaction to one attack.

The Tollgate

The key to any defence of the town is the tollhouse. The portcullis is well maintained, but the iron gates that should close behind it are rusted open. They can be repaired by anyone with the **Smith-craft** speciality or smith's tools.

Train Combatants

There are some twenty men of fighting age in the town, but only a dozen or so have weapons and armour and the training to use them. A character with a suitable Virtue or background can train them in discipline and combat.

Send Explorers

Scouting on the south side of the river lets the company spy on the approaching enemy. On a successful **DC 12 Wisdom (Perception)** check, they spot an advance party composed of Orcs, Wargs, and Orcs riding on Wolves approaching ahead of the main body of the enemy force, with a vanguard trailing them and the main host marching behind.

> ### Collapsing the Bridge
>
> Collapsing the bridge is possible, but extremely difficult. A character would have to swim out into the middle of the river and then smash down the weaker central pillar of the bridge. Doing so requires several hours' work to weaken the bridge enough to collapse it. If the company do collapse the bridge, then the enemy is halted, until they find that they can still ford the river to the east of the town, where the water is shallower, by having Orcs and Trolls throw stones and debris to create a ford: the delay buys the company extra time, corresponding to three additional Preparation dice.

– Part Seven –
The Battle Begins

The enemy reaches the River Running nine days after the company left Dale (two days after they reached Celduin, if they didn't tarry). The sun sets over the Mountains of Mirkwood, falling into the shadowy embrace of the forest. The few defenders prepare for the enemy assault.

From across the river to the south, the company hear the howling of wolves grow louder and louder. Where do the companions make their stand? See the Bridge Map on the back end papers.

On The Bridge

The bridge is narrow enough for two or three characters to hold the bridge and block any enemies advancing across it. A character who is knocked Prone or Pushed on the bridge may be thrown over the side into the river.

The Tollhouse, Ground Floor

Companions using spears can stand behind the portcullis and thrust their weapons through the gaps at enemies who get too close. Characters standing behind the portcullis fight at Disadvantage, but can gain the benefit of three-quarters cover (+5 bonus to **AC** and **Dexterity** saving throws).

The Tollhouse, Upper Floor

The upper floor has the mechanisms to raise and lower the portcullis. The arrow-slits in this room give a commanding view of the bridge and the banks of the river. A narrow ladder leads up to the roof.

The Tollhouse, Roof

Archers on the roof can fire arrows at enemies on the bridge or banks of the river. The trapdoor from the roof leads down to the upper floor.

Banks of the Celduin

Swimming the river requires six **DC 12 Strength (Athletics)** checks to avoid being swept away, with each failure causing 3 (1d6) cold damage. Climbing out of the river is easy enough, and does not require a test, but a character cannot attack while clambering out of the water and up the muddy banks.

The Town

If the enemies break into the town, the companions can take shelter in the wooden huts or the stone buildings.

> ### Inventive Defending
> The players will probably come up with all sorts of plans for the defence of the town and its bridge. You should reward their good ideas with tangible rewards. For example, companions who take up positions at arrow slits or battlements could be harder to hit, giving them half cover. Maybe there's less cover if they take to the battlements rather than the arrow slits below, but the greater height means that their weapons gain range and they can make an additional ranged attack as the enemy closes? If the companions can find some nails and have the time and ability to improvise caltrops, their enemies might take some damage as they cross the bridge. Encouraging and rewarding ingenuity will help bring the encounter to life for your players and lead to a memorable battle, fondly recalled around the fireplace in Fellowship phases to come!

The First Assault – Orcs and Wargs

A host of Orcs and Wargs comes first, with the smaller goblins riding upon the bigger Wolves and scrambling down the valley slope towards the bridge. Heroes from the North recognise them as Orcs and Wolves of the Mountains, probably veterans of the Battle of Five Armies searching for retribution.

Their leader stops in front of the tollhouse, protecting himself with a tall Barding shield defaced by bloody smears. It's a big Orc-chieftain with red burning eyes: he observes the defenders and then sounds his hunting horn.

"Open yer gates, maggots, or you'll hang from them!"

Assuming the gates stay closed, then the outriders charge across the bridge in a horrific tide of slashing fangs and black fur. Some of them make mad leaps from the end of the bridge to the river-bank, while others stop in front of the tollhouse where the Orcs start scaling the outer walls, hoping to climb to the upper storey of the building and open the portcullis and gates from within.

Fighting the First Assault

There are as many Orc Soldiers and Wild Wolves as heroes, along with an Orc-Chieftain and a Wolf Leader.

Some Orc Soldiers try scaling the walls of the tollhouse, while others leap off the end of the bridge and try to reach the bank. The Orcs climbing the tollhouse reach the topmost level in three combat rounds, and then try to storm the upper level and open the portcullis.

If they open the portcullis (and, if they were repaired, the gates), then the wolves on the bridge swarm through into the town.

Defeating the Orcs and Wargs

Once the companions have killed or driven off half the enemies, the remainder either flee or are brought down by the other defenders of the village.

The company have some four hours to rest before the next wave of attackers arrives. They can use this time to take a short rest, recover spent arrows, rally their troops, or improve the defences of the village.

The Second Assault – Hill-Troll Chief

Four hours after the first wave, in the black of night, a monster over ten feet tall lumbers silently into view. The Gibbet King has summoned a Troll-chief out of Mordor, to bring destruction to the North! The monster wears a menagerie of armour from various victims and wields a heavy hammer (see the *Loremaster's Guide*, page 107). He is escorted by a dozen Goblin Archers, whose main purpose seems to be to direct the Troll towards the bridge. One of the goblins points at the river and yelps something at the Troll-chief. The monster suddenly bellows thunderously as if in answer, and charges towards the bridge, raising its titanic weapon to smash the tollhouse down.

- During the battle, the Troll-chief may scream at a target within 20 ft as a bonus action. That target must make a **DC 15 Wisdom** saving throw or become Frightened until the end of the Troll-chief's next turn. (This Troll-chief gains the **Fearsome Bellow** special ability.)

Fighting the Troll-chief

The Troll-chief is a very tough opponent. If allowed to attack the tollhouse, it needs to inflict 50 damage on the gate (**AC 15**) to smash it. If attacked, the stone troll ignores its attackers until it is reduced to half its starting hit points, or it suffers a critical hit. If the Troll-chief succeeds in breaking down the tollhouse and opening the bridge, then the goblins swarm across the bridge and into the town.

The Goblins

While their Hill-troll champion hammers at the tollhouse, the goblins stay on the south side of the river and fire arrows into the town. Some of these arrows are dipped in pitch and set alight to burn the thatched roofs of the cottages; others are soiled with poison. The goblins are cowards, and will not cross the bridge until the way is clear. They flee if the Troll-chief is brought down.

– Part Eight –
The Last Day

The next day dawns with a grey light, and grim clouds hang low over the town. There is an air of impending doom and the joy of the victories of the previous night melts away when the townfolk see the carnage in the full light of day. Worse, to the south, the company can see the enemy army approaching, seemingly as numberless as a tide of ants. With the defeat of the Troll-chief, the companions have several hours to consider their situation. How have the defenders of Celduin fared? If the company drove off the Orcs and the Troll without too much damage, then most of the defenders are alive. If company was hurt badly, then many of the defenders were also severely injured or slain.

If the company sends scouts, they find no sign of any army coming from the north. To the south, across the river, they see the enemy host preparing for battle. The final attack will come tonight. The Master of Celduin suggests that they have done all they can, and that they should flee the town before the enemy attacks again. Heroes that choose to remain can benefit from a long rest.

Fleeing the Town

The company might at this point consider abandoning Celduin. As far as their mission is concerned they have partially succeeded: they have bought Dale enough time to gather an army, but not enough for King Bard to muster his full strength. The battle that will ensue will be much bloodier than it would otherwise be. But there is the safety of the villagers of Celduin to consider: if the companions flee without making sure the town won't fall prey to the bloodlust of the Orcs, they will later discover that the Master didn't succeed in buying the lives of his subjects in exchange for safe passage, and that Celduin was burned and pillaged. Having left the villagers alone counts as a Misdeed, and all the companions deserve at least 2 Shadow points for it.

The Wounded Warrior

A woman of Celduin named Amadisa approaches a member of the company with proficiency in **Medicine**. Her young husband Beoric was struck by a goblin-arrow in the last fight, and he needs help. She leads the companion into the inn, where Beoric lies on a table. Examining the warrior yields a grim result – he is dying, and all that can be done is to make his last hours comfortable. The arrow penetrated his bowels and no surgery could hope to save him. Beoric is delirious with pain and fever, so Amadisa sits by his side and whispers prayers to whatever powers will listen.

The Raven

When the sun starts to set, look-outs spot a black dot in the northern skies, almost invisible in the dying light. Some of the more fearful townsfolk whisper that it is the Dragon returned, but as it comes closer, the company see that it is just a raven from the Mountain. The bird starts to descend towards the town – and then a flight of black darts shoots from across the river - Orcish scouts were hiding from the sun close to the river banks, and just emerged to bring down the bird! The raven is hit by one of the darts, and bloody black feathers rain down on Celduin as the bird plummets to the ground. The Goblin Archers yell in triumph, and run to hide again among the reeds and rushes.

- Call for **DC 15 Wisdom (Perception)** checks; if someone succeeds, they notice that the raven carried a small roll of parchment and let it fall. It was carried briefly by the wind, to finally drop into the river.

If the companions recover the parchment, they discover that it bears the unbroken sigil of King Bard. The message it carries is still readable:

Dale marches south with Esgaroth and the Dwarves of the Mountain! Hold the river through the night. At dawn, look to the North.

Thus Quoth the Raven

If the companions search the area where the raven fell, they find him dying, neatly skewered by the Orc-arrow. There is nothing the companions can do but listen to his last words:

"I am Korun, son of Roäc. I have at last reached the end of my days. Listen to my counsel! Fight the shadow with fire, or water. A foresight is on me, I am warning you."

Voices in the Dark

When the night falls, the villagers of Celduin light lanterns and torches, and ignite bonfires close to the river banks, to better watch for the advancing enemy. But as the preparations for the coming battle draw to a conclusion, the wounded warrior Beoric dies. He shudders as he draws his last breath, then slumps back down on the table. There is a long moment of silence, broken only by his widow's weeping. Then the corpse stirs. An unnatural light blooms in Beoric's dead eyes, and his cold lips part as a lifeless voice emerges.

The Gibbet King has taken Beoric's body as its mouthpiece, and it addresses the company. Any characters who played through *Those Who Tarry No Longer* or *A Darkness in the Marshes* instantly recognises the horrible voice of the spirit.

"Fools! You think Bard the Bowman is coming to save you? Dale is afire, abandoned by Elf and Dwarf alike. No help is coming to you. No hope is left to you. Yield!"

The spirit knows that its forces need to cross the Celduin tonight if it is to catch Dale unawares, so it tries to demoralise the player characters.

- The spirit's baleful influence forces everyone to immediately make a **DC 15 Wisdom** saving throw or gain 1 Shadow Point. Worse, the company must keep making such saving throw (gaining one Shadow Point on a failed test) until one of the company speaks up and defies the spirit, breaking the spell of its evil words.

Once one of the company defies the spirit, it leaves Beoric's body. The dead man falls back and remains still. From outside, the company hear the sound of war-horns.

The Final Assault - Orcs & Worse Things

In the light of hundreds of torches and fires, an army of Orcs swarms across the bridge, if it still stands. If the bridge has collapsed, then they hurl themselves into the river and struggle across, driven by terror of the thing behind them. There are more Orcs than can easily be counted, but the company is outnumbered by at least ten to one. All are Orc Soldiers, Orc Guards and Goblin Archers. Judging from the devices on their shields, a companion with proficiency in **Shadow-lore** or the *Dark Knowledge* ability can identify the bulk of the host as fierce Orcs out of southern Mirkwood, reinforced by the survivors of the Battle of Five Armies and Northeners from the Misty Mountains.

Playing the Onslaught

There is no time for tactics; keep throwing Orcs at the company. For every Orc that falls, more take its place. The company need to hold out for as long as they can. Dawn will only come after they have confronted the Gibbet King (see the next section). As the combat wears on, describe the faint light on the horizon – the heroes should know that they must put every effort into this final stand...

The Gibbet King Comes

Once several of combat have elapsed, a new horror appears on the far side of the river. In the wavering light, the companions see a wooden cart, drawn by a pair of black horses. On the cart stands an iron cage, a gibbet containing a rotting human corpse, little more than a skeleton held together with blackened sinews and rags. The same unholy light that was in Beoric's eyes dances in the skeleton's eye-sockets.

- The skeleton raises one bony hand and points it at the strongest hero, uttering a *Dreadful Spell:* that character must make a **DC 15 Wisdom** saving throw; if he fails he gains 1 Shadow Point and is frozen to the spot, Paralysed and unable to defend or attack for a number of rounds equal to his current Shadow score, unless he spends Inspiration to break the spell.

The skeleton in the cart is the current host body of the Gibbet King, the torturer and jailer of the Necromancer of Dol Guldur. Normally perceived by mortals only as a malevolent shadow, he needs a body to command its followers and affect the material world. Destroying the Gibbet King's body will not kill him, but it will momentarily banish him.

- To throw a torch upon the cart, a hero must make an attack roll as normal; for each torch that hits the cart, roll a d4: the torch sets the cart on fire with a 4. Shooting a flaming arrow puts the attack at Disadvantage, but sets the cart ablaze if it does 4 damage or more.

If the cart is set alight, it takes 2d6 rounds for the flames to reach the Gibbet King (further successful attempts to set the cart alight hasten this process, reducing the number of rounds by one). From that moment on, the Gibbet King loses 2d6 hit points from fire damage every round.

The Gibbet King
Medium undead

STR	DEX	CON	INT	WIS	CHA
10 (+0)	10 (+0)	16 (+3)	17 (+3)	18 (+4)	16 (+3)

Armour Class 13 (Iron Cage)
Hit Points 67 (9d8+27)
Speed 0 ft

Damage Resistances cold, lightning, poison, psychic; bludgeoning, piercing, and slashing from non-magical attacks
Condition Immunities Charmed, Exhaustion, Grappled, Paralyzed, Petrified, Poisoned, Prone, Restrained
Senses passive Perception 14
Languages Westron, Black Speech
Challenge 5 (1,800 XP)

Actions

Dreadful Spells (Recharge 5-6). One nearby foe must make a **DC 15 Wisdom** saving throw. If the character fails, he gains 1 Shadow point and becomes Paralysed for a number of rounds equal to his current Shadow Point total. A character can spend Inspiration to break this spell.
Visions of Torment. As an action, the Gibbet King can force one target within 60 feet to make a **DC 15 Wisdom** saving throw or take psychic damage equal to 2 (1d4) plus their total Shadow score.

Reaction

Feast on Suffering. Whenever a foe suffers a critical hit or is reduced to 0 hit points, the Gibbet King regains 7 (2d6) hit points.

If the bridge still stands, then the cart rattles down the slope towards the tollhouse. The spirit exerts its power on the portcullis, causing the iron wheels to slowly grind backwards and the portcullis to rise as the cart approaches. The company's best chance of victory is to launch a last-ditch attack on the spirit itself, ideally with fire or water, as the last words of the raven suggested.

Attacking the Gibbet King

The cart carrying the Gibbet King is not especially protected, as the Orcs themselves fear to be near it. But to get to it, the companions still need to cut their way through the raging battle.

Fighting the Spirit with Fire

The companions can try to set the cart carrying the Gibbet King on fire: to do so, they can throw torches or shoot flaming arrows against it.

Fighting the Spirit with Water

Another way to destroy the host body of the Gibbet King could be to throw the cart into the Running River. Parts of its waters pass along the Woodland Realm (the Forest

River) and carry with them some of the benevolence of the Fair Folk, a bane for creatures such as the Gibbet King...

- If the cart is upon the bridge, it takes a **DC 25 Strength (Athletics)** check to push it over the edge (inventive players will certainly propose different ways to accomplish the same feat).

Once his host body is immersed in the waters of the River Running, the Gibbet King loses its grip on the material world and is forced to flee.

If the King is Defeated

Destroying the king's body by sword, fire or water scatters the Orc-host. Terrified by the loss of their master, they retreat back south or else flee the battle. The bulk of the army is still on the south bank, so the enemy forces are not wholly broken, but the defeat of the Gibbet King significantly slows the invasion.

If the Company is Overrun

If the company are unable to defeat the Gibbet King, or if they are overwhelmed by the Orcs, then a kind Loremaster can pull them out of the fire by having a group of outriders from Dale arrive, led by Elstan. The First Captain of Dale charges, scattering the Orcs long enough for the company to gather themselves and flee.

The Army of the North

King Bard and his allies meet the Orc-host somewhere south of Dale. Whether the company was successful in holding the bridge or not, the Free Folk of the North are once again victorious – but the amount of time bought by the deeds of the companions heavily influences the nature of this victory.

The Companions were Defeated on the First Night (defeated in Part Seven)

The Gibbet King crosses the River Running early and pushes his army north. Bard is able to meet the enemy forces only when they are already inside the borders of the Upper Marches. The king of Dale is victorious and the Orc-army is scattered, but raiders plague the local farmsteads for months to come. The battle itself is costly and calamitous: of those who marched forth from Dale, less than a third march back home. Bard himself suffers a terrible wound. This will be remembered as a black day for many years to come.

- The companions receive an Experience Award.

The Companions held the Crossings of Celduin for one Night (defeated in Part Eight)

The Orc-host crosses the Celduin and Bard is able to intercept them several miles north of the river, fortunately still outside the most populated areas. The battle is bloody, but in the end the Orcs break and flee. If they weren't led by their dark master, the Orcs might have been routed, for Bard and his men to pursue them and put an end to their menace once and for all. Alas! The Free Folk of the North must be content with a smaller victory.

- The companions receive an Experience Award, and are hailed as heroes of Dale.

The Companions held the Crossings of Celduin for two Nights (victorious in Part Eight)

King Bard reaches Celduin on the morning after the second night of battle. His host crosses the bridge at the Crossings amid the cheers of the exhausted villagers, and falls upon the Orcs before they reorganize themselves. Warriors from Dale, archers from Lake-town and many stout dwarven warriors from the Mountain and the Iron Hills utterly crush the enemy and win a glorious victory.

- The companions receive an Experience Award and are richly rewarded by King Bard (either 100 gold pieces per hero or a suitable item of the Loremaster's creation).

Aftermath

There is one curious and worrisome footnote to the whole affair. Among all the combatants who participated and survived the battle, no one brings back news of the Gibbet King. It is as though the spirit has once again vanished into shadow...

There is no time for a Fellowship Phase after this adventure – the company have a few days to recover before *The Watch on the Heath* begins.

- the watch - on the heath

for heroes of level 6 or higher

- **When:** This adventure takes place shortly after *The Crossings of Celduin*. There is no time for a Fellowship Phase between the two quests.
- **Where:** The company returns to Dale after their defence of the bridge over the Celduin. While the Orcs who served the Gibbet King were defeated, the spirit itself is still at large. From Erebor, the company travel across the Waste into the mountains of the north, and the edge of the Withered Heath.
- **What:** The company are sent to an abandoned dwarven watchtower to investigate.
- **Why:** Before betraying the warriors of Dale, the merchant Lockmand visited the Lonely Mountain and consulted with certain ancient records held in the vaults there. His interest in the old watchtower seemed innocent, but it must conceal a sinister purpose.
- **Who:** The chief foe of this tale is the Gibbet King itself, a spirit of growing power who plots to seize control of a dragon and rain destruction on the Free Folk of the North.

Adventuring Phase

This adventure is divided into six parts.

Part One - Council Under The Mountain
The company are called to Dáin's seat under the Mountain, where he tells them of certain recent troubling events, and commands them to investigate.

Part Two - Across the Trackless Waste
The company set forth from the Lonely Mountain and face the perils of the Waste. There, they meet a strange creature called Witherfinger, who knows much of what transpires in the region. If the company can win her favour, she can help them in their quest.

Part Three - The Grey Mountains
Monsters slumber in the foothills of the Grey Mountains, and the company must tread warily as they find their way to the watchtower.

Part Four - Zirakinbar
The company arrive at the ancient watchtower, and discover that a dire plan is afoot.

Part Five - The Scourge of the North
The companions have the chance to meet Raenar, the plunderer, and strike an uneasy alliance (or die a dolorous death).

Part Six - The Watchtower
Wherein the tower carved on the peak of Zirakinbar is described, and the nefarious plans of the Gibbet King discussed.

Epilogue - A Renewed Spring of Joy
If the companions defeat the Gibbet King, they will have bought Wilderland a few years of prosperity, and finally concluded a threat that started plaguing them long before.

- Part One - Council Under The Mountain

The army of Dale marches home. Whether they have come back in glory, or on their shields, the warriors of the town are welcomed back by their families and friends. The new kingdom has survived another trial, another attack by the forces of darkness. Dale endures. There are no feasts to celebrate this victory, for it was bought at great cost. Help has come from both the halls of Thranduil and from far Rhosgobel to attend to those poisoned by Lockmand or wounded in battle, so all the company are rapidly restored to full health (they get all their hit points and Hit Dice back).

A Secret Summoning
A few days after the battle, the company are contacted by a Dwarf wearing a grey hood. He bows low and introduces himself as Ori, one of the companions of Thorin Oakenshield. (If the company has had dealings with the survivors of Thorin's Company before then Ori recognises them and greets them warmly.) Ori is a well-travelled

and personable Dwarf, friendly even to Elves, and often serves King Dáin as an ambassador and diplomat. Today, though, his mission is more secretive, and he wears a humble, travel-stained cloak (the very same cloak, in fact, that he wore on the Quest of Erebor some years ago) over his fine clothes.

- Ori informs the company that King Dáin wishes to speak with them under the Mountain. He has ponies and horses waiting outside, and the company should come immediately.

To Erebor

On the road that from Dale leads to the gate of the Lonely Mountain, the company pass many Dwarves returning home from the battle, or busy at work on the ancient road that leads between the two cities. Soon, they reach the great cliff-wall where the River Running springs out of the Mountain. Leaving their mounts there, Ori leads them through the Front Gate, into a maze of wide passages, high chambers and halls. Inside the Dwarven fastness, a veritable army of craftsmen are hard at work, and the corridors echo with the din of hammers and chisels.

After a while, the companions lose count of the downward stairs and sloping passages they have passed, and know simply that they must be deep in the roots of the Lonely Mountain. They pass the vast chamber where Smaug lay atop his fabulous hoard - something of the dragon lingers there, a trace of sulphur and greed and heat that will never be washed away. The company are led past the hall down into deeper tunnels. Smaug never despoiled this particular section of the Mountain; he could smell there was no gold down here, and the few Dwarves who did take refuge in this warren of tunnels found themselves trapped here in the darkness, and they starved to death.

Finally, Ori brings the company to a stone door, marked with dwarf-runes. He pushes it open, leading them into the Chamber of Mazarbul under Erebor - the Chamber of Records of the Dwarves of the Mountain. Inside the wide rectangular hall waits Dáin Ironfoot, Lord of the Iron Hills and King under the Mountain.

An Audience with King Dáin

Dáin is a stern and proud Dwarf, perhaps the greatest warrior of the line of Durin in this age of the world. A crown of *mithril* glitters on his head, but on his feet he still wears the iron-banded shoes of a miner. Also in the chamber is a third Dwarf, whose white beard stretches down to the floor. This is one of Dáin's counsellors, a sage named Munin. The Dwarves wait until the companions formally introduce themselves (a **DC 15 Intelligence (Traditions)** check).

Motivation

Dáin seeks heroes he can trust. The dwarf-king is secretive by nature, and loathe to reveal the secrets of his folk to outsiders.

Expectations

+2: The secrets of the Dwarves will never be revealed (gained if the company swear an oath to this effect)
+1: Wisdom and long beards are to be honoured (if there's a dwarf or scholar in the company)
+1: Past deeds reflect future promise (for each relevant deed that the company have already accomplished, like capturing Lockmand or identifying the chain of Thangorodrim)
-1: Deference is a king's due. (Dáin is a stickler for formality.)

Interaction

King Dáin begins by giving a short account of recent events in Erebor.

"Last year, we received the visit of a merchant from Lake-town. He bore letters of introduction from the Master of Esgaroth, and gave his name as Lockmand. He had a treasure to trade with us, a shield that once belonged to Thrór, the grandfather of Thorin Oakenshield. The shield had passed from Thrór to his son Thráin, and it was believed lost since when Thráin disappeared in Mirkwood one hundred years ago. Lockmand claimed to have bought the shield in a market in the far south."

"In exchange for the shield, Lockmand wanted payment in gold, and a fair price was arranged. He also asked, as a favour, for a look in our records. He claimed to be a buyer and seller of treasures and relics, and he hoped that the old books might contain information useful to him. But we do not let foreigners easily in our Chamber of Records, and we deliberated for some time before finally refusing his request."

At this point, Munin takes over the tale. He introduces himself as the keeper of records.

"One night, I was awoken by strange sounds coming from the Hall of Mazarbul. I descended to investigate, and whatever-it-was fled before I could see it. I searched the vaults, but found nothing amiss, and then I soon forgot the matter."

At this point, Munin hangs his head in shame.

"The truth is that I was not diligent enough. One book was out of place, and I did not notice. It was only when news reached the Mountain of Lockmand's treachery in Dale that I recognised the name and made a fuller search of the vault, and found out what happened."

Munin takes a large metal-bound book out of a case and places it carefully on the table. The book is obviously very old, but the dry air of vaults has preserved the parchment almost perfectly. The record-keeper handles the pages carefully.

"This book is one of a great many similar records detailing the building of the works and fortifications of the Kingdom under the Mountain. This particular volume describes a watchtower that our folk built in the Grey Mountains to the north. Its purpose was to keep a watch on the Withered Heath, and send a warning south would one of the great worms that lived there threaten to cross the mountains."

"No Dwarf living today knows if the watchtower was attacked by Smaug before he came to Erebor, or if the warning came too late. In any event, as far we can tell, the watchtower has been deserted for many decades."

Munin shows the company the book. Lockmand cut a page out of it. From its placement in the book, it was likely a map of the watchtower. King Dáin observes the reactions of the companions, then concludes:

"We do not know why this merchant seeks an abandoned watchtower. We don't even know if Lockmand's theft has anything to do with the recent attack on Dale. But I sent a raven north to look for and investigate the watchtower, and the bird has not returned. I worry that danger still hangs over Dale and the Mountain."

We Captured Lockmand!

If the company captured the merchant Lockmand during *The Crossings of Celduin*, then the players may ask why the merchant is not being questioned to find out what he was doing in Erebor last year. Ori shakes his head and tells the company that Lockmand is dead. The merchant was locked in a jail cell in Dale, but was found dead a few days ago. His body was icy cold, and there was an expression of utter terror on his face. Whatever evil killed him, it passed by all the guards and watchmen in King Bard's hall without being seen.

The King under the Mountain needs counsel. What do the company say? Various topics are addressed below.

The War
The companions can speculate (correctly) that the recent attack on Dale may have been a diversion, to allow the enemy to slip past the Mountain and head for the northern wastes. The Orc army was too small to conquer Dale, and the enemy does not squander forces without purpose.

The Chain
If the company mention the chain they saw on the Dwimmerhorn during *A Darkness in the Marshes*, then both Dáin and Munin stroke their beards thoughtfully. The connection between the chain and the watchtower is a mystery to them, but the chain is another significant factor that should be considered.

Where Exactly is the Watchtower?
The book that Lockmand perused and vandalised is unclear about the location of the watchtower. If Lockmand is still at large, this might lead the companions to the conclusion that if the watchtower is involved in the next stage of the merchant's plans he cannot have too much of a lead on them, as he is probably still searching the mountains.

- Scholarly companions can try to locate the watchtower by spending a fortnight studying with Munin in the Chamber of Mazarbul and making a **DC 15 Intelligence (Lore)** check. On a success, they find additional details in a volume about the construction of

Dwarven roads: the watchtower has been dug into the tip of a mountain peak called *Zirakinbar*, this isolated horn of rock rises about eighty miles north of Erebor, in the southeastern arm of the Grey Mountains.

Conclusions

Make a Final Audience Check using **Traditions**, **Lore** or **History**. Compare the margin of success to the list below:

Failure: Dáin is dismayed by the lack of initiative from the companions. The king doesn't comment, but he certainly hopes that they make better adventurers than diplomats!

0-2: The King under the Mountain offers the company a fine reward from his armoury once they return from the quest. If there is at least one Dwarf in the company, the king allows them to take the book describing the watchtower with them, *but only if they expressly ask for permission*.

3-5: As 0-2 above; additionally, the king allows the company to take the book even without a Dwarf.

6+: King Dáin is positively impressed. Apply the results above; additionally, the king directly proposes that the company carry the book with them, and permits the characters to take their reward from his armoury before departing for the watchtower. (See *Epilogue* on page 142.)

If there are no Dwarves in the group, or if the companions do not ask to take the book and the king doesn't tell them

Secrets of Mazarbul

Dwarven records can be written in the secret language of the Dwarves, but also in the Common speech, using dwarf-runes or various Elvish scripts. The book describing the watchtower is written in a dense, hard-to-read style that combines the Common Speech with Khuzdul terminology.

A character can try reading the book while travelling, at night by the light of a campfire. Doing so costs one level of Exhaustion, but allows the character to make a Intelligence (Lore) check each night. The difficulty for the roll is DC 15, or DC 10 if the reader is a Dwarf.

Each successful check reveals one of the following secrets:

1. **Secret Entrance:** There is a concealed entrance into the cellars of the watchtower. The key to the door is "a polished axe, thrice".

2. **Traps:** The Great Hall is guarded by a mighty stone. Should enemies breach the gate, the stone can be lowered to block the entrance tunnel, protecting the watchtower from the mightiest foes.

3. **Treasure Vault:** A secret vault was built when the tower was carved out of the mountain. It is in the last bedchamber on the left, and the entrance is hidden in the floor.

4. **Dangers of Dragons:** Light no fire when in the Grey Mountains, and keep your gold out of the wind. Dragons can smell gold.

5. **Chamber of Winds:** The upper level of the watchtower is a great chamber where eight tunnels meet and eight windows look out over the world. Each of the tunnels has a separate door that can be opened or closed independently. When the wind blows, the tunnels become musical instruments and the mountain produces powerful sounds, originally used by the watchmen in the case of the direst emergencies. But the ingenious device can prove very dangerous: when the wind blows from the north, make sure not to open the north, south and north-east doors simultaneously, or the mountain's howl is so loud as to be dangerous!

6. **Raven's Perch:** For ordinary communications, at the very top of the watchtower is a small chamber where the Dwarves kept raven messengers. It looks down onto the Chamber of Winds. It is reached by a spiral staircase that opens off the main stairs.

If the companions do not take the book, then Munin's research reveals one of the secrets (roll a d6 to decide which) before the company leaves Erebor.

to do so, then Munin promises to study the volume as much as he can before the group departs, but he fears that the dense tome will take too long for him to unlock all its secrets. See *Secrets of Mazarbul*, on the previous page.

The Last Night

Once the company have agreed to undertake the quest, Dáin tells them they will depart at first light tomorrow. They will be provided with such supplies and travelling gear as the Dwarves can muster; Ori will see to their needs. The king departs, and leaves the company in Ori's care. Ori brings the company back up to the first level of the Mountain, and shows them to a dining hall where they are treated to the Dwarves' hospitality. The company may also visit the smithies and storehouses of the dwarves (each hero may select 100s of gear before leaving).

- Part Two -
Across the Trackless Waste

The company leave the Mountain by the North Door, a postern gate only recently opened after some one hundred and fifty years buried under fallen stones. The view from the Mountain's northern flank is not as pleasant as the view from the Front Gate. Instead of the lights of Dale, the green valley, and the bright waters of the river running away into the south, the company look out upon miles of empty, trackless wasteland. Beyond the Waste they see a dark ridge of mountain peaks - the Grey Mountains.

"Good luck", says Ori, *"I rather wish I was going with you. You might see a Dragon along your quest. You may not believe it, but during our adventure I never laid my eyes upon Smaug, and some people from Lake-town described his wrath as being terrible and beautiful at the same time. Is that not strange? Well, good luck and safe travels."*

The Journey

The companions must journey across miles of broken land to reach the Grey Mountains. The Waste is a trackless wilderness, full of strange twisted shapes of stone and blind canyons. Little grows there except thorny bracken and weeds. No travellers go there and no folk dwell there.

- This journey to the Grey Mountains covers eighty miles across trackless, hard terrain. The journey takes eight days on average. The Peril Rating for the Journey is 3 and it provokes 1d2+1 Journey Events at DC 15.

Once across, the company will have to find and ascend the peak of Zirakinbar.

Corruption Checks

The Waste is a Shadow Land, so a **DC 15 Wisdom** saving throw is required every day to avoid gaining a point of Shadow. The endless piles of stone and looming tors seem almost like gravestones, and as weariness takes hold, the companions seem to glimpse impossible shapes lurking in the stones or swirling in the fog.

From Erebor to the Grey Mountains

Unlike the Desolation of Smaug, the Waste is a land that is forever tainted. The Desolation is a fresh scar that may heal cleanly; this land is a rotten corpse, a gangrenous wound. Nothing seems to live here, amidst the tumbled hills and the reeking pools of foul water.

129

Searching for Signs

As the company travel, they make a grim discovery. They find the corpse of an Orc at the bottom of a gully. From his gear and weapons, the Orc seems to have been part of the same band that attacked Dale. Searching around nearby, the companions find some tracks in a soft patch of ground. Judging from the tracks, they are hunting a dozen or more Orcs, and some of the Orcs were carrying a very heavy burden.

- As the company examine the tracks, call for a **DC 10 Wisdom (Perception)** check. Anyone who succeeds notices an eerie glow in the eyes of the Orc-corpse. The characters are being watched by the Gibbet King! If anyone reacts, the spirit departs, slithering out of the corpse and then vanishing into the north like a shadow.

Witherfinger

On the fifth day of travel into the Waste, the company come upon a stagnant pool of brown water. By the side of the pool is a figure. At first, it looks like a spindly, leafless tree covered in dead moss and ivy, but as they draw closer, they realise that it is an immensely old woman. Her skin is brown and wrinkled, and her thin body is hunched over with a lifetime's work. Her eyes are old and sad and utterly mad. She stands with her feet immersed in the brown water, and sways gently back and forth, sometimes trailing her thin fingertips in the pool. She does not move while speaking with the company.

This strange creature calls herself Witherfinger. Whether she is human, Elf or something stranger, it is impossible to say. What is certain is that Witherfinger has a terrible fear of Orcs and fire, a legacy of some ancient tragedy, and so she dwells in the Waste where there is no-one to threaten her. She roams the land endlessly with only her own thoughts and memories for company.

Playing Witherfinger

Witherfinger is a mystery in Middle-earth. She might be an incredibly old Entwife, or an incarnate spirit, or just a crazed old hermit. She is nervous and fearful, and is utterly terrified of Orcs and the shadow. She lives in the Waste to hide from these enemies, and worries that the presence of the company may draw the enemy to her. At the same time, she seldom has the opportunity to speak to anyone, and thus she cannot resist talking to them. Only listen to half of what the company say. Pay more attention to the hobbit's shiny buttons than the elf's tales of impending doom. If someone mentions Orcs, panic! Mutter to yourself. Stand with your legs straight together, and sway back and forth when talking.

Motivation

Witherfinger is nervous, and fearful of strangers, but she's also terribly lonely.

Expectations

+2: Elves woke us up, long ago. (if there is an Elf or any Elf-friends in the company)
+1: A little kindness for an old woman. (If the company are especially gentle and polite to her)
-1: I don't like hasty words. (If rushed or questioned forcefully)
-2: Strangers bring trouble. (If threatened)

Introduction

"I am... well, I had a name once. It went away, like all the rest. Hmm. Call me Witherfinger. Come close, child, let me smell you and touch you."

She beckons the company closer with her long black fingernails. Witherfinger wants to know what the company are doing here, who they are and, most importantly, she wants to make sure they are not Orcs. They could be Orcs, after all. They may look like Free Folk, but Orcs are tricky – maybe they are Orcs who peeled the faces off their victims and are now using them as masks! She wants the company to come close enough for her to touch them. If everyone refuses, then Witherfinger assumes they are Orcs and panics – see *Witherfinger's Fear*, below. If a companion submits, then Witherfinger runs her withered fingers over the companion's face. It is a disconcerting experience – her fingers are covered with wispy hairs or tendrils or worms that wriggle and writhe, and force their way into the companion's ears, nose and mouth. The hero must make a **DC 15 Wisdom** saving throw to remain calm. Once satisfied that this hero is not an Orc, she agrees to talk to the company.

Interaction

Witherfinger looks askance towards all strangers; the DC for the Final Audience Check with her is **DC 14**, or **DC 16** if the character(s) she touched failed their saving throws.

For her part, Witherfinger wants to know who the company are and what they are doing. She knows little of the 'southlands', as she refers to everything south of the Lonely Mountain; Smaug's conquest of the Mountain counts as recent news to her, let alone the Dragon's death. If the company mention Orcs, she shivers and says:

"Orcs! You brought Orcs here! I saw them! Orcs are bad, bad, awful things. Don't bring Orcs here! No Orcs here!"

The company must immediately calm her with a **DC 10 Charisma (Persuasion)** check, otherwise, the audience comes to an abrupt end as Witherfinger panics. If they calm her, they can question her about the Orcs she saw.

"They passed by here a few days ago. I hid. I'm very clever at hiding. I hid long ago, long ago, in a place where no-one would ever find me. I saw them, and they did not see me.

I... what was the question again, dearie? Oh yes, what I saw, I saw. Orcs! I saw Orcs, such Orcs as I have not seen in an age. They were going north towards the mountains. They were carrying a heavy chain. And I could smell dark magic upon it."

To convince Witherfinger to help them, the companions may persuade her they are ready for the challenges, or beg for her help. Alternatively, they can address her fears by telling her that there is now peace and friendship between the Free Folk of the North, how the Bardings and Woodsmen are allied with the Elves and Dwarves, how there is a King under the Mountain again and a King in Dale, and that the Orcs will be defeated by their new alliance. If asked about the chain, she knows little. She could tell it was evil, and powerful. If asked for directions, Witherfinger shudders again.

"The Orcs went north, yes, but that way leads into a dangerous land, where no one in their right mind should go! Huge Snow-Trolls prowl there, fighting and eating each other! Snow-Trolls are horrible, dangerous things, creatures made by the Enemy in the Elder Days! They'll eat you in two bites, and come after me for dessert. No, it is much safer for you to stay here and hide with me."

Conclusion

Make a Final Audience Check using **Persuasion** or **Riddle**. Compare to the results below.

Failure: Witherfinger is easily scared, and by the end of the audience she starts fearing she should have not spoken to these foreigners. A sudden gust of wind throws dust in the eyes of the companions, blinding them for an instant: when they recover, Witherfinger is nowhere to be seen.

0-2: Witherfinger fears for the safety of the companions. She teaches them how to avoid attracting the unwanted attention of the Snow-Trolls. The creatures slumber during most of the day, but they can be awoken by the smell of prey. Each Troll sleeps in a different cave inside a deep valley. If you stay downwind of the caves' entrances, and avoid getting too close, you can creep past the Trolls without waking them. Tread softly!

3+: As above, but Witherfinger adds an additional warning; once the companions climb the Grey Mountains and look out over the Withered Heath, they should light no fire and carry no gold! Flame and treasure may both draw dragons down upon unwary travellers. All that is bright is death in the Withered Heath.

Witherfinger bids the company farewell. If the company return to the brown pool later, there is no sign of her.

> ### Witherfinger's Fear
> If the company attack Witherfinger, or if they alarm her, then she calls up a windstorm that whips dust and small stones into the company's eyes. Everyone in the company takes 1d6 damage and is Blinded for a moment. When they can see again, Witherfinger is gone.
>
> Worse, from that moment on, it is as though the whole of the Waste turns against the company. Stones work their way into boots, the weather switches from torrential rain to howling wind and back again, and every path seems to twist and double back on itself. The characters are at Disadvantage on all rolls for the rest of the journey.

– Part Three –
The Grey Mountains

Once the company have crossed the Waste, they have another day or so of slow travel across the foothills of the Grey Mountains. The terrain climbs steadily, as all the paths wind among the peaks and mountain tops.

- To find the peak of Zirakinbar and climb it the company must travel for ten miles on broken paths and dangerous terrain.

Corruption Tests
While travelling toward Zirakinbar, the companions can sometimes espy the Withered Heath through gaps in the mountains. The heath was once a green valley, but it was despoiled by the great worms long ago, and now it is a dead land. Its surface is scorched black, and the terrain itself has been rent for centuries by the claws of fighting dragons. There are always great smoky clouds above the Heath, and the companions cannot shake the impression that there is something moving within the clouds. There is a smell of ash on the wind. This region ranks as a Dark Land, and the companions must make a **DC 15 Wisdom** saving throw twice a day, gaining a point of Shadow on a failure. See page 181 of the *Adventures in Middle-earth Player's Guide* for more information.

The Snow-Trolls
On their way to the watchtower the company enters a deep, shadowy gorge, with high rock walls punctuated by openings. This gully is the lair of the Snow-Trolls, and each opening is a cave that might contain one of them. Luckily for the company, there are no storms brewing, and the Snow-Trolls are asleep in their caves (see the description of Snow-Trolls below).

Scent of Prey
To navigate around the sleeping Snow-Trolls, the company need to stay downwind of their caves and to tread lightly. Normally, that would be easy enough – but inside the gorge the direction of the wind is not easy to divine, and every sound echoes against the sheer surface of the gully walls.

- Crossing the gorge without waking a Troll requires three **DC 10 Dexterity** (**Stealth**) checks from each companion. Every round represents crossing in front of the mouth of a cave. If one hero fails a test, then the Troll inside the cave merely stirs and does not awaken. Two failures in the same round– or one failure with a natural 1 awakens a Troll.

The Snow-Troll Wakes
If the company are unlucky enough to wake a sleeping Snow-Troll, then they are sent sprawling as the monster emerges from the cave charging and roaring, stones tumbling from the mouth cave like an avalanche. A Stone-Troll is a ferocious beast, ten feet tall, entirely covered by shaggy white hair and with a head the size of a barrel.

When fighting the Troll, there are two added dangers.

- The path used by the company is narrow and steep: each round, one character in the group is at Disadvantage when attacking. The players may choose which character is inconvenienced at the start of each round, with the proviso that no character can be chosen two rounds in a row.

- There are other sleeping Snow-Trolls in the vicinity. If the company flee in the wrong direction, or if the fight disturbs a sleeping Troll, then they may awaken another one.

Snow-Trolls

He would go out by himself, clad in white, and stalk like a snow-troll into the camps of his enemies, and slay many men with his hands.

Snow-Trolls are smaller than many of their brethren, but their ferocity makes up for the difference in size. They are usually found in caves, where they slumber waiting for a snowstorm to arrive. When the wind blows and snow reduces the visibility to mere inches, they go out to hunt in great numbers. Despite their size, Snow-Trolls are silent hunters, capable of creeping upon their prey and catching them completely by surprise.

Snow-Troll
Large Giant (Troll-kind)

STR	DEX	CON	INT	WIS	CHA
18 (+4)	12 (+1)	20 (+5)	7 (-2)	9 (-1)	7 (-2)

Armour Class 16 (natural armour)
Hit Points 84 (8d10+40)
Speed 30 ft

Skills Perception +2, Stealth +4, Survival +2
Senses passive Perception 12
Languages Orkish
Challenge 5 (1,800 XP)

Camouflage. Snow-trolls have Advantage on all **Stealth** checks in snowy terrain.

Actions

Multiattack. The Snow-troll makes three attacks: one bite and two with its claws.
Bite. *Melee Weapon Attack:* +7 to hit, reach 5 ft, one target. *Hit:* 9 (2d4+4) slashing damage.
Claw. *Melee Weapon Attack:* +7 to hit, reach 5 ft, one target. *Hit:* 11 (2d6+4) slashing damage.

- Part Four -
Zirakinbar

Once past the gorge of the Snow-Trolls, the company emerges in sight of the watchtower. There it stands, carved by the Dwarves out of the living rock, atop the peak of Zirakinbar. A narrow mountain road leads up to the main gate of the watchtower. As the company approaches, they see the many empty windows of the tower. Smoke issues from the upper levels. The watchtower is occupied, and there is a risk the company is being observed.

- The companions must immediately make **DC 10 Dexterity** saving throws to take cover before the Orcs spot them. If successful, the company can sneak up on the watchtower. Otherwise, the enemy knows they are there.

As soon as the companions begin to move towards the tower they find their way blocked by the shade of a Man who beckons them to stop.

The Old Master

The shade is that of a middle-aged Northman, dressed in tatters. He stands motionless, but his clothes move as if touched by intangible winds. Heroes from the local area (Bardings, Men of the Lake, Dwarves of Erebor) will recognise the apparition as the old Master of Lake-town, who many years ago fell prey to the Dragon-sickness and fled from Esgaroth with the city's share of the gold of Smaug, only to die in the Waste deserted by his accomplices. His visage is a mask of sadness and distress - if the companions address him, the old Master speaks.

"They took my treasure, my share of gold thrice-cursed. They brought it all here, my coins, my cups, my strings of rings. Thrice-cursed, I call it. First, it made the Dwarves greedy and drew their doom upon their heads. Then, it consumed Smaug the Dreadful and made him weak. Finally, it made me blind to the joys of life, and turned me into an oath-breaker."

"Now my graven silver and carven gold will be offered to the plunderer, the slithering death. A precious lure to call him, an iron trap to chain him, and then unleash him upon the North. My betrayal is complete. I already feel his cold breath blowing from the North. Here he comes!"

With his last words, the shade raises an emaciated arm and points a finger towards the Withered Heath - there, a faint plume of dust can now be seen. Judging from the distance, whatever is causing the disturbance must be very large, and it is advancing at great speed. Then, the ghost of the old Master disappears.

What should the Companions Do?

The next two parts of the adventure aren't necessarily presented in chronological order. The first, *Part Five: The Scourge of the North*, details the great Cold-drake Raenar and how the company may deal with him. The following section, *Part Six: The Watchtower*, concerns what is inside the tower and the plans of the Gibbet King. Since the two parts are closely connected, the Loremaster should be familiar with the contents of both sections, and be prepared to inter-mingle them depending on the choices of the players.

– Part Five –
The Scourge of the North

When there was a Dragon under the Lonely Mountain, Gandalf the Grey feared that the Dark Lord could use Smaug the Dreadful as a weapon, and send him to burn the North in wrath. Bard the Bowman put that fear to rest, but there are still Dragons in the North...

A Forgotten Threat

Far off in the Withered Heath, a great Cold-drake slept. More than three hundred years ago he plagued the Grey Mountains, killing and stealing from the Dwarves who lived there. They called him *Raenar*, the Plunderer, for he had smashed the gates of many halls since the reign of Náin the Second. In 2589 he killed King Dáin the First, together with Frór his second son, but was grievously hurt in the battle. Soon after that, he abandoned the region.

But Raenar didn't die of his wounds. He settled in a frozen cave to heal, and slowly fell into a slumber. His sleep would have lasted an age or more, if something didn't wake him up. His long sleep has diminished him in size and strength, but it hasn't robbed him of his wicked cunning or of his ability to catch the scent of gold and precious things...

A Precious Lure, an Iron Trap

Inside the watchtower, the Gibbet King has built a huge bonfire in the middle of the chamber at one of the topmost floors; he has also reopened the furnaces of the fortress, and he is melting the gold of the Master of Esgaroth. The firelight and smoke has been pouring out of the eight windows of Zirakinbar for days now, to be carried by the winds towards the Withered Heath. It didn't take long for Raenar to catch the scent of molten gold, and he soon started to swiftly travel south...

With the Cold-drake unable to resist the scent of gold, the Gibbet King has started to tap into the baleful power of the Chain of Thangorodrim to enslave the monster to his will: by the time Raenar arrives at Zirakinbar, he will be fully under the spell of the Chain, ready to be attached to it and enslaved to the Gibbet King's will.

A Dangerous Conversation

If the company has figured out the plot of the Gibbet King, they might want to face Raenar, to warn him of the plans of the spirit. Hopefully, he won't like the prospect of slavery and will either return to his frozen lair, or even resolve to help the company to destroy the Gibbet King as a punishment for his attempted treachery. But it takes a lot of courage to face a living Dragon, and the companions will understandably be very uncertain about the prospect!

- It's possible to have an audience with a dragon: after all, the famous Bilbo Baggins had a nice conversation with Smaug – at least before the dragon tried to burn him! Naturally, the success of the task will depend on how the conversation is led, and who will be doing the talking: good sense should suggest they avoid sending forward a Dwarf or an Elf spokesman!

A Date with Death

To approach Raenar, the companions must head down the northward slopes of the mountains towards the Withered Heath. The Great Worm advances swiftly, and they see the dust cloud he raises in his march getting bigger and bigger, until they meet while still upon the foothills of the Grey Mountains. The Cold-drake's arrival is heralded by an almost overpowering stench. Raenar is a terrifying sight, a vast silver-grey serpent, wingless, with a huge head set upon a thick neck. He advances walking on four short and robust legs, sometimes slithering on his slime-covered belly. From his beak-like muzzle and powerful, saw-toothed jaw emerge wisps of venomous cold vapours. Even reduced in size by centuries of slumber, Raenar is one of the greatest calamities that might befall the North, should his wrath be unleashed upon it.

If the companions do not hide from the Cold-drake, Raenar sees them from afar, and slows his advance, curious to discover what this is about. If they hide, he stops when close, and hails them: his keen sense of smell has revealed their presence from miles away...

Motivation

Raenar values little apart from murder, gold and precious stones, but he feels that something is not right, and he wants to discover what it is.

Expectations

+2: Flattery will get you eaten last.
+2: That flattery is especially obsequious. Keep talking.
+1: Riddles amuse me.
+1: Is that a smell I do not know? (if there is a Hobbit or something equally strange to Raenar in the party)
+1: Forewarned is forearmed (if they tell him of the Chain)
-1: Thieves are tricksters. (If he suspects the company are trying to stall or fool him)
-2: Do not doubt my will! (Raenar is irritated if anyone claims he's under the influence of the Chain already)
-4: I! AM! RAENAR! (if anyone implies that he is anything less than the mightiest dragon in this age of the world)

Introduction

Raenar is as vulnerable to flattery as any of his kin. Moreover, his latest deeds and his sleep have made him eager for a good duel of wits - the Dwarves he attacked before he retreated north weren't usually keen on making conversation! If the company chooses a Dwarf or an

---

Playing Raenar

Dragons are among the most powerful creatures to walk upon Middle-earth. This notion once made you impetuous and proud, even by the standards of dragons. But the axe of Dáin I and the rune-scored sword of his son Frór have taught you that you are not invincible. Moreover, during your rest in the frozen north you have seen the fall of Smaug in your dragon-dreams. You are not sure it really happened, but to exercise some caution in the presence of keen weapons will do no harm, especially until you'll be properly fed and grown to full size once again - and when that day comes, the Scourge of the North will be back!

Finally, there is something you secretly hold precious above all else, even your life, and that is freedom. In distant ages you were born in thralldom, and long suffered the whip of your Master. That will never happen again, no matter the cost...

Elf as their spokesman, Raenar will try to kill the chosen representative right away, then resume the conversation where it was interrupted. This introduction requires a DC **20 Intelligence (Traditions)** check. Dragons view everyone other than Elves and Dwarves as Askance at best.

For his part, Raenar humbly presents himself as the greatest of all Cold-drakes, the Dragon-king, the plunderer of a hundred Dwarf-halls, the slayer of Kings, the Great Worm of the Frozen Waste, the Scourge of the North, and so on.

Interaction

The companions now face the difficult prospect of convincing a dragon not to kill them, and possibly to help them. Luckily for them, Raenar has only awoken recently and feels weak, and he has also known too many dragons who died because they underestimated the strength of armed and armoured warriors...

Each of the following entries could raise the modifier for the Final Audience Check or lower it. As the Loremaster, it is up to you to judge if the heroes have answered the dragon politely enough but not angered him with any unfortunate truths.

There are a number of clues that the companions can pick up to pursue their cause.

Spellbound

Heroes who have learned the Gibbet King's plans might realise that the dragon is being dragged forward against his will. Raenar does not realize it though, so the companions need to convince him that he is being summoned by sorcery.

Former Slave

Raenar wears an iron-banded collar around his powerful neck. Was he a slave before? The companions could fire up his anger against the treasonous spirit who is trying to put shackles on him again.

Smaug is Dead

The company can tell Raenar that Smaug has been killed. They do not need to roll to convince Raenar this time - inside himself he knows it's true. What the companions have to decide is to what end they want to use the information.

Do they want to daunt Raenar, telling him that in Dale now sits a Dragonslayer? Or do they want to flatter him, telling that now he is the Chiefest and Greatest of Calamities?

Conclusions

Make a Final Audience Check and compare the results to the entries below:

Failure: The dragon decides that the company are plotting against him. He might attack them, or decide that they're just trying to trick him into leaving the treasure of the watchtower for them to take. Furious, he rushes past them – unless the characters hurry, Raenar will get to the tower before they do, and they will have only moments to stop him from falling under the spell of the Gibbet King.

0-1: The great Cold-drake has been convinced that something is suspicious about this treasure he smells in the air, but he can't be bothered with helping the company - he doesn't feel confident enough, and turns his tail and heads north, saying that one day he will return. The company has to deal with the Gibbet King on their own.

2-4: Raenar hears what the companions say, but he cannot believe someone will be able to subjugate him. He commands the companions to return to the watchtower, promising that he will take the Orcs and the spirit by surprise. He secretly intends to kill everyone once there, including the heroes, but he will fall under the Gibbet King's spell if the companions do not prevent it (see The Chain of Thangorodrim, at page 95).

5+: The Cold-drake sees the wisdom in the words of the companions. He accepts this strange alliance, but with his conditions: the companions will return to the watchtower alone, and he will come later to take the spirit by surprise. Once there, he will attack the spirit who intends to enslave him before it can work its sorcery upon him, and take the tower as his new lair and the treasure of the Master of Esgaroth as his hoard.

Raenar the great Cold-drake

Raenar is a monster bred in another age of the world. Once grown back to full stature, there will be no match for his strength in the North, now that Smaug is dead.

Raenar
Huge dragon (Venerable Cold-drake)

STR	DEX	CON	INT	WIS	CHA
24 (+7)	18 (+4)	20 (+5)	14 (+2)	13 (+1)	18 (+4)

Armour Class 21 (natural armour)
Hit Points 241 (21d12+105)
Speed 30 ft

Saving Throws Con +10, Int +7, Wis +6
Skills History +7, Intimidation +9, Perception +6
Senses darkvision 60 ft, passive Perception 16
Languages Westron, Black Speech, Sindarin
Challenge 14 (11,500 XP)

Legendary. Raenar may take two legendary actions each turn. Each legendary action allows him to attack with his Bite, Rend or Tail-Lash attacks.
Resistance. (1/day) If the dragon fails a saving throw, it can choose to succeed instead.
Horrible Strength. If Raenar makes a successful melee attack, he may use his bonus action to cause 7 additional damage of the same type.
Weak Spot. If Raenar uses a special ability that uses an action (Mesmerise, Multiattack, Poison Blast), any heroes that are within reach may use their reaction to make a single melee attack. For this attack only, Raenar is considered vulnerable to piercing, slashing and bludgeoning damage.

Actions

Multiattack. Raenar makes two attacks biting once and then either rending or using his tail attack.
Bite. *Melee Weapon Attack:* +12 to hit, reach 5 ft, one target. *Hit:* 20 (3d8+7) piercing damage.
Rend. *Melee Weapon Attack:* +12 to hit, reach 5 ft, one target. *Hit:* 17 (3d6+7) slashing damage.
Tail-Lash. *Melee Weapon Attack:* +12 to hit, reach 10 ft, one target. *Hit:* 14 (3d4+7) bludgeoning damage and the target is knocked Prone.
Mesmerise. Raenar may use his action and target one creature, who must make a **DC 18 Wisdom** saving throw. On a failed save, the target becomes Charmed until Raenar leaves the area or attacks the Charmed creature.
Poison Blast (Recharge 5-6). As an action, Raenar exhales poisonous bile in a 40 ft cone. Each creature in that area must make a **DC 18 Dexterity** saving throw, taking 30 (4d4+20) poison damage and becoming Poisoned for 2d4 rounds on a failed saving throw. A successful saving throw reduces the damage by half, and the target is Poisoned for only 1d4 rounds.

Reaction

Draconic Resistance (Recharge 6). Dragons are notoriously tough and free-willed. Raenar may activate this ability as a reaction to failing a saving throw. He automatically succeeds at the saving throw instead.

- Part Six - The Watchtower

The watchtower is divided into four levels, carved into the living rock of Zirakinbar. When the company arrives, the Gibbet King is on the third level, bent on using the Chain of Thangorodrim to enslave the dragon. His servants are mostly on the second level, ready to attack anyone who dares disturb their master.

- If the company head straight to the main door, then they walk into a fight (see *The Battle of the Great Hall* below). A better alternative is to enter the fortress by stealth, either by the hidden side door or by climbing up the side of the mountain.

Climbing the Mountain

Climbing the sides of Zirakinbar requires a **Strength (Athletics)** check. They can either make two tests at **DC 10** if they take their time, or one test at **DC 15** if they climb in haste.

Exploring the Watchtower

If the companions enter the watchtower stealthily they can explore it. Moving silently inside the fortress requires **Dexterity (Stealth)** checks, with the DC set by the area, see the entries overleaf.

The Watchtower

1. The Road (DC 10): This road zig-zags up the mountain to the main gate. Parts of the road are badly damaged, but the mountain keep itself is untouched.

2. Main Gate (DC 10): Two great doors of stone stand proud, engraved with runes of defiance and watchfulness. The doors swing open when touched if they are unlocked, but could not be pushed open by a dragon if locked. The doors are unlocked, and one is ajar.

3. Secret Entrance (DC 10): This is a side portal, disguised using dwarven artistry so it looks just like a rock face. The outline of the door can only be seen in a mirror or some other reflection. To open the door, a Dwarf must knock three times with a hammer or axe-head. The secret entrance opens into a narrow tunnel that leads to the cellars.

4. Guardrooms (DC 15): Orcs lurk in these rooms. Each guardroom contains from 1d6+1 Orc Soldiers. If the company's presence is known, then the Orcs are alert and patrolling nearby rooms, or getting ready to attack. If the company have managed to approach the watchtower without being spotted, however, then the Orcs are mostly lazing around, sleeping or grumbling about being dragged here to the end of the world by 'Bloodybones'.

5. Great Hall (DC 20): This hall was made using cunning stonework. The ceiling arches so high up that the roof is lost in shadow. Hidden vents in the floor and

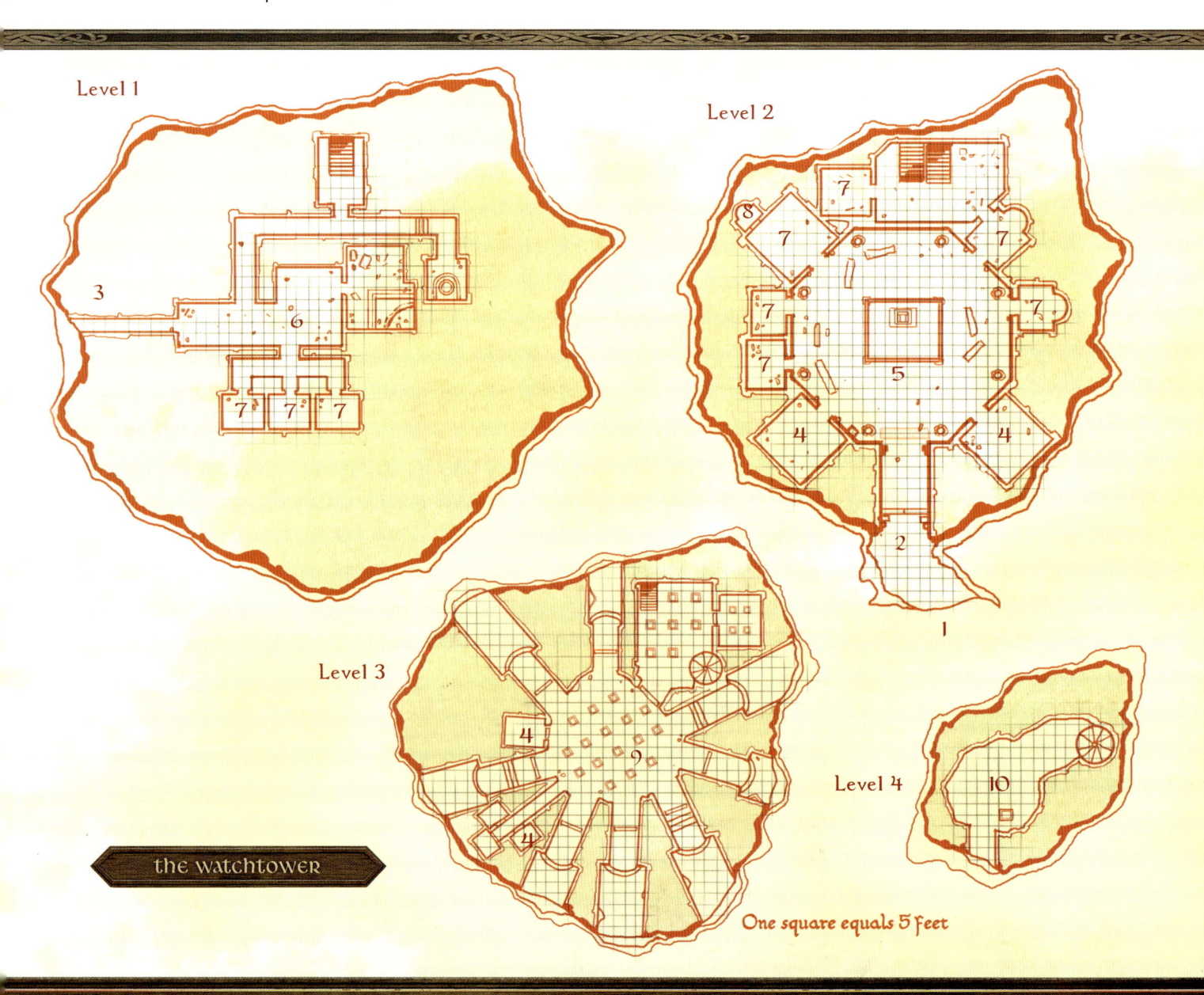

Level 1

Level 2

Level 3

Level 4

the watchtower

One square equals 5 feet

walls connect to furnaces in the cellars, so that the hall was once warm and welcoming even when the blizzards howled on the mountain outside. Most of the furnaces are dark and dead now, and the hall is icy cold. There is a massive central platform where the Dwarves met in council, a stone throne upon it. Around the edge of the hall are benches, nooks for study and craft, and a kitchen.

Directly over the entrance is a huge block of stone suspended by chains. The Dwarves put this in place to block the entrance should the main gates ever be breached. A huge wheel next to the entrance corridor controls the raising and lowering of the block. If the wheel is allowed to spin freely, the block falls and crushes anyone or anything beneath it. The company can use this trap in their fight if they spot it, or learned of its existence by consulting the dwarven records.

The Gibbet King ordered his defenders to make their stand here. A huge Troll lurks in the shadows. There are Goblin Archers crawling in the darkness overhead. Meanwhile, the Orcs in the two adjoining guardrooms are ready to rush out and join the fray once battle begins. See *The Battle of the Great Hall*.

6. Cellars (DC 15): The old cellars are lightless and abandoned. Most of these rooms were old store-rooms; others were furnaces used to heat the halls above. Two of these have been opened and are being used to melt the gold of the Master of Esgaroth. Two trusted servants of the Gibbet King have been set to the task: a Messenger of Lugbúrz and a lowly Snaga Tracker.

7. Empty Chambers (DC 10): These rooms were once inhabited by Dwarves, but no longer. Most are entirely empty; others contain the shattered remains of furniture and other debris. They have long since been picked bare of any treasure or useful items.

8. Secret Vault (DC 10): The entrance to this vault is cleverly concealed. A trap door opening onto steps leading downward can be found with a **DC 20 Intelligence (Investigation)** check, unless the searcher is a Dwarf or the heroes know about the vault, in which case it is **DC 10**.

- The vault contains the part of the treasure of the Master of Esgaroth that is not being burned in the furnaces: gemstones, necklaces, carved idols, worth hundreds of gold pieces all told. Getting this hoard across the wastes and back to Erebor may prove tricky.

9. Chamber of Winds (DC 25): This chamber is the heart of the watchtower. Eight portals look out on the mountains from this vantage point. From here, a watcher can look north into the Withered Heath. Looking south, the observer can see the sunlight gleaming off the snowy peak of the Lonely Mountain on the horizon. East and west, the mountain chain stretches off into the distance. There is a door halfway along each tunnel, so the eyes of the watchtower can be closed in a particular direction to shelter observers from the wind. The Dwarves wrought these doors and tunnels in such a way that they can be left partially open. When the wind blows in the right way, and the correct combination of doors are open or half-open, then the whole chamber resonates with the howling of the wind, becoming a mighty musical instrument. The peak of Zirakinbar *sings*.

10. Raven's Perch (DC 10): The raven's perch is a small room at the very top of the watchtower. Once, a colony of ravens of the mountain lived here, and carried messages between the outpost and Erebor. They are gone now. There is a trapdoor in the floor of the perch that looks down on the Chamber of Winds below.

> ### The Howl of the Mountain
>
> The Chamber of Winds holds a deadly secret — the Dwarves calculated long ago that the right combination of winds could cause the whole watchtower to resonate, creating a thunderous dirge so loud that it would crush the skull of anyone in the chamber. Left for long enough, it could even cause the very walls to crack and break. Creating the Howl of the Mountain requires the wind to blow from the North, and for the companions to close all the doors except the south, north and north-east doors. If this is done, then the Howl begins to build. It takes six rounds of combat for the noise to reach a dangerous intensity. After this, anyone in the Chamber of Winds takes 2d8 thunder damage each round. Any character who suffers more than 20 points of damage in this fashion is permanently deafened.

The Battle of the Great Hall

If the company dare defy the defences of the enemy, they will find that their forces in this chamber are considerable. The main danger is the Cave-Troll lurking on the far side of the room, but there are also Goblin Archers hiding in the ceiling — twice as many as the number of heroes.

Entering the Hall

When the company enter the hall, spotting the Cave-Troll requires a passive Perception score of 14 or higher. Otherwise, the company only realise they are not alone when the Troll attacks.

The Battle Begins

The troll begins the fight by leaping onto the middle platform, grabbing the throne, and throwing it at the company. This is an improvised attack: +5 to hit, range 20 ft, two adjacent targets. *Hit:* 13 (2d10+2) bludgeoning damage. At the same time, the Goblins on the ceiling start loosing arrows at the company, while the Orcs in the side rooms (area 4) will join the battle next round. The Orcs try to surround the company, blocking their retreat down the tunnel to the main doors.

Escape but No Retreat

While the company cannot flee out the main gate if the tunnel is blocked by Orcs (or by the stone block), there are other ways out of the chamber. A character could flee up or down the stairs, or jump into one of the heating vents and tumble down to the old furnace in the cellars below.

Dropping the Stone Block

To use the stone block trap, the company must:

- **Know about the trap:** If the company read the dwarven records at Erebor, they may know about this trap. Otherwise, any character looking around the hall will notice the block of stone hanging from the ceiling, and the control wheel can easily be found by a character who goes looking for it.

- **Move their enemies under the block:** This can be done by shoving or grappling their foes, or by clever footwork.

- **Drop the block:** A successful **DC 15 Strength (Athletics)** check unlocks the wheel. Alternatively, a character can cut the chain with a weapon attack and spending Inspiration.

- **Get out of the way:** Any companions under the block must make **DC 14 Dexterity** saving throws to dodge out of the way. Anyone under the block is crushed to death when it falls.

Entering the Chamber of Winds

The first thing the companions see if they enter the Chamber of Winds is the blazing bonfire. Next to the bonfire, in a cage, stands another mummified corpse like the ones they saw at Dwimmerhorn and at the Crossings of Celduin – another mouthpiece for the Gibbet King.

The Gibbet King is accompanied by five Black Uruks of Mordor, his bodyguards of choice; two of them carry the heavy weight of the Chain of Thangorodrim, and cannot join the fray.

The Last Debate

Once the company enter the Chamber of Winds and the spirit detects them, he mocks them and bids them to lay down their weapons.

"This is the hour of my triumph. In ages past, the Dragons were weapons of terror, wrought by the Lord of Middle-earth to enslave all the Mortal races. Now, this weapon will once again be in the right hands. No sword nor shield can withstand the fury of the Great Worm! Lay down your weapons and I shall grant you a quick death. Refuse, and your souls will be my playthings until the ending of the world!"

Assuming the company do not surrender, then battle is joined. The Gibbet King orders the Black Uruks to engage the company. The two Uruks holding the chain wait in reserve, and only join the fight if the company are clearly winning the battle.

Battling the Orcs

The Orcs try to drive the companions away from the Gibbet King, ideally by forcing them down one of the side tunnels towards another window.

Sorcery

The Gibbet King does not attack physically, but every round he targets a companion, either with *Dreadful Spells* or *Visions of Torment*, to open them to the attack of his Black Uruk bodyguards. He uses his paralysing spell on the most dangerous companions. He can only cast spells before the Dragon arrives – if Raenar is present, the Gibbet King must bend his will towards controlling the drake, and cannot continue to weave his sorcery against the company.

Reinforcements

More Orcs may arrive from the lower levels of the watchtower during the fight, especially if the company avoided the battle in the great hall below.

The Chain of Thangorodrim

If the company didn't warn Raenar of the plans of the Gibbet King, the Dragon arrives on Zirakinbar not expecting a trap. If this happens, the spirit successfully bewilders the Great Worm long enough for the remaining Uruks to carry the Chain forward and place it around Raenar's neck. To keep the Dragon quiescent, the Gibbet King must turn all his power towards the dragon, and thus cannot target the companions.

- The company must stop the Orcs from placing the chain on the Dragon. If they fail to do so, then the Gibbet King gains complete control over Raenar. The Gibbet King's first command is to order the Cold-drake to destroy the companions. With no way to stop the Gibbet King or to defeat the dragon, the company are likely doomed.

If the company slay the Orcs, then they have a chance to defeat the Gibbet King once and for all before more Orcs arrive from the lower halls.

Raenar

When he arrives, the Dragon creeps upon the mountain outpost. The company catch a whiff of his foul stench carried by the wind. Suddenly, they hear a roar that is louder than thunder, louder than an earthquake. Raenar climbs the north face and scrabbles at the windows, his claws ripping chunks of stone asunder as a man might tear paper. What the Cold-drake will try to do depends on whether the company encountered him or not.

The Power of a Dragon

The spirit that animates Raenar can be considered to be at least as powerful as the Gibbet King. If the Great Worm were to breathe his poison upon the Gibbet King, it would not only dissolve the bones and melt the cage bars, but it could also send the spirit into oblivion, consuming away so much of the King's spiritual essence as to reduce it to a bodiless, wordless spirit of hate. The dragon attempts to annihilate the Gibbet King only if the companions were able to inflame the Dragon's fear of being enslaved once again.

Defeating the Gibbet King

As the Gibbet King is an incorporeal spirit, the company cannot attack him directly. Barring the unexpected help of Raenar (see the *The Power of a Dragon* sidebar on the previous page), there are two main ways that the company can defeat him.

Ruining His Plans

Stopping the Gibbet King from enslaving the great Cold-drake is enough to temporarily defeat the spirit. The Dwimmerhorn is empty, his Orc-host was destroyed by the army of Dale, and now the Chain of Thangorodrim has proven useless.

The Gibbet King may still be abroad in the world, but his power base is depleted. The spirit may return to trouble the Free Peoples once again in the future, but the company have ruined his plans, and it will take him many years to rebuild.

Using the Chain of Thangorodrim

The Chain of Thangorodrim enslaves the will of whoever wears it, making them subservient to the Gibbet King. If the companions place the chain upon the Gibbet King, they create an endless loop. The spirit will be trapped within the confines of the chain, beyond all darkness, unable to give itself commands, endlessly waiting for orders from its own dead lips.

– Epilogue –
A Renewed Spring of Joy

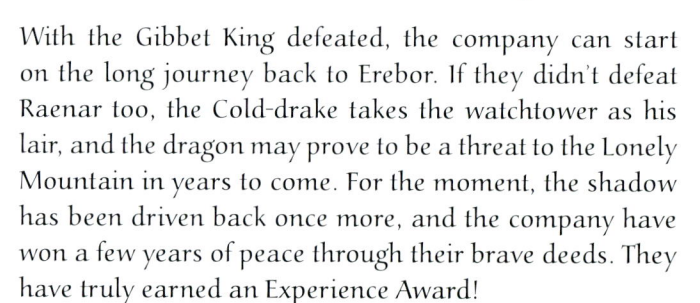

With the Gibbet King defeated, the company can start on the long journey back to Erebor. If they didn't defeat Raenar too, the Cold-drake takes the watchtower as his lair, and the dragon may prove to be a threat to the Lonely Mountain in years to come. For the moment, the shadow has been driven back once more, and the company have won a few years of peace through their brave deeds. They have truly earned an Experience Award!

- King Dáin is generous once he hears of the company's deeds, and rewards them each with one Dwarven-crafted Legendary item each (each item has a single Enchanted Quality). He also gives them a cask of silver and gold – enough coin to last several years, unless the companions squander it. A feast is held in the company's honour in Dale, and their names are spoken of with respect throughout Wilderland.

Fellowship Phase

The year after the defeat of the Gibbet King is a prosperous one. The company may open Dale or Erebor as a sanctuary, and can easily win the patronage of Dáin or Bard should they wish. Any companions who wish to settle in Dale will be given land by King Bard, who knows the value of having trusty allies nearby.

- Appendix -

Introduction to the Journey Rules

The Journey rules in *Adventures in Middle-earth* are designed to offer a varied selection of possible encounters in the Wild, called Journey Events. These Events are intended to be both well-suited to Middle-earth, and to reduce the burden of work on the Loremaster. Each offers a set of suggestions on what the company may have encountered, along with the rules to resolve the Event.

In this appendix you will find a section for each of the 12 possible outcomes on the Journey Events table. The basic event description appears first in each numbered section for reference.

Below that standard Event description each adventure has some customised Events specific to the locale and events that are occurring at that point in the campaign.

Loremasters should feel free to use these suggested encounters or to work with the basic Event description to create Events best suited to their group of Player-heroes.

You have the most direct knowledge of your players and what they enjoy, or what would make an entertaining, engaging and challenging event at any given moment.

Should any Journey Event come up more than once or twice, the Loremaster should feel free to select another event. If there is an event on one of the tables you feel your players will especially enjoy, then you should also feel able to run it, regardless of the dice rolls. The Journey Rules are there to help you make a great adventure, but you need not feel bound by them.

Note that *"A Darkness in the Marshes"* has two journeys. Two different options are provided where necessary for that adventure, to reflect both river-based and mountainous terrain.

Adventure	Events DC
Don't Leave the Path	15
Of Leaves and Stewed Hobbit	13
Kinstrife and Dark Tidings	varies
Those Who Tarry No Longer	13
A Darkness in the Marshes	14
The Crossings of Celduin	14
The Watch on the Heath	15

Journey Event Table Entry 1

Standard Journey Event Table Entry

1. (or less) A Chance Encounter
The company meet a fellow traveller or a group of travellers. The Scout may either make a **Dexterity (Stealth)** ability check to lead the company past the travellers undetected or any member of the company may attempt a **Charisma (Persuade)** ability test if they choose to interact with them.

If the Persuasion test is successful the company gains information concerning the path ahead of them; the first roll of their next travel event is made with Advantage.

If the Persuasion test is unsuccessful the company has made a poor impression on the travellers and the information they receive is inaccurate or misleading; the first roll of the next event is made with Disadvantage.

◆ Don't Leave the Path
The company hear enchanting singing coming from the forest at the edge of the path. A band of Wayward Elves are feasting in the woods, and the company can almost smell the delicious food on the breeze. The wise thing to do is to soldier on and not leave the path. Follow the standard Journey Table entry above to deal with the encounter.

◆ Of Leaves and Stewed Hobbit
When making camp for the night, the travellers are approached by a ragged figure, a battle-hardened old traveller with rotten teeth and a pock-marked face. Without so much as a by-your-leave, he sits down by the fire, pulls off his old boots and sticks his stinking, rotten feet out. If the companions question him, he introduces himself sullenly as 'Shanker'. If feeling inhospitable, the companions can convince him to leave by threatening him with weapons in hand, or with a successful **Charisma (Intimidation)** check.

If they allow Shanker to stay by the fire, though, he produces a clay pipe and a bag of excellent pipe-weed. Any Hobbit recognises it as Longbottom Leaf from the Shire. Shanker tells the characters that he bought it a few days ago from a caravan up in the mountains. The caravan was led by one of the 'little folk' who sold him the pipe-weed. Shanker then laughs cruelly – the fools did not know that the Goblins had come back to the High Pass. If that caravan makes it down the hills intact, it will be a miracle.

This tale brings the company both hope and fear – Dindy's caravan is only a day or two ahead at most, but there are indeed Goblins nearby.

◆ Kinstrife and Dark Tidings
The company come across the wreckage of a trader's caravan that was ambushed by bandits. Blood on the Road, trampled grass, torn sacks and broken crates – and the corpse of a man feathered with three arrows. Crows found the body before the adventurers did, and few clues remain. The event forewarns the presence of bandits in the wood, but could also mislead. Follow the standard Journey Table entry above to deal with the encounter, substituting **Intelligence (Investigation)** for the **Charisma** check.

◆ Those Who Tarry No Longer
An Elven messenger, Miriel, approaches the company with great haste, hoping to catch Irimë before she travels intro the West. Irimë and the envoy will speak in quiet tones on a secret matter that will not be shared with the company. There is no chance to avoid this meeting, but otherwise follow the standard Journey Table entry above to deal with the event. If the company impress the envoy she will impart information on shortcuts for the road ahead. If they do not impress the envoy, then she speaks only in incomprehensible riddles before departing.

◆ A Darkness in the Marshes
On the way to the Marshes, the company encounters Marcha, one of the fabled Wild Hobbits, the inhabitants of the Gladden Fields who are distant kin to the Shire-Hobbits. The young Hobbit hides from the travellers, vanishing as only Hobbits can into the rushes and undergrowth. Only characters with a passive Perception of 14 or more have a chance to spot her as she hides. If persuaded through kindness to talk, Marcha can give the characters directions to the Dwimmerhorn.

◆ The Crossings of Celduin
The company encounter a lone shepherdess who has cared for her sheep in these meagre pastures alone for many years. She may be glad of the meeting, or hostile towards the appearance of unexpected strangers. She grew up in Celduin, and can relate any of the information in the description in the section "The Town" on page 116. Follow the standard Journey Table entry above to deal with the encounter.

◆ The Watch on the Heath
Our heroes come across a wild eyed, disheveled old man who calls himself The Crowherd. He has lost his wits, and is barely surviving in The Waste. The Crowherd might give the company useful information on the whereabouts of their final destination. Or he may not. Follow the standard Journey Table entry above to deal with the event.

Journey Event Table Entry 2

Standard Journey Event Table Entry

2. Of Herbs and Stewed Rabbit

The company finds signs of easily foraged food or useful herbs at a fortuitous moment, perhaps as their own supplies are running low. The Hunter must make a **Wisdom (Survival)** check in an attempt to take advantage of this.

If successful, they may choose to either gather food (in which case they may prepare a meal which will restore 1 Exhaustion level or 1 Hit Die to each member of the company) or they may collect herbs (Selected by the LM). If they fail this roll, the Guide's Arrival roll will incur a -1 penalty.

The roll made during this task is subject to Disadvantage/Advantage if the Guide's Embarkation roll was either 6 (Meagre Supplies and Poor Meals) or 7 (Feasts Fit for the Kings of Ancient Times).

◆ Don't Leave the Path

The Hunter spots a flock of juicy fat black pheasants on a branch. Follow the standard Journey Table entry above to deal with the event, although there are no useful herbs to be gathered in Mirkwood.

◆ Of Leaves and Stewed Hobbit

In their search for food, the Hunter passes one of Beorn's flower-strewn meadows filled with honey-bees. They could try to acquire some of Beorn's honey; this requires a **Wisdom (Survival)** check, and if successful the company may remove one level of Exhaustion. If the Hunter fails, then the company must flee a swarm of angry bees, provoking a -1 to their Arrival Roll.

◆ Kinstrife and Dark Tidings

This area is rich in opportunities to catch fish, and the riverbanks are lined with fragrant green herbs. Follow the standard Journey Table entry above to deal with the event.

◆ Those Who Tarry No Longer

Irimë has a deep knowledge of all things that grow, and if persuaded can help the company's Hunter find nutritious fruits, vegetables and useful herbs to sustain them while on the road. Follow the standard Journey Table entry above to deal with the event, substituting a **Charisma (Persuasion)** check for the **Wisdom (Survival)** check.

◆ A Darkness in the Marshes

Follow the standard Journey Table entry above. The Vales of Anduin are full of rabbits, and verdant herbs. The Misty Mountains is home to various wiry goats that offer good eating if they can be caught.

◆ The Crossings of Celduin

Many fat rabbits graze the sweet herbs of the region without interference from men-folk. Follow the standard Journey Table entry above to deal with the event.

◆ The Watch on the Heath

Food is hard to come by in this place. But a sharp-eyed Hunter will spot the stringy goats that eke out a meagre living here, amid brackish pools in which grows a strain of Hagweed. Follow the standard Journey Table entry above to deal with the event.

Journey Event Table Entry 3

Standard Journey Event Table Entry

3. An Obstacle
Fallen trees, a fast flowing river, a rockslide, or a fallen bridge block the path ahead. The company must work together to clear their path. The Guide must make a **Wisdom (Survival)** ability check and each of the other company members must test against their choice of **Survival** or **Athletics**.

If the company has horses or pack ponies, one of the company must instead test against **Wisdom (Animal Handling)**.

All these tests are subject to Disadvantage/Advantage if the Guide's Embarkation roll was either 4 or 9. If all of the tests are successful, the company has worked well together, clearing the route and feeling a sense of satisfaction from their unity. As a result, the Guide's Arrival roll will benefit from a +1 modifier. If half or more of the tests are successful, the route is cleared with some difficulty and no bonus or penalty is incurred.

If less than half of the rolls are successful, but not all fail, the company has struggled to overcome the obstacle and each of them gains a level of Exhaustion.

If all the rolls fail, the company is forced to backtrack to bypass the obstacle. Each of them gains a level of Exhaustion and the Guide's Arrival roll is subject to a -1 penalty.

🔶 Don't Leave the Path
The company enter a region of the forest where thick spider-webs criss-cross the path. Follow the standard Journey Table entry above to deal with the event.

🟢 Of Leaves and Stewed Hobbit
Streams running down from the Misty Mountains have turned the road into a morass of mud. It might be faster - and cleaner - to go cross-country over a rocky hillock and find the road again a few miles easy. Follow the standard Journey Table entry above to deal with the encounter.

🟩 Kinstrife and Dark Tidings
Blood-sucking insects from the marshes descend on the company. These swarms are an obstacle to be overcome. Follow the standard Journey Table entry above to deal with the event.

🔷 Those Who Tarry No Longer
Heavy rain over the last few days has washed away an ancient bridge spanning a fast flowing river. Irimë sees this as an event of dark portent. Follow the standard Journey Table entry above to deal with the event.

🔶 A Darkness in the Marshes
Pea Soup! A thick fog descends, and the company risk separation. Follow the standard Journey Table entry above to deal with the event, with the company having to use their wilderness savvy or their athletic ability in order to stay together, or backtrack and find their lost companions.

🔷 The Crossings of Celduin
A heavy rain has fallen for an entire day, and the terrain ahead is now muddy and dangerous. Follow the standard Journey Table entry above to deal with the quagmire.

🔶 The Watch on the Heath
The company lose their way as the path peters out. The guide cannot find an easy way into the mountains, and the companions are forced to retrace their steps several times. They must exert themselves, using all their combined wits and sinews to get back on track. Follow the standard Journey Table entry above to deal with the event.

Journey Event Table Entry 4

Standard Journey Event Table Entry

4. In Need of Help

The company discover a band of travellers who have suffered some misfortune, or a small settlement beset by woes. The company may choose to help them, or not. If they choose not to, they must make a **Wisdom** saving throw to avoid gaining a point of Shadow. If, instead, they choose to help, the company must make three tests, chosen by the Loremaster, to reflect them aiding the innocent souls. Each test must be made by a different character (unless there are fewer than 3 Player-heroes in the company) and will typically be selected from: **Survival, Traditions, Insight. Persuade, Animal Handling, Medicine** or **Nature**.

It is possible that the same skill may be called upon more than once, in which case it must be attempted by two different Player-heroes.

If all of the tests are successful, each member of the company gains Inspiration. Additionally, the company will receive a +1 bonus to the Guide's roll upon arrival at their destination.

If half or more of the rolls are successful, the company may select one of its number to become Inspired and the company receives a +1 bonus to the Guide's Arrival roll.

If one of the rolls is successful, the company receives a +1 bonus to the Guide's Arrival roll.

If all the rolls fail, the company is slightly despondent and receives a -1 modifier to the Guide's Arrival roll.

Don't Leave the Path

Some movement in the woods at night startles the ponies, who are already nervous in the forest gloom. All characters make **DC 15 Wisdom (Animal Handling)** checks. (A kind Loremaster might allow players to use **Survival, Medicine** or **Nature** instead.

If everyone succeeds, the ponies are calmed, and the company get a +1 bonus to their Arrival roll. If half or more succeed, there's no further benefit or consequence. If less than half of the company succeed, then one of the ponies runs off into the woods and vanishes; recovering it means the company gains 1 level of Exhaustion. If everyone fails, then the pony is gone for good: everyone gains 1 level of Exhaustion and their eventual payment is reduced to 20 silver pennies each.

Of Leaves and Stewed Hobbit

The company encounter a family of settlers from the southland, who came north along the Anduin in search of hope, having heard tell that Wilderland was becoming peaceful and prosperous. Their wagon is stuck in the mud, and they cannot get it out - will the characters help them? Follow the standard Journey Table entry above to deal with the encounter.

Kinstrife and Dark Tidings

Late in the afternoon, the companions come across a band of three Beornings. One of their number, Angund, has been wounded by Goblin arrows while collecting firewood. He needs help or he will die. His friends are fiercely suspicious of these strangers in their land. Follow the standard Journey Table entry above to deal with the event.

Those Who Tarry No Longer

Irimë is afflicted by a deep sense of despair. Her mood is fey: she sees only the doom of the last of her people and thinks back on those who have fallen over the long Ages. She yearns for the sea and the uttermost West, yet finds no hope in this desire. The Player Heroes may choose to try to help her lift her dark mood, but in doing so, run the risk of being drawn into the melancholy that afflicts her. Follow the standard Journey Table entry above to deal with the event, encouraging the company to be creative in their choice of skill check in their attempt to raise Irimë's spirits.

A Darkness in the Marshes

The company encounter a band of Woodmen travellers, carrying stone or wooden carved goods for sale at the market in Woodman Town. They have been beset by a Swarm of Insects that sting and bite. Follow the standard Journey Table entry above to deal with the event.

The Crossings of Celduin

One of the company's horses throws a shoe, or becomes lame after a hard day's ride. Follow the standard Journey Table entry above to deal with the lame mount.

The Watch on the Heath

The company come across a juvenile Eagle flapping in the dust of the Waste. It has been wounded by a wickedly barbed Orc arrow. The noble creature is starved and giving up hope. Follow the standard Journey Table entry above to deal with the event.

Journey Event Table Entry 5

Standard Journey Event Table Entry

5. Agents of the Enemy
Hostile scouts or hunters cross the company's path, this may even be a sharp eyed Creban, gathering news for the Enemy.

The Look-out must make a **Wisdom (Perception)** check to spot the enemy before they become aware of the company.

If successful, the company has seized the initiative and may decide how to proceed. They may either sneak past the hostile force or ambush them, in which case their enemies are Surprised.

If the Look-out's Perception roll fails, the hostile scouts set an ambush and the heroes are Surprised.

If combat ensues, the Loremaster may resolve it as normal, setting out the combat abilities of the small enemy party to give a small to moderate challenge to the company.

All rolls made outside of combat during this task are subject to Disadvantage/Advantage if the Guide's Embarkation roll was either 3 or 10.

◆ Don't Leave the Path
A band of Attercops plots to snare the company with webs. The look-out may make a **DC 15 Wisdom (Perception)** check to spot the danger. If successful, the company avoid the spiders. Otherwise, they blunder into the webs, and must battle the spiders. See page 105 of the *Loremasters Guide* for details of the Attercops. There is one Attercop for every two heroes, rounding up if necessary.

◆ Of Leaves and Stewed Hobbit
Early during the journey, the companions misread the weather, and they are caught in a torrential summer downpour. If the company's Scouts cannot find shelter with a successful **Wisdom (Survival)** check, then the company suffers a -1 penalty to the final Arrival roll.

◆ Kinstrife and Dark Tidings
The company cross the hunting grounds of a band of outlaws. Follow the standard Journey Table entry above to deal with the event. There are as many Thugs as there are heroes and one Outlaw that is their nominal captain (see pgs 73-75 of the *Loremaster's Guide*).

◆ Those Who Tarry No Longer
The day has been especially long and hard, and every step walked can be felt as a deep weariness in the bones. Irimë on the other hand seems completely unaffected by any sign of fatigue. The Look-out must make a Charisma (Persuasion) check. If successful, Irimë will share with the Company a flask of Miruvor. This will remove 1d4 levels of Exhaustion and returns 1 Hit Die.

If the check fails, Irimë is struck only by the frailty of the Company and will not share the cordial with them. Each member of the Company gains a level of Exhaustion.

◆ A Darkness in the Marshes
Will the Look-out spot the scouting party of Snaga before they are ambushed? There are two Snagas for each member of the company. These Snaga Trackers are direct servants of the Gibbet King. Replace their Coward ability and replace it with Bloodthirsty.

◆ The Crossings of Celduin
A flock of suspiciously large black crows crosses the sky in the company's path. Follow the standard Journey Table entry above to deal with the encounter. If the Look-out is successful then the company may drive off the flock with 3 successful ranged attacks. If the Look-out fails their **Perception** check, the crows attack the company's mounts before flapping off, leaving the heroes to calm and tend their horses and with a -1 to their arrival roll.

◆ The Watch on the Heath
The huge piles of stone in the waste seem to move at night. The Look-out must make a **DC 15 Wisdom (Perception)** check to become aware of this.

If the test fails, the company suffers -1 to their Arrival roll as the Look-out uses one of the stone piles as a landmark, and ends up contributing to the Guide leading the company around in a circle. Worse, the company are now surrounded by these stone piles, which seem to be drawing closer every day. Another **DC 15 Wisdom (Perception)** check is required of the Look-out to thread a course between the piles.

If this second test is failed, then the company is forced to climb over one of the stone piles. The pile is made up of thousands of jagged rocks and pebbles, and soon everyone in the company has banged a shin or cut a foot on a piece of sharp rock, gaining a level of Exhaustion. Weirdly, there is no blood on any of the stones – it is as though the stones drank the blood that was spilled on them!

Journey Event Table Entry 6

Standard Journey Event Table Entry

6. The Wonders of Middle-earth

The company finds itself presented with a spectacular vista. A sunset, a forest glade, a mountain range. Each member of the company must make a **Wisdom** check or **Investigation (Intelligence)** check (their choice). If successful, they see the beauty of the scene and feel invigorated, recovering from a level of Exhaustion. If unsuccessful, they instead see brooding clouds, hard paths yet to be walked or steep and daunting hills to be climbed and suffer a level of Exhaustion. If all members of the company are successful, they receive a +1 bonus to the Guide's Arrival roll.

If all fail, the Guide's Arrival roll incurs a -1 penalty. Rolls made for this task are subject to Disadvantage/Advantage if the Guide's Embarkation roll was either 5 or 8.

◆ Don't Leave the Path

A flock of huge purple butterflies flutter down from the treetops and nest on the sleeping company. These butterflies are like a velvet shroud; a wonderful sight, but also potentially a claustrophobic and unsettling encounter. Follow the standard Journey Table entry above to deal with the event.

◆ Of Leaves and Stewed Hobbit

The setting sun casts a glow of honey gold across Beorn's lands. It is a beautiful and wild place, and the company have a great distance to travel, and an important mission to complete. Follow the standard Journey Table entry above to deal with the event.

◆ Kinstrife and Dark Tidings

The great Anduin River stretches before the company. Deep, wide and fast flowing, it is both an invigorating and daunting sight. Follow the standard Journey Table entry above to deal with the event.

◆ Those Who Tarry No Longer

Upon the road Irimë is most often quiet and reserved but this night, as the Company settle into their camp she seems content to engage in conversation. Any member of the Company may choose to sit and talk with her. Irimë will speak about the setting sun, of how, like her, it falls to the West. She will talk of the lives of the Elves in Middle-earth as long summer's days, now reaching their twilight hour. She will speak of the lives of Men and Dwarves as fleeting, the last flash of sunlight before it dips below the horizon. Follow the standard Journey Table entry above to deal with the event.

◆ A Darkness in the Marshes

Follow the standard Journey Table entry above. The rolling lands around the Great River, or the sheer rise of the Misty Mountains can both daunt and inspire the weary traveller. Follow the standard Journey Table entry above.

◆ The Crossings of Celduin

From the backs of their mounts, the company are struck by the early morning mist burning off across the ancient barrows and fallen stones that pepper the vales around the Running River. This may be an uplifting sight or an ill portent. Follow the standard Journey Table entry above to deal with this event.

◆ The Watch on the Heath

The company pass through an incredible valley of wind carved rocks, twisted into incredible shapes. Whether this is an inspiring and beautiful sight, or an unnerving experience is down to the dice. Follow the standard Journey Table entry above to deal with the event.

Journey Event Table Entry 7

Standard Journey Event Table Entry

7. A Hunt

The Hunter sees signs or tracks left by some game that would likely prove a far better meal than their travelling rations, perhaps at a point in the journey where the company's supplies are running low, or when their spirits seem to be flagging.

The Hunter must make a **Wisdom (Survival)** ability check to hunt down this game.

If the check is successfully made by 5 or more, the prey is brought down and a great feast is had, restoring 1 level of Exhaustion and giving a +1 bonus to the Guide's Arrival roll.

If the check is successful, the company enjoy a hearty meal and each may remove a level of Exhaustion.

If the check fails, the hunt was unsuccessful and the company spend a hungry night, resulting in each gaining a level of Exhaustion.

◆ Don't Leave the Path

The company finds a good place to camp and rest, but there's a complication - the huntsman finds a gigantic paw-print in the mud. It is definitely that of a wolf, but it is incredibly large and heavy – the beast must be at least the size of a bear! The prospect of encountering such a beast makes resting here less appealing.

The hunter must make a **DC 15 Wisdom (Survival)** or **Intelligence (Investigation)** check. If successful, the character correctly determines that the print is old, and that the wolf is no longer nearby. The company can rest in comfort, recovering a level of Exhaustion. If the character succeeds by 5 or more, the investigation also discovers a cache of supplies left by some previous traveller that was partially destroyed by the wolf. The remaining supplies, including a good bottle of wine, give a +1 bonus to the Arrival roll.

If unsuccessful, the hunter mistakenly determines that the print is fresh and that a gigantic wolf is lurking in the woods nearby. If the company continue on they fail to find a good camp site. If they choose to stay anyway, disturbing sounds during the night frighten Balder and Belgo, who repeatedly wake up the company with cries of "Wolf! Wolf!" Either way, the company gain 1 level of exhaustion. If the hunter fails by 5 or more, Baldor panics and urges the caravan to travel all night, giving a further -1 penalty to the Arrival roll.

◆ Of Leaves and Stewed Hobbit

The Hunter spots a wild sheep on a nearby hillside. It's completely out in the open, an easy shot that means a delicious mutton dinner - but then the shadow of an Eagle passes overhead. The Hunter isn't the only one hunting this prey! Does the character shoot or not?

If the character does nothing, then a huge Eagle swoops down, grabs the sheep, and flies off.

If the character shoots it requires a **DC 14 Wisdom (Survival)** check. Succeed, and the sheep is felled with one blow, and the characters have a +1 bonus on their Arrival roll. Fail, and the eagle gets the sheep. Fail by 5 or more, and the character nearly hits the Eagle - and Eagles, like elephants, never forget. If the unlucky hunter ever visits the fabled Eyrie of the Eagles, he or she is treated with Mistrust.

◆ Kinstrife and Dark Tidings

The hunter spots a huge silver salmon in either the great river or a tributary. Either the company will feast like kings, or someone is getting soaked to the bone. Follow the standard Journey Table entry above to deal with the event.

◆ Those Who Tarry No Longer

The Vales of Anduin are home to many tufted boar. Follow the standard Journey Table entry above to deal with the event.

◆ A Darkness in the Marshes

Follow the standard Journey Table entry above.

◆ The Crossings of Celduin

The Hunter spies a tasty lowland goat that is all alone. Follow the standard Journey Table entry above to deal with the hunt.

◆ The Watch on the Heath

The hunter comes across an unusual sight - a prodigiously meaty mountain sheep growing on the thin grass of the waste. How it grew to such a large size is a mystery. But it looks like mutton is back on the menu. Follow the standard Journey Table entry above to deal with the event.

Journey Event Table Entry 8

Standard Journey Event Table Entry

8. A Fine Spot for a Camp

The Scout has spotted a place to make camp. Perhaps it is a sheltered glade, or an existing campsite, used by travellers. It may even be an ancient building, allowing the company to rest a little easier on their journey. The Scout must make an **Investigation** check as the company draw close to the site.

If the check succeeds by 5 or more the camp site is all the company could have hoped for, and they may benefit from a long rest in addition to recovering a level of Exhaustion. As an added bonus, the Guide will receive a +1 modifier to their Arrival roll. If the check is simply successful, the company has an undisturbed night, and if needed each may recover a level of Exhaustion.

If the check fails, the company spend a restless night. They awake weary and dispirited and suffering from a level of exhaustion. If the check failed by 5 or more, the camp is already occupied by something hostile and dangerous; a Troll, sheltering from the sun, an Orcish war party, a band of Evil Men, intent on dark deeds, perhaps even a bear. Whatever the nature of the threat, the company have blundered into its midst and combat will surely ensue.

Regardless of the result of the combat, assuming the company survives, the night is a poor one at best and the only memories they carry with them of the camp are those of hard knocks and a final, unfulfilling rest. In addition to any damage sustained the Guide's Arrival roll is subject to a -1 modifier.

Don't Leave the Path

The company has need to make camp in a region where the trees are rotten and dead. Huge rotten branches hang low over the path, and could break at any time. Follow the standard Journey Table entry above to deal with the event: the easily harvested wood may provide shelter and warmth, or perhaps falls unexpectedly close to sleeping heroes. The dead wood might be home to a number of Attercops equal to that of company members. (See the *Loremaster's Guide* page 105 for Attercops). The battle may also make use of the Rotten Trees scenery feature (see page 93 of the *Loremaster's Guide*).

Of Leaves and Stewed Hobbit

The company chances upon the campsite of some of Beorn's followers. A successful **DC 12 Charisma (Persuasion)** check from the Guide lets the company stay the night in a hay-loft; failing to express common courtesy means the company finds no welcome and must sleep in the open. The companions sleep miserably and are not considered to rest properly for the rest of the journey, and so all suffer a level of Exhaustion.

Kinstrife and Dark Tidings

Long has this region been home to bandits. On finding a well-used campsite it is hard to tell if it is still dangerously occupied, or a highly convenient place in which to make a new camp. Follow the standard Journey Table entry above to deal with the event. There is a possibility that the Thugs will return to their camp. Use the statistics on page 73 of the *Loremaster's Guide* for the thugs.

Those Who Tarry No Longer

The company come across a regularly used hunting camp of the Woodmen, apparently sheltered by ancient trees, and thick banks of bracken. But it may prove less than it first appears, perhaps having been long abandoned as draughty and uncomfortable. The presence of Irimë means there is no chance of being attacked by enemies at this time. Otherwise follow the standard Journey Table entry above to deal with the event.

A Darkness in the Marshes

The company sets camp in a mouldering ruin, slowly sinking into the landscape. While it may prove the best campsite in the region, it could also be home to Wild Wolves (two per hero). Follow the standard Journey Table entry above. Use the statistics on page 111 of the *Loremaster's Guide* for the Wolves.

The Crossings of Celduin

A sheltered cave in a rocky outcrop looks like a perfect campsite. It may have a freshwater spring, or it may be home to a Cave or Hill-troll (See pages 107-108 of the *Loremaster's Guide*). Follow the standard Journey Table entry above to deal with this event.

The Watch on the Heath

The temperature drops, and all the company are tired and wet by the time darkness falls and they must make camp. Do they light a fire, or do they heed Witherfinger's warnings? If the company do not light a fire, then everyone must immediately make a **DC 15 Wisdom (Survival)** check or gain a level of Exhaustion. If they do light a fire, there is no need for a test, but something huge and reeking of death flies low over the campsite in the middle of the night. All characters must make a **DC 15 Wisdom** saving throw; if half or more of the company fail then they suffer -1 to their Arrival Roll.

Journey Event Table Entry 9

Standard Journey Event Table Entry

9. A Lingering Memory of Times Long Past
The company discovers a relic of past ages. A statue, a building, or the remains of an ancient settlement. It is even possible that they witness a travelling company of Elves, making their way towards the Grey Havens.

With good fortune and a light heart, the company will be uplifted by this sight, sensing something hopeful for the future in this glimpse into the past. With poor fortune, the company will be filled with a sense of doom, seeing the decay of lost glory and the end of hope.

Each member of the company should make a **Wisdom** check. If successful, they are filled with hope regarding their journey and their struggles against the Shadow and gain Inspiration. If they make the roll by 5 or more they are so positively affected by the sight that they may also remove a level of Exhaustion. Additionally, if at least half of the company is successful, a +1 modifier may be applied to the Guide's Arrival roll. With a failed roll, they see only the fleeting nature of life and the fall of all that is good, and must make a Corruption check (a **Wisdom** saving throw) to avoid gaining 2 points of Shadow.

If they fail the roll by 5 or more, they feel morose and wearied by the scene and suffer a level of Exhaustion in addition to the Shadow points. Additionally, if more than half of the company fail (since we're talking about individual rolls) their roll, a -1 modifier must be applied to the Guide's Arrival roll.

Don't Leave the Path
The oppressive darkness of the woods drains the company's spirits. In a drift of skeletal leaves they come across a web strewn skeleton, wearing a piece of beautifully wrought jewellery - surely the work of Elves, or the ancient men from across the sea. Follow the standard Journey Table entry above to deal with the event. If the company attempt to take the necklace it crumbles to powder, and they gain the ill effects of the event, however they rolled.

Of Leaves and Stewed Hobbit
In the distance the company see a procession of silver-clad Elves, heading West toward the Grey Havens and the sea. The Elves are too far away to reach, but brief snatches of their song are borne on the wind. Whether the song is uplifting or saddening is up to the dice. Follow the standard Journey Table entry above to deal with the event.

Kinstrife and Dark Tidings
The heroes find a ruin of elder days, featuring carvings of men-like figures battling monstrous foes, which could be orcs or trolls. Follow the standard Journey Table entry above to deal with the event.

Depending on the rolls, the company are either buoyed up by this ancient story of the battle against evil, or are daunted by the numberless perils ahead.

Those Who Tarry No Longer
Pausing for a rest by the side of the road, the company realise they have sat amidst not boulders, but huge fragments of an ancient statue, made long ago by Men. Follow the standard Journey Table entry above to deal with the event, with Irimë adding to the sense of wonder at what Mannish folk may achieve in their short span of years, or the despair of how quickly everything falls to ruin.

A Darkness in the Marshes
By the River: Elves in graceful, silver boats pass silently by. Depending on how the company roll, the elves are either deep in quite contemplation, or under a heavy pall of sadness.

Away from the River: The company stumble into the ruin of an ancient Dwarven waystation, the stone work is still sharp, but all woodwork is long gone and blue green lichen covers everything. Is this a reminder of enduring craftsmanship, or the slow decline of all things?

Follow the standard Journey Table entry above to deal with the event.

The Crossings of Celduin
The company realise they have made their camp in the midst of an ancient burial site. Follow the standard Journey Table entry above to deal with the event. If a creature is discovered, then use the *Night Wight* on page 27.

The Watch on the Heath
In the dust of the Waste the company discover an ancient artefact. It appears to be some kind of map from long ago, carved into a black stone with a hole for a cord, perhaps carved by a Dwarf. Is this a cause of inspiration, or a dismal reminder of times past? Follow the standard Journey Table entry above to deal with the event.

Journey Event Table Entry 10

Standard Journey Event Table Entry

10. A Place Touched by the Shadow

The essence of something dark and terrible lingers here. However even the darkest of Shadows may hide something bright and good.

The Scout must make an **Intelligence (Investigation)** check to become aware of the darkness surrounding this area before the company blunders too deeply into it.

If the roll is a success by 5 or more, the company witness some sign that reaffirms their hope in the struggle against the Enemy. Each member of the company may remove one point of Shadow and gains Inspiration. Additionally, the Guide will receive a +1 bonus to their Arrival roll. On a successful roll, they manage to avoid the pervasive sense of corruption that lingers here and may count themselves lucky. Accordingly, the Guide receives a +1 bonus to their Arrival roll.

If the Scout fails their roll, the company has wandered into the heart of the area and feels the dark nature of the place touch their hearts. Each hero must make a Corruption check to avoid gaining a point of Shadow. If the Scout's roll fails by 5 or more, some dark thing still lurks here, ancient and evil, and the company have disturbed its slumber...

◆ Don't Leave the Path

This area is filled with pits of brackish water covered with deep layers of ancient blackened leaves. Over thousands of years these pits have swallowed hundreds of unfortunate travellers. The air around them is thick with menace. Follow the standard Journey Table entry above to deal with the event. Spotting the pits before falling in is inspiring; coming close to falling in will remind the company of the dangers ahead; Failing the check by 5 or more means the company fall into the pits, and spend a miserable time dragging one another out, gaining a level of Exhaustion in the process.

◆ Of Leaves and Stewed Hobbit

The company stumble into a darkened dell, littered with what appear to be large wolf skulls. Follow the standard Journey Table entry above to deal with the event. If the Scout fails by 5 or more then an ancient Warg that has been gnawing on the old bones of its fellows is awoken from its slumber. (LMG, pg 111)

◆ Kinstrife and Dark Tidings

The company's route finds them crossing a boggy, backwater lake that is draining away to an evil-smelling marsh. With the disappearance of the water something foul is being revealed, and an evil atmosphere is gathering in this place. Follow the standard Journey Table entry above to deal with the event.

◆ Those Who Tarry No Longer

The Company passes through an area of ancient ruins, perhaps once inhabited by Elves in ages long past. Little tangible remains, save a single graceful archway and a low wall but, despite this, the beauty of the architecture is striking. Irimë will begin to speak of the greatest artisans of the Noldor and will speak of Celebrimbor and the wonders he wrought. Follow the standard Journey Table entry above to deal with the event, replacing **Intelligence (Investigation)** with **Charisma (Persuasion)** to bring out the best of this brush with the past in the company of such an awe-inspiring guide. In this instance there is no chance of disturbing an ancient evil.

◆ A Darkness in the Marshes

A nearby body of water, or the river itself, boils and froths with a foul grey foam. The companions struggle to overcome their fear and maintain control of their boats. A breed of grey skinned Marsh Hags (LMG, pg. 99), (one per hero) call these treacherous waters home and seek to drown any interlopers. Follow the standard Journey Table entry above to deal with the event.

◆ The Crossings of Celduin

The company's route takes them through a glade of sinister-looking trees that have unnerving, agonised faces in their gnarled boles. Follow the standard Journey Table entry above to deal with the encounter. Hiding under the skeletal leaves choking the glade are sleeping Hobgoblins, one per hero, (see page 98 of the *Lormaster's Guide*).

◆ The Watch on the Heath

The company's scout finds one of the old dwarf-roads that once crossed the Waste. This road does not head in the exact direction of the watchtower, but the characters could choose to take a longer but easier route by following the road for a while instead of going cross-country. The company must decide. If the company chose not to follow the road they feel suddenly uplifted as if they have escaped a threatening situation, and may remove a point of Shadow, or recover 1 Hit Die. If they choose to follow the road, the company proceed along the straight, flat road. However, when it comes time to leave it, something strange happens. They feel an unnatural compulsion to keep following the road. The company must make a **DC 15 Wisdom** saving throw to leave the road willingly. Those who fail are unable to step off the road, and must be dragged off by their companions. If everyone fails, the whole company can try again a day later, but must make a Corruption check (a **DC 12 Wisdom** saving throw) or gain a Shadow point.

(Whatever dark force reached out for the companions is not part of this scenario. Brave companions can return to the road after completing their current quest, to investigate the matter further.)

Journey Event Table Entry 11

Standard Journey Event Table Entry

11. The Enemy is Abroad

Evil Men, Orcs, Goblins or other servants of the Enemy are moving through the area. Avoiding them will be challenging.

If the Guide's result on the Embarkation roll was a 3, a confrontation is unavoidable. In spite of this, a successful **Wisdom (Perception)** ability check from the Look-out will allow the company time to prepare and will grant them a round of surprise in the combat.

A failed **Perception** roll in this instance will indicate that the company has little time to prepare and receives no such bonus. If the Guide received a 10 on the Embarkation roll, the Lookout may make a **Wisdom (Perception)** or **Dexterity (Stealth)** ability check (player's choice) to allow the company to find a path that will bypass the enemy force unnoticed.

◆ Don't Leave the Path

A host of Spiders gathers near the path. If the Embarkation roll was a 3, then the Attercops have been following the company since they left the Elf-King's halls, and there is no way to avoid the Spiders. If it was a 10, then the company can sneak past the Spiders with a **DC 15 Dexterity (Stealth)** or **Wisdom (Perception)** check from the Look-out.

If the Embarkation roll was neither a 3 nor a 10, then the company as a whole can try to sneak past the Spiders with a Dexterity (stealth) test. If anyone fails, the Spiders attack. See page 105 of the Loremasters Guide for details of the Attercops. There is one Attercop for every two heroes, rounding up if necessary.

◆ Of Leaves and Stewed Hobbit

The company passes a pair of Woodman trappers, who stop and ask if the companions have heard of a new Inn in these parts, said to be run by 'wise children'. A successful **DC 13 Wisdom (Insight)** check suggests that the trappers intend to rob the inn, and the companions can confirm this by sneaking after the trappers with a **DC 13 Dexterity (Stealth)** check and listening to their conversation at the campfire. Challenging the trappers dissuades them from their planned larceny, while killing them outright to prevent their crime without trying to discourage them is a despicable act and qualifies as a Misdeed worthy of at least 3 points of Shadow.

◆ Kinstrife and Dark Tidings

A pack of wolves has crossed the Gladden River and are now hunting in the vales. While they are unlikely to attack a band of armed adventurers, a lone Look-out might be easier prey, especially if he is a toothsome morsel like a Hobbit or a fat Dale-man. Follow the standard Journey Table entry above to deal with the event.

◆ Those Who Tarry No Longer

The Company has strayed into an area where a powerful servant of the Enemy dwells. Perhaps some great Troll, maybe an old and mighty Orc chieftain. Regardless of the nature of the threat, such is Irimë's power that she has caught the attention of this creature and it will attempt to seek her out, drawn to the brightness of her spirit. Follow the standard Journey Table entry above to deal with the event.

◆ A Darkness in the Marshes

A pack of wild wolves shadows the company (one Wild Wolf per hero with a Wolf Leader). For a while they stay out of bowshot, and can be heard howling at night. Eventually they attack. Follow the standard Journey Table entry above to deal with the event.

◆ The Crossings of Celduin

Shortly after the sun sets, a group of Goblins come grumbling and spitting across the company's path. There are two Misty Mountain Goblins for every member of the company. One has the Call for Aid special ability. See page 102 of the *Loremaster's Guide* for the Goblins statistics.

◆ The Watch on the Heath

There are steep shafts like dry wells scattered across the Waste, and an unwary companion might accidentally fall into one. There are loose stones and scree around the lip of each shaft, so putting a foot wrong may send the character tumbling down.

The Look-out and Guide must both make **DC 15 Wisdom (Perception)** checks to to avoid the shafts; if both tests are failed, then the company tumble and slide into a hidden pit. The company suffer a level of Exhaustion from the delay and effort of rescuing themselves.

If one test succeeds then some of the company fall in; everyone must make a either a **Dexterity (Acrobatics)** or **Strength (Athletics)** check. Those who fail fall in. After being forced to extricate their comrades from the pit, the company suffer a -1 to their Arrival Roll.

Journey Event Table Entry 12

Standard Journey Event Table Entry

12. (or more) Many Meetings? Fly you Fools!
The company has encountered a traveller upon the road, but all may not be as it at first appears.

If the Embarkation roll was a 1, the encounter will automatically be with a servant of the Enemy. Conversely, if it was a 12 the company has encountered one of the great powers for Good. The outcome of such a meeting however, will depend on how the company approaches matters.

If neither a 1 or a 12 was rolled on the Embarkation table, the Look-out must make a **Wisdom (Perception)** check.

If the roll succeeds by 5 or more, the company has encountered a person of great standing, and sees them for what they are.

Each member of the company may immediately remove one point of Shadow. They may also seek an Audience (see page 192 of the *Player's Guide*) with them and, if successful, they may gain great knowledge of their path ahead which will grant them advantage on the initial rolls on their next encounter, and will also bestow a +1 bonus to their Arrival roll. If the Audience goes particularly well, the Loremaster may decide that the company have gained a Patron.

If the Look-out's roll succeeds, they have spotted the traveller, but do not realise who they may truly be. The initial description of this encounter should then be played out as if it was a result of 1 on this table (A Chance Encounter).

Should the company choose to interact with the traveller, successful **Wisdom (Insight)** rolls or some demonstration that the company has true and good purpose should lead to the true identity of the person they have met. Should this happen, the encounter should then play out in much the same way as detailed above.

If the Look-out's roll fails, the company have encountered a dark and powerful foe way beyond any of them. For low-level companies this could be a superior force of Orcs, a pack of Wargs, or perhaps a particularly large and fierce Troll. At higher levels it could be something much darker and more powerful – a warband of Uruk-hai, or even a Nazgûl about his master's dark bidding.

Companies must immediately make a Corruption check to avoid gaining 2 points of Shadow and they must seek to avoid further confrontation by each making a **Dexterity (Stealth)** check (with a single additional **Animal Handling** check if the company has horses or pack ponies) to slip away unnoticed.

Should more than half fail, they will need to flee in haste for fear of their very lives. All gain an additional level of Exhaustion, additionally the arrival roll will be subject to a -1 modifier.

If the Look-out's roll fails by 5 or more they are automatically spotted, with no chance to sneak away. They must flee in haste for fear of their very lives. They automatically gain 2 points of Shadow, and an additional level of Exhaustion, additionally the arrival roll will be subject to a -1 modifier.

◆ Don't Leave the Path
If the company meet an ally here, they they encounter King Thranduil and his court, out hunting the fabled White Deer of Mirkwood. The stag has vanished, much to the king's consternation, but at least this gives the company a chance to pay their respects, and possibly make amends if their Audience with Lindar went awry.

If the company encounter a foe, then they meet Tauler the Hunter, one of the most dangerous of the fabled Great Spiders of Mirkwood. Big enough to suck an Oliphaunt dry, Tauler is a foe far beyond the company. All they can do is run or hide while he horrifically consumes one of their ponies.

⬢ Of Leaves and Stewed Hobbit
The company encounter an old man, with a long white beard, bent almost double as he walks along the Road. He leans on a gnarled staff of wood, and bright eyes glitter beneath his battered hat. His raiment is grey, but keen-eyed companions might spot the flash of white robes beneath his travel-soiled cloak. The old man's boots are caked with thick mud, as if he has been walking in the marshlands near the Great River. The old man does not stop as he walks south, but he makes a strange gesture of benediction with one hand as he passes the company. The blessing of Saruman the White is a potent one – each companion may reroll one skill check at any point in this adventure.

◆ Kinstrife and Dark Tidings
Beorn – in the form of a bear – walks near the company. They might glimpse the shadow of a tremendous bear watching over their camp at night, or find signs that some of the bandits pursuing them met with a gory end. Beorn's protection ensures that the company have a +1 bonus to their Arrival roll. However, the chieftain avoids directs contact with the player characters on the journey – he prefers solitude in his bear shape.

Those Who Tarry No Longer

Irimë is powerful and ancient beyond the reckoning of mortal Men. Her memories are long and deep and, though intangible, hold great power. As the Company take their rest, she begins to speak of one such memory, a momentous occurrence from an Age long since past. Companions have the choice to listen or to absent themselves from the ensuing event.

Such is the power and allure of Irimë that any Player-Hero listening will find themselves drawn into this tale, witnessing it as if they were actually there. To see such sights will be a huge challenge and may leave the witness feeling utterly drained. Conversely it has the potential to grant huge insight and wisdom.

Irimë remembers a conversation long ago with Lord Elrond in Rivendell, when it was but newly built. She recalls how amid the singing and feasting they engaged in a lively conversation about the fate of the world.

Companions should now make a **Charisma (Persuasion)** check at the DC of the journey to test their ability to hold their own in the conversation as Irimë relates these ancient events.

If the check is passed, they are filled with hope as Irimë remembers a younger, brighter time. This grants them Advantage on the initial rolls on their next encounter, and will also bestow a +1 bonus to their Arrival roll.

If the check is failed, then Irimë's memories are soured, and she recalls a bitter argument when Elrond expressed his darkest fears for the future.

If the check is failed by 5 or more, then Irimë's reminiscences have also lit a beacon for all servants of the Shadow, who begin to converge on the camp from miles around, the first large band of goblins arriving within moments. The company must immediately make a Corruption check to avoid gaining 2 points of Shadow, and they must seek to avoid further confrontation by each making a **DC 13 Dexterity (Stealth)** check (with a single additional **Animal Handling** check). if the company has horses or pack ponies) to slip away unnoticed by the converging orcs, trolls and worse creatures.

A Darkness in the Marshes

Suddenly, the company all feel terribly cold, as something icy claws at their bones. A shadow passes over them – the Gibbet King is on the wind, moving from one corpse to the next. In this spirit form, it is invisible and immaterial, existing only as a shade of horror. Still, the feeling of terror and oppressive evil is unmistakable. All characters must immediately make a **DC 14 Wisdom** saving throw to avoid gaining 2 points of Shadow.

The Crossings of Celduin

Gandalf the Grey left Dale before the company did. The Wizard is on his own errand – Radagast has warned him of the threat posed by the Gibbet King, and he intends to confront the spirit when the time is right. He urges the company to travel onto Celduin as swiftly as they can, and hold the Crossings for as long as they can. *"I will come as soon as I can,"* he promises, *"but all roads go awry this day."* The promise of a Wizard carries great weight – if all hope seems lost in the Battle of the Crossing, Gandalf might arrive in the nick of time to save the company.

The Watch on the Heath

Suddenly, the company are in the grip of biting cold, and the frozen wind seems to take on a dreadful voice, howling incomprehensible imprecations. A shadow passes over them – the Gibbet King is abroad, exerting his will across the Waste. In this spirit form, it is invisible and immaterial, existing only as a shade of horror. Still, the feeling of terror and oppressive evil is unmistakable. All characters must immediately make a **DC 15 Wisdom** saving throw to avoid gaining 1 point of Shadow.

- Index -

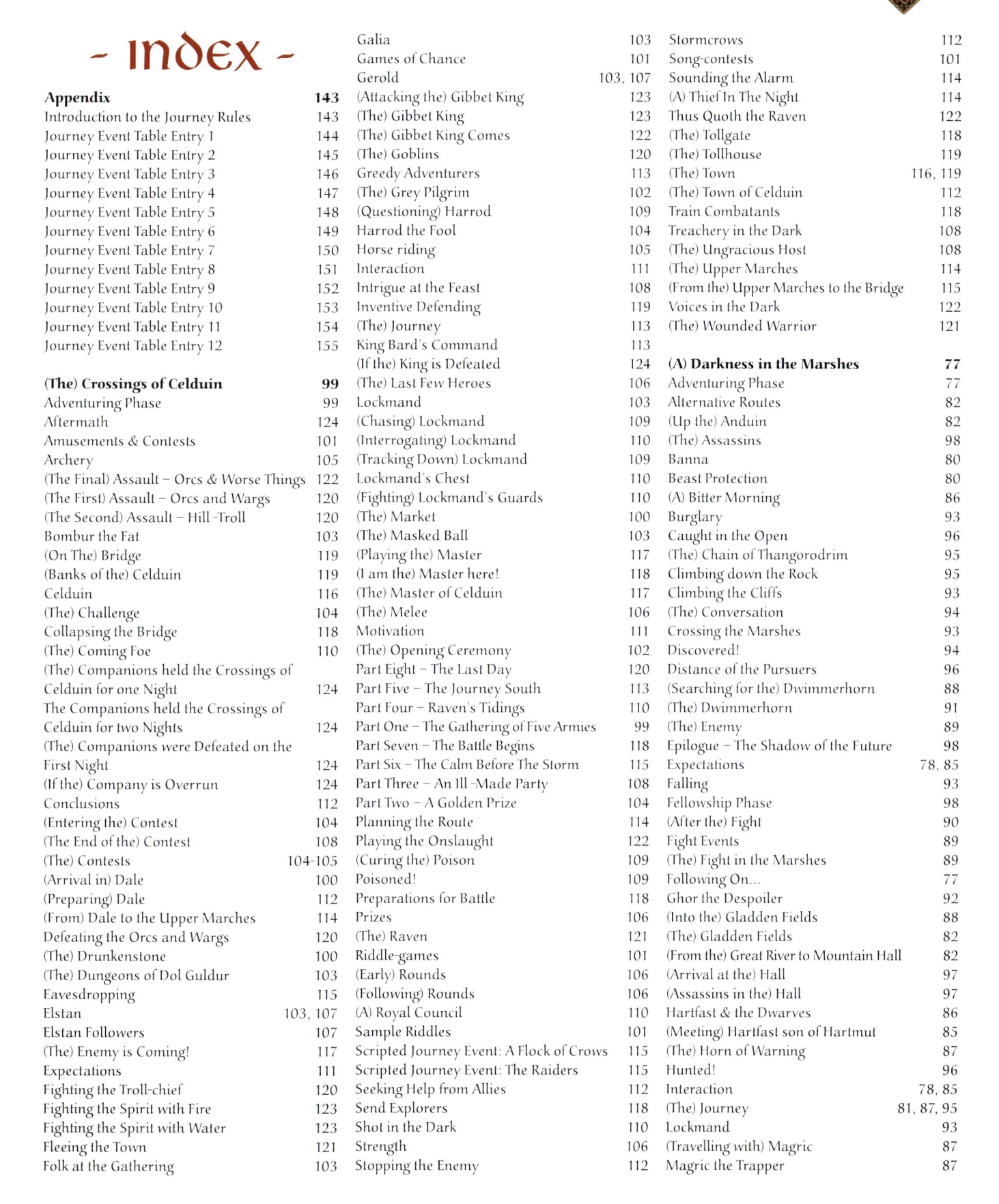

Appendix 143
Introduction to the Journey Rules 143
Journey Event Table Entry 1 144
Journey Event Table Entry 2 145
Journey Event Table Entry 3 146
Journey Event Table Entry 4 147
Journey Event Table Entry 5 148
Journey Event Table Entry 6 149
Journey Event Table Entry 7 150
Journey Event Table Entry 8 151
Journey Event Table Entry 9 152
Journey Event Table Entry 10 153
Journey Event Table Entry 11 154
Journey Event Table Entry 12 155

(The) Crossings of Celduin 99
Adventuring Phase 99
Aftermath 124
Amusements & Contests 101
Archery 105
(The Final) Assault – Orcs & Worse Things 122
(The First) Assault – Orcs and Wargs 120
(The Second) Assault – Hill-Troll 120
Bombur the Fat 103
(On The) Bridge 119
(Banks of the) Celduin 119
Celduin 116
(The) Challenge 104
Collapsing the Bridge 118
(The) Coming Foe 110
(The) Companions held the Crossings of Celduin for one Night 124
The Companions held the Crossings of Celduin for two Nights 124
(The) Companions were Defeated on the First Night 124
(If the) Company is Overrun 124
Conclusions 112
(Entering the) Contest 104
(The End of the) Contest 108
(The) Contests 104-105
(Arrival in) Dale 100
(Preparing) Dale 112
(From) Dale to the Upper Marches 114
Defeating the Orcs and Wargs 120
(The) Drunkenstone 100
(The) Dungeons of Dol Guldur 103
Eavesdropping 115
Elstan 103, 107
Elstan Followers 107
(The) Enemy is Coming! 117
Expectations 111
Fighting the Troll-chief 120
Fighting the Spirit with Fire 123
Fighting the Spirit with Water 123
Fleeing the Town 121
Folk at the Gathering 103
Galia 103
Games of Chance 101
Gerold 103, 107
(Attacking the) Gibbet King 123
(The) Gibbet King 123
(The) Gibbet King Comes 122
(The) Goblins 120
Greedy Adventurers 113
(The) Grey Pilgrim 102
(Questioning) Harrod 109
Harrod the Fool 104
Horse riding 105
Interaction 111
Intrigue at the Feast 108
Inventive Defending 119
(The) Journey 113
King Bard's Command 113
(If the) King is Defeated 124
(The) Last Few Heroes 106
Lockmand 103
(Chasing) Lockmand 109
(Interrogating) Lockmand 110
(Tracking Down) Lockmand 109
Lockmand's Chest 110
(Fighting) Lockmand's Guards 110
(The) Market 100
(The) Masked Ball 103
(Playing the) Master 117
(I am the) Master here! 118
(The) Master of Celduin 117
(The) Melee 106
Motivation 111
(The) Opening Ceremony 102
Part Eight – The Last Day 120
Part Five – The Journey South 113
Part Four – Raven's Tidings 110
Part One – The Gathering of Five Armies 99
Part Seven – The Battle Begins 118
Part Six – The Calm Before The Storm 115
Part Three – An Ill-Made Party 108
Part Two – A Golden Prize 104
Planning the Route 114
Playing the Onslaught 122
(Curing the) Poison 109
Poisoned! 109
Preparations for Battle 118
Prizes 106
(The) Raven 121
Riddle-games 101
(Early) Rounds 106
(Following) Rounds 106
(A) Royal Council 110
Sample Riddles 101
Scripted Journey Event: A Flock of Crows 115
Scripted Journey Event: The Raiders 115
Seeking Help from Allies 112
Send Explorers 118
Shot in the Dark 110
Strength 106
Stopping the Enemy 112
Stormcrows 112
Song-contests 101
Sounding the Alarm 114
(A) Thief In The Night 114
Thus Quoth the Raven 122
(The) Tollgate 118
(The) Tollhouse 119
(The) Town 116, 119
(The) Town of Celduin 112
Train Combatants 118
Treachery in the Dark 108
(The) Ungracious Host 108
(The) Upper Marches 114
(From the) Upper Marches to the Bridge 115
Voices in the Dark 122
(The) Wounded Warrior 121

(A) Darkness in the Marshes 77
Adventuring Phase 77
Alternative Routes 82
(Up the) Anduin 82
(The) Assassins 98
Banna 80
Beast Protection 80
(A) Bitter Morning 86
Burglary 93
Caught in the Open 96
(The) Chain of Thangorodrim 95
Climbing down the Rock 95
Climbing the Cliffs 93
(The) Conversation 94
Crossing the Marshes 93
Discovered! 94
Distance of the Pursuers 96
(Searching for the) Dwimmerhorn 88
(The) Dwimmerhorn 91
(The) Enemy 89
Epilogue – The Shadow of the Future 98
Expectations 78, 85
Falling 93
Fellowship Phase 98
(After the) Fight 90
Fight Events 89
(The) Fight in the Marshes 89
Following On... 77
Ghor the Despoiler 92
(Into the) Gladden Fields 88
(The) Gladden Fields 82
(From the) Great River to Mountain Hall 82
(Arrival at the) Hall 97
(Assassins in the) Hall 97
Hartfast & the Dwarves 86
(Meeting) Hartfast son of Hartmut 85
(The) Horn of Warning 87
Hunted! 96
Interaction 78, 85
(The) Journey 81, 87, 95
Lockmand 93
(Travelling with) Magic 87
Magic the Trapper 87

Wilderland Adventures

(The) Mine	84
Mirkwood Cordial	80
Motivation	78, 85
Mountain Hall	83
(Night at) Mountain Hall	96
(From) Mountain Hall to the Gladden River	88
Overtaken!	96
Other Routes?	96
Part Five – Slave & Hunters	89
Part Four – The Passage of the Marshes	87
Part One – Wizard's Counsel	78
Part Seven – Fly, You Fools!	95
Part Six – By Secret Ways	90
Part Three – The Harrowed Hall	82
Part Two – Across the River	80
Planning the Route	81, 88
Radagast's Magical Boons	79
(Leaving) Rhosgobel	80
(From) Rhosgobel to the Great River	82
(A) Rude Awakening	86
(The) Sanctum	94
(The) Shadow in the Temple	93
Sneaking Around the Fortress	93
Spell of Concealment	80
Storm Bag	80
(Entering the) Temple	93
(Exploring the) Temple	94
Travel Blessing	80
Treachery!	97
Waking in the Night	98
(The) Wizard	78

Don't Leave the Path 7

Adventuring Phase	7
(The) Ancient Wood	17
(Following) Baldor	13
(Playing) Baldor	8
(Saving) Baldor	8
Baldor's Error	12
Baldor's History	9
Baldor's Offer	9
(Playing) Belgo	8
Belgo's Talisman	12
(The) Castle	13
Climbing the Wall	14
(The) Creature Attacks	19
Doomed!	15
Dreams and Intuitions	18
(Guests of the) Elves	10
Epilogue – The Forest Gate	19
Escape!	15
Expectations	11, 16
Fellowship Phase	19
Fighting the Thugs	9
Gathering Darkness	15
(Encountering the) Hermit	16
(Playing the) Hermit	16
(The) Hermit's Tree	16
Interaction	11, 17
Intimidating the Thugs	9

Introduction	11, 16
(The) Journey	9, 11
(The) Journey Begins	11
Loading the Ponies	11
March of the Spiders	14
Motivation	10, 16
(The) Old Well	18
Outcomes	11, 17
Part Five – The Hermit	15
Part Four – Castle of the Spiders	12
Part One – Where Rivers Run With Gold	7
Part Six – The Well in the Wood	17
Part Three – The Long Road	11
Part Two – The Edge of the Woodland Realm	10
(The) Thing in the Well	19
(The) Thunderstorm	15
(The) Tower Stairs	14
Under the Spell	18

Introduction 4

Experience Awards	6
(The) Gibbet King	5
How to Use this Guide	6
(The) Passing of Years	6

Kinstrife & Dark Tidings 37

Adventuring Phase	37
After the Battle	56
Aftermath	58
Arrangements for the Night	42
(The) Bandit Camp	51
Barred From The Village	45
Battle is Joined!	56
(The) Battleground	56
(Encountering) Beorn	40
Beorn! Beorn!	56
Beyond the Gate	39
Brunhild & Helmgut	57
Brunhild's Crime	48
Clouds Gather	55
Dinner	41
Event Suggestions	44
Exchange of News	41
Expectations	40, 45, 54, 57
Faron, the Trapper	53
Fellowship Phase	58
Forced March	55
Foreshadowing	38
(The) Foster-Father's Tale	46
(The) Funeral	43
(Across the) Great River	48
Ignoring the Dead	39
In the Fray	56
Interaction	40, 45, 54, 58
Introduction	40, 45, 58
(The) Journey	55
Judgement	58
Motivation	40, 45, 54, 57
(The) Next Day	42
(A) Nightly Adventure	42

Oderic	54, 57
(Capturing) Oderic	54
(Speaking to) Oderic	54
(Watching for) Oderic	51
Oderic guides the outlaws against the Beornings	56
(Playing) Oderic Kinslayer	52
Oderic is a prisoner	56
Oderic tricks the outlaws	56
Oderic's Fate	55
Outlaw Archers	51
Outlaw Patrols	51
Outlaw Warriors	51
(The) Outlaw Watchman	53
Planning the Route	44
Searching for the Fugitive	44
Sending Word to Beorn	52
Telling the Tale	41
Part Eight – Grim Tidings	55
Part Five – The Chase Continued	48
Part Four – Kinstrife	44
Part Nine – Judgement at the Carrock	57
Part One – A Funeral Boat	38
Part Seven – The Outlaw Boy	52
Part Six – Cruel, Ill-Favoured men	49
Part Three – The Chase	43
Part Two – Beorn's Hall	39
Planning the Route	48
Signs of a Host	49
Signs of the Prisoner	48
Sorrows Old & New	46
Success or Failure	55
(The) Trial	57
(Encountering the) Village Elders	44
Valter and the Spirit	50
Valter the Bloody	49-50, 57
Village Stories and Rumours	46
(The) Widow's Tale	47

Of Leaves & Stewed Hobbit 20

Adventuring Phase	20
(The) Adventure Begins	22
Alarums!	33
Battle!	30
Battle Events	30
(Andy) Blackthorn	29
(Bill the) Bowman	29
(Agatha) Brandybuck	22
(Dindy) Brandybuck	22
(The Hobbit Dinodas) Brandybuck	28
(Dody) Brandybuck	22
(The) Caravan	28
Cave Spiders	32
(The) Chain	34
(The) Challenge	29
Cooking Time!	34
Darkness and Light	32
(Rescuing) Dinodas	36
Dodinas' Plea	23
Dread Ubhurz	30

Index

(From The) Easterly Inn to The Old Ford	25	Aldor's Sickness	73	(The) Watch on the Heath	125
(The) Enemy	29	(The) Alehouse	69	Adventuring Phase	125
Epilogue – Back To The Inn	36	(The) Assault	64	(The) Battle of the Great Hall	140
Escape!	36	Awakening	74	Battling the Orcs	141
Event Suggestions	32	(The) Battle of the Hill top	65	(The) Chain of Thangorodrim	141
Expectations	23	Blessed by the First-born	76	(Using the) Chain of Thangorodrim	142
Falling Rocks	32	(A) Chance Meeting	60	(Entering the) Chamber of Winds	140
(The) Feast	35	Conclusions	61	Climbing the Mountain	137
Fellowship Phase	36	(A) Darkness in the Present	63	Conclusions	128, 131, 136
Folk of the Inn	22	Departure	67	Corruption Checks	129, 132
Frier	22	(The) Dream Begins	68	(A) Dangerous Conversation	134
Getting Stuck	32	(The) Eagles	65	(A) Date with Death	135
(The) Goblin Hall	34	(The) Eagles are Coming!	66	Dropping the Stone Block	140
Goblin Sentinels	33	Easterling Warriors	72	Epilogue – A Renewed Spring of Joy	142
Goblin Skirmishers	30	Escape?	73	(To) Erebor	126
(The) Goblin Song	31	Expectations	61, 66	(From) Erebor to the Grey Mountains	129
(The) Goblin Tactics	29	Fellowship Phase	76	Expectations	126, 130, 135
(A) Homely House	21	(The) Final Challenge	75	Fellowship Phase	142
Interaction	24	Flight to the Pass	64	(A) Forgotten Threat	134
Introduction	23	(Healing) Gaerthor	67	Former Slave	136
(The) Journey	25	Galion	60	(Defeating the) Gibbet King	142
(The) Journey Through the Tunnels	32	Geb the Servant	73	(The) Howl of the Mountain	140
Journeys in the Dark	32	Geb the Trickster	74	Interaction	126, 131, 136
(Averting the) Kidnapping	31	Geb's Betrayal	73	Introduction	131, 135
(The) Kidnapping	30	(A) Glimpse of Irimë	72	(The) Journey	129
Letters of Introduction	24	(Saving) Haleth	74	(An Audience with) King Dáin	126
(Tom) Lumpyface	29	Haleth's Death	74	(The) Last Debate	141
(Iwgar) Longleg	28	(Rumours in the) Inn	70	(The) Last Night	129
Motivation	23	(Siege of the) Inn	71	(We Captured) Lockmand!	127
(The) Mountain Ruins	26	(The) Inn	69	Motivation	126, 130, 135
(The) Night-Wight	26-27	Interaction	61, 66	(The) Old Master	134
(From The) Old Ford to The High Pass	25	Introduction	61	Part Five – The Scourge of the North	134
Outcomes	24	(Playing) Irimë	63	Part Four – Zirakinbar	133
Part Five – Prisoner of the Goblins	33	Irimë failed	76	Part One – Council Under The Mountain	125
Part Four – Into The Mountains	31	(If) Irimë fails	75	Part Six – The Watchtower	137
Part One – The Easterly Inn	20	Irimë succeeded	76	Part Three – The Grey Mountains	132
Part Three – Battle at the Ringfort	27	(If) Irimë succeeds	75	Part Two – Across the Trackless Waste	129
Part Two – Searching the High Pass	25	Irimë's Dream	68	(The) Power of a Dragon	141
(A) Rain of Arrows	30	(The) Journey Home	76	(A) Precious Lure, an Iron Trap	134
(The) Ringfort	27	(The) Journey South	72	(Playing) Raenar	135
Rumours at the Inn	23	(The) Lady's Request	60	Raenar the great Cold-drake	136-137, 141
Sabotaging The Feast	36	(The) Long Memory of the First-born	59	Ruining His Plans	142
Searching For The Caravan	27	Motivation	66	Scent of Prey	132
Shadrach	22	(The) Orcs Assemble	64	Searching for Signs	130
Stealing The Key	36	Part Five – The Ruins	67	(A) Secret Summoning	125
Surprise Attack	36	Part Four – A Guest of Eagles	66	Secrets of Mazarbul	128
Tactics	29	Part One – The Borders of the Forest	60	Smaug is Dead	136
Tap-Tap-Tap	32	Part Seven – Dawn in the West	75	(The) Snow-Troll Wakes	132
Their Plight	29	Part Six – Dark Dreams	72	(The) Snow-Trolls	132-133
Their Tale	29	Part Three – The Hill of Woe	64	Spellbound	136
Treacherous Footing	33	Part Two – Weary of the World	62	(Exploring the) Watchtower	137
(The) Tunnels	31	(The) Shadow of the Past	62	(The) Watchtower	138
Victory!	30	Slain Companions	71	What should the Companions Do?	134
Wandering Troll	32	Set between Worlds	68	Witherfinger	130
(The) Wolves Beyond The Walls	30	(The) Spirit	74	(Playing) Witherfinger	130
		Supper by the Forest Eaves	62	Witherfinger's Fear	132
Those Who Tarry No Longer	59	Those Who Kneel	73		
Adventuring Phase	59	Twilight	67		
(Fate of the) Alderman	70	Undead Warriors	71		
(Return of the) Alderman	70				

159

OPEN GAME LICENSE Version 1.0a

The following text is the property of Wizards of the Coast, Inc. and is Copyright 2000 Wizards of the Coast, Inc ("Wizards"). All Rights Reserved.
1. Definitions: (a)"Contributors" means the copyright and/or trademark owners who have contributed Open Game Content; (b)"Derivative Material" means copyrighted material including derivative works and translations (including into other computer languages), potation, modification, correction, addition, extension, upgrade, improvement, compilation, abridgment or other form in which an existing work may be recast, transformed or adapted; (c) "Distribute" means to reproduce, license, rent, lease, sell, broadcast, publicly display, transmit or otherwise distribute; (d)"Open Game Content" means the game mechanic and includes the methods, procedures, processes and routines to the extent such content does not embody the Product Identity and is an enhancement over the prior art and any additional content clearly identified as Open Game Content by the Contributor, and means any work covered by this License, including translations and derivative works under copyright law, but specifically excludes Product Identity. (e) "Product Identity" means product and product line names, logos and identifying marks including trade dress; artifacts; creatures characters; stories, storylines, plots, thematic elements, dialogue, incidents, language, artwork, symbols, designs, depictions, likenesses, formats, poses, concepts, themes and graphic, photographic and other visual or audio representations; names and descriptions of characters, spells, enchantments, personalities, teams, personas, likenesses and special abilities; places, locations, environments, creatures, equipment, magical or supernatural abilities or effects, logos, symbols, or graphic designs; and any other trademark or registered trademark clearly identified as Product identity by the owner of the Product Identity, and which specifically excludes the Open Game Content; (f) "Trademark" means the logos, names, mark, sign, motto, designs that are used by a Contributor to identify itself or its products or the associated products contributed to the Open Game License by the Contributor (g) "Use", "Used" or "Using" means to use, Distribute, copy, edit, format, modify, translate and otherwise create Derivative Material of Open Game Content. (h) "You" or "Your" means the licensee in terms of this agreement.

2. The License: This License applies to any Open Game Content that contains a notice indicating that the Open Game Content may only be Used under and in terms of this License. You must affix such a notice to any Open Game Content that you Use. No terms may be added to or subtracted from this License except as described by the License itself. No other terms or conditions may be applied to any Open Game Content distributed using this License.

3. Offer and Acceptance: By Using the Open Game Content You indicate Your acceptance of the terms of this License.

4. Grant and Consideration: In consideration for agreeing to use this License, the Contributors grant You a perpetual, worldwide, royalty free, non exclusive license with the exact terms of this License to Use, the Open Game Content.

5. Representation of Authority to Contribute: If You are contributing original material as Open Game Content, You represent that Your Contributions are Your original creation and/or You have sufficient rights to grant the rights conveyed by this License.

6. Notice of License Copyright: You must update the COPYRIGHT NOTICE portion of this License to include the exact text of the COPYRIGHT NOTICE of any Open Game Content You are copying, modifying or distributing, and You must add the title, the copyright date, and the copyright holder's name to the COPYRIGHT NOTICE of any original Open Game Content you Distribute.

7. Use of Product Identity: You agree not to Use any Product Identity, including as an indication as to compatibility, except as expressly licensed in another, independent Agreement with the owner of each element of that Product Identity. You agree not to indicate compatibility or co adaptability with any Trademark or Registered Trademark in conjunction with a work containing Open Game Content except as expressly licensed in another, independent Agreement with the owner of such Trademark or Registered Trademark. The use of any Product Identity in Open Game Content does not constitute a challenge to the ownership of that Product Identity. The owner of any Product Identity used in Open Game Content shall retain all rights, title and interest in and to that Product Identity.

8. Identification: If you distribute Open Game Content You must clearly indicate which portions of the work that you are distributing are Open Game Content.

9. Updating the License: Wizards or its designated Agents may publish updated versions of this License. You may use any authorized version of this License to copy, modify and distribute any Open Game Content originally distributed under any version of this License.

10. Copy of this License: You MUST include a copy of this License with every copy of the Open Game Content You Distribute.

11. Use of Contributor Credits: You may not market or advertise the Open Game Content using the name of any Contributor unless You have written permission from the Contributor to do so.

12. Inability to Comply: If it is impossible for You to comply with any of the terms of this License with respect to some or all of the Open Game Content due to statute, judicial order, or governmental regulation then You may not Use any Open Game Material so affected.

13. Termination: This License will terminate automatically if You fail to comply with all terms herein and fail to cure such breach within 30 days of becoming aware of the breach. All sublicenses shall survive the termination of this License.

14. Reformation: If any provision of this License is held to be unenforceable, such provision shall be reformed only to the extent necessary to make it enforceable.

15. COPYRIGHT NOTICE
Open Game License v 1.0a Copyright 2000, Wizards of the Coast, LLC.

System Reference Document 5.1 Copyright 2016, Wizards of the Coast, Inc.; Authors Mike Mearls, Jeremy Crawford, Chris Perkins, Rodney Thompson, Peter Lee, James Wyatt, Robert J. Schwalb, Bruce R. Cordell, Chris Sims, and Steve Townshend, based on original material by E. Gary Gygax and Dave Arneson.
Adventures in Middle-earth Player's Guide Copyright 2016 Cubicle 7 Entertainment Ltd/Sophisticated Games Ltd; Authors: James Brown, Paul Butler, Walt Ciechanowksi, Steve Emmott, Gareth Ryder-Hanrahan, Jon Hodgson, Shane Ivey, Andrew Kenrick, TS Luikart, Dominic McDowall, Francesco Nepitello, James Spahn, Ken Spencer.
Adventures in Middle-earth Loremaster's Guide Copyright 2017 Cubicle 7 Entertainment Ltd/Sophisticated Games Ltd; Authors: Walt Ciechanowski, Steve Emmott, Jon Hodgson, TS Luikart, Dominic McDowall, Francesco Nepitello, David Rea, Jacob Rodgers, Gareth Ryder-Hanrahan and Ken Spencer.
Adventures in Middle-earth Wilderland Adventures Copyright 2017 Cubicle 7 Entertainment Ltd/Sophisticated Games Ltd; Authors: Gareth Ryder-Hanrahan, Francesco Nepitello, Jon Hodgson, and Steve Emmott.

END OF LICENSE

Adventures in Middle-Earth™

The Road Goes Ever On

The Road Goes Ever On™: a beautiful collection of 4 journey maps for **Adventures in Middle-earth**, along with a 32 page supplement packed with setting information, rules and guidance on making the most of your journeys.

The double sided, large format maps cover the greater part of known Middle-earth: Eriador, Wilderland, Rohan, Gondor and Mordor. With Player maps and hexed Loremaster maps, these provide an invaluable play aid for planning your **Adventure in Middle-earth** journeys.

The accompanying 32 page softcover supplement gives Loremasters even more support, inspiration and systems for generating even more engaging and exciting journeys.

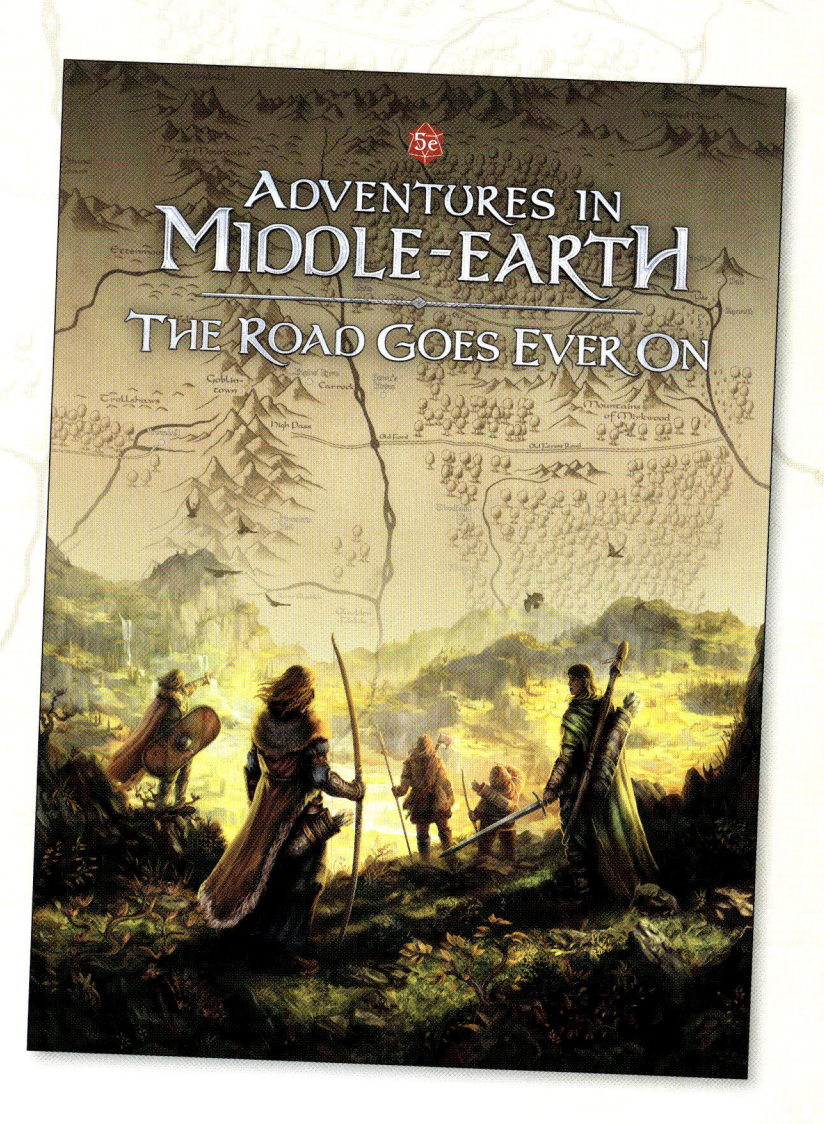

CB72305
$29.99
£19.99
www.cubicle7.co.uk

CUBICLE 7 SEVEN

Hill of Woe Map
Scenery (page 91, LMG)

- Boulders
- Steep slope
- Shallow slope

Inn Map
Scenery

- Tables (treat as boulders, page 91, LMG)
- Stairs (page 94, LMG)
- Steep slope (page 91, LMG)
- Scattered crocks, pots, flagons and pans (treat as scattered rocks, page 91, LMG)

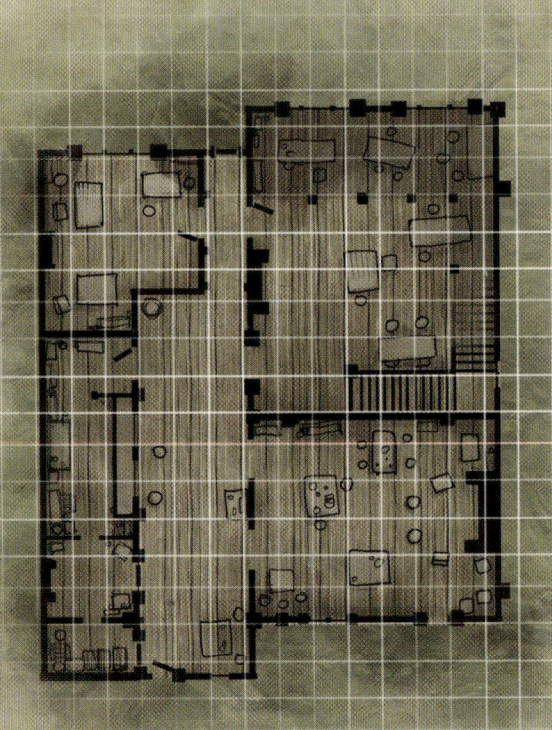

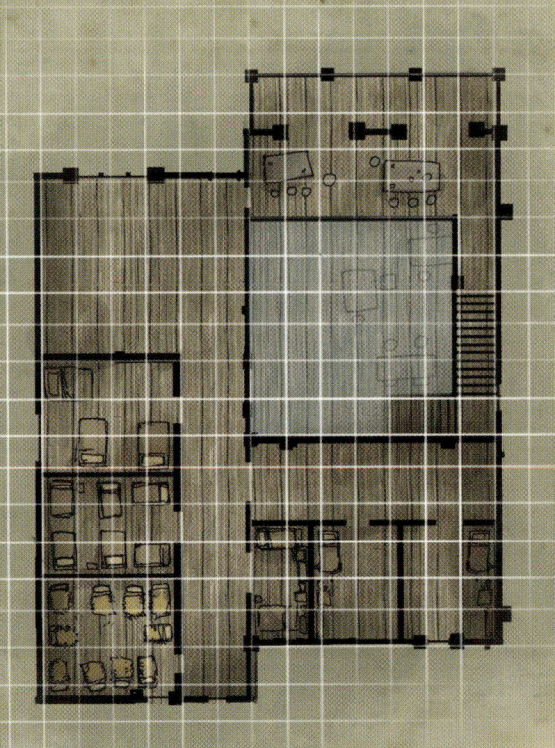

Ground floor

Upper floor